ALL HELL BROKE LOOSE

The story of how young Minnesota people coped with the November 11, 1940 Armistice Day storm — the worst blizzard ever to hit Minnesota.

by William H. Hull, M.A.

T0164248

All Hell Broke Loose
by William H. Hull

Copyright ©1985 by William H. Hull

Published by
Thunder Bay Press
West Branch, MI

Twenty-fifth printing, 2023

ISBN: 978-1-882376-96-4

Printed in the United States of America

CONTENTS

(Note: These 167 experiences are selected from 512 different ones by Minnesotans in 166 different Minnesota communities.)

INTRODUCTION

After going through all the thousands of hours it takes to write a book, an author sometimes asks himself why he did it? That's a fair question.

I wasn't even in the state of Minnesota on that fateful day of November 11, 1940. I was a graduate student at Southern Methodist University in Dallas and a steady reader of the Dallas Morning News. The story must have been covered by that fine newspaper but, if so, it made no impression on me. Later when I became a Minnesotan I began to hear stories of this horrible storm that killed so many people. Through the 39 years I have considered myself a Minnesotan I have frequently thought what a shame that all of those stories about this particular storm weren't written, so I decided to act for the good of history and before these people died. After all, that storm was 45 years ago at this writing.

It seemed to me that people would want to know what it was like to be living on a farm with cattle and chickens to take care of, to be facing possible death on a small island in the Mississippi while duck hunting, to fight for survival in snow that seemed to be up to the armpits in northern Minnesota while deer hunting, and to be immovably caught in the "loop" of a big city like Minneapolis or St. Paul with no place to spend the night and no way to get home. These are the experiences about which these many Minnesotans have written. Speaking for all of them, I hope you enjoy their tales and realize how agonizing it was for many people — those who were fortunate enough to live through it.

My only regret is that so many of the 500 + experiences received and edited had to be eliminated to restrict the physical size of the book. After repeatedly selecting from the anecdotes received, the final cutting eliminated sixty percent of those I wished to include.

William H. Hull, M.A.

AND ALL HELL BROKE LOOSE
by William H. Hull
Edina, MN

December 31, 1984

It's two degrees below zero this morning and I decided, as a city man, that I should get out to plow my short driveway before the city snowplow came down the street and filled in my driveway entrance with a mass of snow. We had three inches of new snow overnight with a fifteen mph wind, resulting in a wind chill of 32 below zero. That's cold!

I should have had more breakfast but I wanted to get this done quickly so I started dressing. I donned a pair of balbriggan pajamas instead of long underwear because I didn't expect to stay outside that long. Next came a couple of soft shirts and the heaviest blue jeans I could find. My insulated rubber boots and my dear old red deer hunting jacket topped it off. My ski mask, used only for this snowblowing detail, had disappeared and had to be forgotten. For gloves, I used a pair of what Minnesotans call "choppers", so named because woodsmen used them for chopping wood. They are heavy leather mittens with removable heavy wool liners. These will usually keep the fingers warm in any weather; I have used them for years when hunting deer in subzero weather.

The first job was to move the van from the driveway so I could plow it. Not wanting to pack down too much snow, I swept an informal path to the van and used the broom to push off much of the three inches of new snow atop the vehicle. I had run an extension cord to the van and had placed a lighted electric bulb atop the motor block to make starting easier. To remove it I had to peel off a glove for thirty seconds, in which time my fingers almost froze solid. My ears were getting brittle so I lowered the flaps on my heavy hunting cap and pulled the extension cord back into the garage. Rushing back to the van, I ripped off one mitten, folding it over so cold air couldn't get in, and quickly unlocked the door and inserted the key in the ignition. Damn! It was cold. The van started immediately, thanks to the light bulb heat, so I moved it to the street as quickly as possible. Of course I had immediately replaced the glove. I also was wishing I had a contracted snow removal service, as did my neighbor, whose snow was removed at three o'clock that morning. But I knew I couldn't do that because the van had to be in the driveway; it is too tall to go into the garage.

My fingers were excruciatingly cold. My breath was freezing around the collar of my jacket. But I had to go on.

Back at the garage, only fifty feet away, my quick-start snowblower turned over immediately. In those very few seconds when the garage door was open, I though I could hear my held-over geraniums at the rear of the garage screaming in agony from the wave of cold from the open door. As I shut the garage door and started plowing I thanked God for a situation which, two years before, had forced me to buy an excellent two-stage, five-horse self-propelled snowblower. I put it in high gear and went practically racing up and down the driveway, rooster-tailing snow from the below-ground level of the drive to the higher lawn. Of course I was getting colder every second.

Half way through the job I wanted to quit—but knew I had no alternative. I could not avoid thinking of the people caught in that horrible November 11, 1940, blizzard—people who froze to death—some even standing up.

Of course I finished the job because we are that way and ran the blower into the garage, pressed the button to close the door, all the time saying "Oh, My God, I'm cold. Oh, Lord, this is unbearable." Maybe it was a prayer meaning "Lord, don't let me freeze my fingers doing a simple, routine job like this."

At this point I realized that I hadn't even touched the forty feet or so of winding steps from the driveway to the front door, but that would have to wait. I had had enough and that was a shovel job, not a blower job. I was going inside.

Inside the house, off the garage, I realized I couldn't see because my eyeglasses had fogged from the warm and humid inside air. The water from the nearby laundry tub hose helped warm my hands but it had to be done gradually. The ends of the fingers had turned white from the intense cold; sometime I must have frostbitten them. But now they gradually thawed.

I looked at the clock when I could put on my glasses again. It had only been thirty minutes since I first went outside.

That's what it's like being in a northern state on a fairly normal winter day. Contrast that with the evening and the morning following that fateful November 11, 1940 blizzard when snowfall measured from 16.2 inches upward in the Twin Cities to 26.6 inches in Collegeville. When winds up to 63 miles-per-hour helped kill a lot of people and animals. It was a time when all hell broke loose.

SITUATION PRIOR TO ARMISTICE DAY

World War II was at its height in Europe, but without USA formal involvement yet. The streamer headline of the Minneapolis Morning Tribune on Saturday, November 9, 1940 was "FIGHT ON, HITLER EXHORTS NAZIS; SCOFFS AT U.S. ARMS PRODUCTION." Obviously the Nazis thought they were in control and that the USA could not hurt them. The very next day the same paper headlined that "RUSSIA WILL JOIN IN AXIS PARLEY. DUCE'S CRACK DIVISION WIPED OUT." What was happening was that there was a lot of talk that the Russian Premier Molotoff was going to visit Berlin for a tri-government conference with leaders of Germany and Italy. Obviously the leaders of these three countries thought that "the visit may mark the turning point of the war . . . and would dash all hopes of alienating Russia from the Axis and 'indirectly deal a heavy diplomatic blow at Britain and also the United States.' "

The war had broken out and developed into a global conflict between the Axis and the Allies. Although the United States had not yet become a warring nation (Germany and Italy were to declare war on us on December 11, 1941 — a year from our story — just four days after Japan bombed Pearl Harbor), Congress had already voted a billion dollar naval building program. That was in 1938. In 1939 American neutrality had been pledged but our cash and carry policy allowed us to export arms to the combatants. Later, the Lend-lease Act of March 1941 would help prospective allies in need of aid.

"The course in 1940 was mapped by rapidly passing events. The April and May invasions of Norway, Denmark, Holland, Belgium, Luxembourg, and France triggered American actions. In his Chicago speech of 1937, President Franklin D. Roosevelt had promised to quarantine aggressors. In his Charlottesville, Va., speech on June 10, 1940, he went further. He not only indicted Germany's new partner, Italy, but also issued a public promise of help to "the opponents of force." In June also, he assured himself of bipartisan political support by appointing the Republicans Frank Knox and Henry L. Stimson to head the Navy and War departments. Military expansion began in earnest."*

One of the first actions Congress took was to pass "the draft" as it was called. It was officially the Burke-Wadsworth Bill or The Selective Service and Training Act of September 16, 1940. This was the nation's first peacetime program of compulsory military service. Just two months before our fateful Armistice Day, men realized that going to war was soon going to be a reality.

Perhaps just as upsetting was the Presidential election which had been held just a few days earlier — on November 5, 1940. Families were divided over the choice between Franklin Delano Roosevelt and Wendell Willkie. Democrat FDR was seeking a highly controversial third term. He had been elected in 1932 with a 57.4% popular vote over Herbert Hoover and again in 1936 with a 60.8% overwhelming victory over Alf Landon. Now, in 1940, with a 54.7%

*Dictionary of American History, Charles Scribner's Sons, New York, 1976, Volume VII, page 334.

margin, he had overcome Wendell Willkie. He was destined to win a fourth term in 1944 with a 53.3% defeat of Thomas E. Dewey and, although FDR died in office, he remains the only president to win more than two elections to that position.

In November 1940 the country knew it was dangerously close to involvement in the war and the people wanted no part of it. The 1940 Democratic platform and Roosevelt, its candidate, were pledged against participation in foreign wars, except in case of attack. That was the very attitude that made critics a year later claim that Roosevelt had permitted Pearl Harbor to happen, because it gave him justification for us to enter the war. FDR's opponent, Republican Wendell Willkie, had stressed that Roosevelt's third term threatened democratic government but it wasn't a sufficiently strong argument to stop the Roosevelt train.

So, in 1940 the people had been pulled back and forth by the war in Europe, by the controversial third term election and the populace was in need of an emotional release. This Armistice Day, particularly for duck and deer hunters, was anticipated to be just that.

The weather had been deceptively mild. There was no precipitation on November 8, the temperature range was 31–43 degrees and the total precipitation for year-to-date was only 22.45 inches. By Sunday, November 10 (1940) the official U.S. Weather Bureau forecast read "Cloudy, with snow flurries, considerably colder Sunday; Monday cloudy and continued cold. 24 hour high: 42 at 4 p.m.; low 40 at 2 a.m." (Those were for November 9 as reported in the November 10 issue of the Minneapolis Morning Tribune.)

But the deer hunters were ecstatic because there was a promise of snow and they needed/wanted a light snow cover to make deer tracking easier, as well as to give better visibility in the woods. The duck hunters thought that birds would be easy to find. For example, the sports page (p. 11) of that same November 10 paper carried a headline reading: "CHANGE IN WEATHER HERALDS GOOD DEER SEASON". So the hunters flocked into the woods, particularly the northern woods. In the south they headed for the river bottoms.

Then came Armistice Day itself—*the* Armistice Day to Minnesota people—as well as to those in other areas. That Monday's Minneapolis Morning Tribune, November 11, 1940, talked about the usual accidents (28 people having died in a collision between two boats near St. John's, Newfoundland) but the big stories concerned such things as plans for Armistice Day services to be held in the Twin Cities. Radio stations were to carry the American Legion Armistice Day program from Arlington National Cemetery in Washington, D.C. The newspaper carried the summary of weather to date and again we point out that the total annual precipitation through November 10, in Minneapolis, had only reached 22.91 inches—*for all year*.

Now the stage was set for all hell to break loose. And it did.

THE DAY DAWNS DARK AND GLOOMY

The day started with misty rain which had fallen almost constantly over the week-end, sleeted for a while and then became snow. Although snow had been forecast, no one had any inkling the amount would be more than a few inches at the most. No one thought this would be a record event.

This Armistice Day was just another one in some people's thinking. True it was full of memories for men who had fought in the war to end all wars and for families whose sons and fathers were about to be involved in the present world war, but Armistice Day was not solely a day of great mourning. In Minnesota it is deer hunting season, when thousands of hunters, mainly men, head for the woods for their great sporting challenge. In Minnesota that usually meant going "up north" to the northern woods from Cloquet on up to the Canadian border. For many others it meant going to the rivers for the elusive mallard ducks. It meant getting away from job difficulties, from world war worries, from the bitterly fought Presidential election. People hoped to step aside from the mad world for a day or so.

It was a Monday — for many people just another Monday. City and town people got up and went to work, realizing as the day progressed that something severe might be coming their way.

During the day the wind increased to 32 mph with gusts in the 60s. The situation was fast deteriorating and downtown Minneapolis and St. Paul workers were concerned about getting home. Many didn't make it.

"Drifts were piled up with such suddenness that thousands of cars became stalled to block roads. At 3:30 p.m. and later the visibility for drivers was virtually nil. Cab companies suspended operations and late in the day at 9 p.m. the street car company gave up attempting to maintain schedules. Train service was seriously hampered and to some points in the south and west was stopped. Bus lines out of the city (Minneapolis) were stopped completely. Airplanes were grounded . . ."*

People all over the state started holing up simply to live through the blizzard. They had experienced bad storms before and Minnesota people are known as a tough and hardy group of survivors. But they knew they needed to find shelter. And find shelter they did. Downtown hotels in the Twin Cities were quickly filled to overflowing. People ganged up to occupy every possible sleeping space. Four to a room, more if necessary. People slept in their offices, on desks, on the floors. Travellers were happy to find a small town gymnasium with pads and blankets. All over the state Minnesotans were trying to keep alive.

It was bad. Just how bad they didn't yet know.

For example, in south Minneapolis divorced Percy W. Young had an evening date with a lady, Lola Bender, whom he had been dating for some time. Lola and "P.W.", as he was known to all of his friends, returned to Lola's apartment on Girard Avenue after having dinner nearby and spent the evening listening to radio music and the ten o'clock radio news—at which time he and Lola realized the storm outside had escalated dramatically. P.W. said his goodbyes and went out to get into his car, parked in front of Lola's on the street. He said later "I couldn't find the damned thing. There were all of these lumps of snow and I could see that even if I found it, it would be impossible to drive through all that snow to reach my place. So I said the heck with it and went back to Lola's."

At that point one of his friends, also in the Men's Garden Club of Minneapolis, said "Well, P.W., I suppose you stayed all night there too?" "Of course", replied the ninety year old man (who had been sixty-one in 1940). "There was nothing else I could do." Then, to his friends' snickers, he added . . . "But we got married soon after that and have had a darned good life together."

What P.W. and hundreds of thousands of other people found out the next morning was that the Armistice Day of 1940 Blizzard had dumped a record amount of snow in 24 hours on Minneapolis—an all-time record. And the temperature had dropped to six above zero at eight o'clock that Tuesday morning.

It was as if all nature were on a rampage, unleashing its raw power on the universe.

The whole state was hit, as were other states. At first count there were ten people dead in Minnesota and three in Wisconsin plus many known to be missing. The United Press quickly put the dead at 52 in the midwest and noted that the storm "battered furiously at the eastern seaboard . . . Fifty-mile-an-hour winds tore at property in New England and the middle Atlantic states as temperatures dropped to freezing levels. Icy squalls and snow pounded at the Rocky Mountain region for the fourth day."*

It had been a hell of a day.

*Minneapolis Star Journal, November 12, 1940, page 1.

HOW COULD IT HAPPEN?

How could such a terrible storm come about and so many people be killed? What were the causes?

Unpreparedness.

A large number, if not most, of the fatalities would have been prevented today by better weather forecasting and alert, more numerous and efficient road clearing vehicles, the interstate highway system, heat efficient and water protective outerwear, modern airlift capabilities.

It is hard for us to realize that the nation was just coming out of a severe depression, that jobs were scarce and that people didn't have disposable income. Many houses had no central heating system—or storm windows, or weather stripping, or even insulation. Some rural areas still had no electricity or telephone service or running water in the house.

The mild weather had lulled people into complacency. They had not laid in a winter supply of coal or heating oil, much less groceries. With antifreeze being so expensive they planned to add the cheaper alcohol to their auto radiators when the weather got cool. If put in too soon it could overheat and boil away and be lost.

So Minnesotans were just not prepared. Furthermore, they were not forewarned by the weather forecasters via radio. Weather services were very inadequate compared with today's highly technical equipment.

Time and again through the stories herein we hear people talking of inadequate personal clothing. Even though it was a mild morning and they dressed lightly, their footwear and outer clothing in no way approached the effectiveness of today's parallels. Many of us can remember how cold and wet we were in our best wool hunting clothes in those days, compared to today's synthetics, greater use of goose down filler and water resistant hats and jackets.

The storm also offers a study in human nature. Those were not the good old days, as we have said. As a result, some people were generous and compassionate. Others made money from the misfortunes of storm victims; some refused to share; some took and thoughtlessly neither paid nor thanked their benefactors. It was a strain on personal budgets, food supplies and emotions.

YES IT WAS MINNESOTA'S WORST STORM

As the storm subsided the public became increasingly aware of just how horrible it had been. A 24-hour all-time record snowfall was reported in the local newspaper as being 16.2 inches, but reported as being 16.8 inches in the Minneapolis Star & Tribune by meteorologist Bruce F. Watson, on November 11, 1983 (39 years later). Watson also pointed out snowfall totals of 22 inches at Orr, 19.3 at Milaca, 16.7 at Bird Island and a whopping 26.6 at Collegeville, near St. Cloud, which also stands as a state single-storm record for November.

Does this storm remain the champion? In 1985 does it still hold the all-time snowfall record in the Twin Cities? Yes, if you use similar measuring techniques, says Earl Kuehnast, Minnesota State Climatologist at the Deaprtment of Natural Resources, University of Minnesota campus. Kuehnast points out that the 1940 figure of 16.7 inches was surpassed on January 20, 1982 (17.1") and two days later on January 22, 1982 (17.2"). *However*, "if we had used the old system of measuring snowfall in 1982, as we used in 1940, 1940 would retain its record."

He then explained that in 1940, under the old measuring system, snowfall readings were taken by National Weather Service officials at 24-hour intervals. In 1982, under the new measuring system, readings are taken hourly. Thus, he continues, the 1982 readings were taken when the snow was fresh and fluffy and the 1940 after it had settled to a more compact mass.(1) Thus, those people who experienced the storm and insist it is indeed the worst they have ever seen, the storm of the century, are justified. They are right.

The death toll was staggering. The first count for Minnesota, just two days after the storm, put the figure at 37 (2) but later it was set at 59 (3) within the state. Bruce Watson, meteorologist, writing 39 years later in 1983, put the figure at 49. (3) Another reliable source says there were 144 dead nationwide.(4) If we apply the 59 figure to that 144, it is obvious that Minnesota's 41% of the total dead put it at the heart of the storm.

They took refuge wherever possible. Fifty passengers of a stalled street car fled from the cold into the John Swanson grocery store at 2400 East 25th Street, Minneapolis. Many accepted the invitation of the Minneapolis House Furnishing company to stay the night — after reading a banner put up by the store. The downtown hotels had quickly filled to overflowing. Everything was so jammed that businesses had reserved blocks or floors for their personnel, doing so early in the day. The Minneapolis Morning Tribune reported that cots and mattresses were placed every place possible — dining rooms, clubrooms, lobbies, hallways with patrons eventually sleeping on blankets only. One hotel reported that at midnight calls were coming at the rate of ten per minute.

"J.W. Nordquist, room clerk at the Sheridan hotel, said the night was the busiest he had seen in 25 years . . . The Minneapolis Athletic club . . . said the demand was the greatest ever seen there by the manager of 16 years . . . An estimated 2,000 people jammed every sitting and standing place (in the

Nicollet hotel). The Curtis was full at noon and Luella Olson, chief operator, said the switchboard was the busiest in the 14 years she has been at the hotel. The Radisson, Dyckman, Andrews and other hotels all had similar accounts of record-shattering business."

People simply couldn't move. Streetcar service soon came to a halt; snow-plows were bogged down; 226 of the 460 circuits leading out of Minneapolis were out of service; there were 25 breaks in the wires and 200 telephone poles known to be down.

But it wasn't just the Twin Cities. Twenty-three Minnesota cities were without telephone service on the twelfth. Many calls had to be rerouted through other cities, if they were successfully made at all.

Near Savage a newborn child died in a farmhouse when the physician and ambulance couldn't get through the snowdrifts. At the Lohman farmhouse near Lake Elmo the Great Northern quartet from St. Paul entertained about 40 snowbound travelers. The Twin Point tavern near St. Elmo, sheltered 54 persons who lived off canned soup and sandwich makings until the snowplows rescued them.

"Another 54 persons crowded a tavern at county road D and highway #8, where the worst jam occurred. Mrs. Mabel Philbrook, the tavern proprietor, and Leroy Linder, who runs an adjoining filling station, spent the night making sandwiches and hot coffee as car after car crashed into the pileup and became hopelessly entangled. Motorists and bus passengers who remained at the tavern slept in chairs, on beer cases and kegs, on the floor and on the bar." (Minneapolis Morning Tribune, Nov. 13, 1940).

But the highway snowplow drivers and others were trying hard to open the roads and to save people. The department had 14 rotary plows, 300 "V" plows and 230 smaller plows and extra crews working. It was a tremendous and apparently futile job they were attempting. They succeeded in rescueing many like the hundreds marooned in the New Brighton town hall. One of the heroes was highway maintenance engineer C.L. Motl who loaded his car with 500 pounds of sand and a Tribune Newspaper reporter and photographer, plus two more highway employees, to supervise the opening of some of the bad stretches. It was touch and go everywhere.

Back in town three prominent ladies of the James Ford Bell family were marooned with a chauffeur and maid in the Oak Hill grocery store in St. Louis Park, and spent the night sleeping on the floor of the store. In another event, Municipal Judge Joseph A. Poirer was the only one to hold court—but to little avail. Of the cases he heard, he sentenced about 20 drunks to the workhouse but they couldn't be transported there because of no available buses. On a lighter note, University of Minnesota students were stalled in a train at the edge of Farmington and, in typical youthful exhuberance, danced to radio music in the baggage car. The meeting of the Minnesota Horticultural society and the

Minnesota Beekeepers' association, scheduled to meet Wednesday night, had to be cancelled and rescheduled, typical of many such planned events.

Meanwhile, in the rural areas things remained very difficult. The bodies of 14 duck hunters were found Tuesday night in the Winona area, seven having perished from drowning, seven from freezing. Ten cars piled up in a single accident near Faribault, 100 duck hunters took over every bed possible in Parkers Prairie, a bus from Waterloo, Iowa to Minneapolis called it quits in Austin, — and farmers and ranchers began to count their dead animals. A turkey farmer near Henning reported that 2,000 of his 3,000 turkeys died in the storm; Ross Bryant, near Buffalo, lost almost his entire flock of 300 turkeys. H.G. Pester of Crookston lost 1,500 sheep valued at $6,000. It was not only costly in human life but also in animal life and equipment. How many cars were worthless after crashes? How many engine blocks were frozen solid and cracked beyond repair? How much misery and how many broken dreams? Much, much too much.

"The Twin Cities high temperature (on November 11, 1940) was only 38 while in extreme southeastern Minnesota it was in the 60s . . . Trees were uprooted by the gale-force winds — 63 miles per hour was recorded by the weather service in Duluth." (4)

Nationwide it reached $6,000,000 in damages and was labelled "one of the most destructive snowstorms ever". (5) Minnesotans, however, have always called it "The Great Minnesota Armistice Day Storm" or "The Storm of the Century" or "The Time When All Hell Broke Loose".

(1) Interview January 16, 1985.
(2) Minneapolis Morning Tribune, Nov. 13, 1940.
(3) Minneapolis Star, Nov. 12, 1970.
(4) Minneapolis Star & Tribune, Nov. 11, 1983
(5) The 1979 Hammond Atlas.

LORD, HAVE MERCY AND GIVE US COURAGE (1)

In Glencoe, a hundred cars, carrying an estimated 250 men, women and children, broke through to warmth and safety Wednesday, November 13, after a bitter day and night spent two miles west of Glencoe in the drifts. Bob Seiberlich, former state boxing commissioner, led the caravan. Scores of the marooned were hunters. Others were visitors and travelers from the Twin Cities. A number of others were visitors from South Dakota. A number were suffering from cold and exposure. Sieberlich appealed for help of the highway department in a call to the Star Journal, reporting that there were scores sick from the cold. One man's hands were badly frozen, he reported. The refugees trooped into Glencoe, seeking warmth and shelter in the town's cafes and stores. The highway department reported plows were bucking the drifts between Norwood and Chaska on highway #212. This section was blocked by drifts and stalled cars but crews were battling to clear the way for the Glencoe storm victims to get into the cities.(2)

In Fergus Falls, Hans Bardson, an 80 year old man living alone, was believed to have died when his house burned to the ground during the storm.(2)

In Minneapolis, stranded people went to General Hospital and hitched rides on ambulances when they were dispatched on emergency trips. Five rides accommodated fifteen people.(3)

Approximately 250 out-of-town students at Technical high school were given shelter at the St. Cloud hotel on Armistice day when they were unable to return to their homes, while others from Central and junior high schools were taken care of in private homes.(3)

(1) From Litany used in Christ Presbyterian Churcn (Edina, MN) services.
(2) Minneapolis Star Journal, November 13, 1940, page 1.
(3) Minneapolis Morning Tribune, November 12, 1940.

CARRYING OUT AN EXHAUSTED HUNTER

The saga of how two St. Paul hunters perished was told the day after the storm by the men who braved the elements to find them.

E.V. Hanson, who lives on a farm in Prairie Island near lower North lake, near Red Wing, said he had just tended the morning fires when two duck hunters drove into the yard; it was 6 AM. They had a letter from a mutual friend permitting them to use a boat the friend had left there for the season. Soon they left in the rain and headed across what was once Chain lake but is now a part of the dam pool, with Miley's run their destination. That run is a narrow channel that connects Chain lake with the Mississippi river and is about one mile in a direct line from the Hanson farm.

When the rain turned first to sleet, then to snow, Hanson realized that the two hunters would never be able to make their way back to his place against the northwest wind. The only possible way to get out of Miley's run was by boat. Hanson wanted to help but knew it was suicide to try to cross at night on account of the stumps in the dam pool, particularly now that there were white caps on North lake that no small boat could survive. Not being able to help, the Hanson family retired late Monday night, leaving their door unlocked and a light in the window—just on the slim chance that the lost men might find their way to the farm.

At 8:30 AM Hanson left for Miley's run, crossing on the thin ice over an old road, now several feet under water. One hour later he discovered some tracks near the water's edge and followed them. He found Roberts, one of the hunters, standing near the body of his companion, Iverson, which lay face down in the bushes.

Roberts was standing in a small pool of water, attempting to get the frost out of his feet. He was not delirious but was completely exhausted, according to Hanson. "I told him I'd take him home and warm him up," said Hanson; "he agreed and we started back. We walked about a quarter of a mile with him stumbling and grabbing to tree trunks for support. Finally I saw that we were not making any headway, so I stopped and built a fire for him; then I gave him a drink of brandy to stimulate him some."

Hanson then returned home, reaching there at 12:15 noon. He called Jesse Samuelson, a neighbor, to help him bring in the hunter, and the two left at 2 PM. They returned to the spot where Hanson had built the fire and they found Roberts lying face down near the fire, which had by this time died down. Apparently Roberts had not put any fuel on it.

"We tried to give him hot coffee," Samuelson said, "and he seemed to want it all right, but he just couldn't manage to swallow it very well."

Hanson and Samuelson realized by this time that the exhausted Roberts would never reach the Hanson home on his own, so they made a stretcher from some saplings and loaded him onto it. They had carried him in this manner for one-half a mile, when Roberts died. At this point Earl Flynn, Bud Flynn,

Richard Johnson, Ted Samuelson, and Fritz Brescamp, all neighbors, arrived to help, and they carried Roberts' body back to where Iverson lay, on Miley's run. Then they marked the spot with a ladder so it would be possible for a searching party to find the bodies from the river.

"When I first found them near the run," Hanson related, "the wind was making so much noise I didn't notice a steamboat that went up, and was quite a ways past me by then. If I had seen it in time, I would have hailed it, and had them take Roberts on to Hastings for medical care."

"Another thing, if I had known that the sheriff planned to come up to Miley's run by boat, I would have kept Roberts right there and whopped up the fire. As it was, my first thought was to get him back to a warm place."

According to Mr. Hanson, it was apparent both from what Roberts said and from the position of Iverson's body that Iverson had given up without more struggle. A small piece of light canvas, used to cover the duck boat, was stretched between two saplings for shelter.

"If they had moved fifty feet farther back from the river shore" Samuelson told the Daily Republican, "they would have been snug and safe."

(Adapted from the November 13, 1940 edition of the Red Wing, MN Daily Republican by special permission of the editor.)

DRY MATCHES WOULD HAVE SAVED HIS LIFE

Had Bror Kronberg, 36-year old St. Paul man, had dry matches in his pocket when he was lost in the storm on Prairie Island, he might be alive today.

The lifeless body of Kronberg, last of the missing duck hunters who perished that day on Prairie Island, was discovered Thursday afternoon after the Monday storm, by E.V. Hanson, Prairie Island farmer who had led searching parties in that region since early Tuesday morning.

Kronberg was found lying face down, 20 feet from a haystack approximately three-fourths of a mile north of the Prairie Island Lutheran church. The lone hunter's boat was beached a few hundred feet away on the east shore of John Larson lake, three miles south of Miley's cut, where four others died in the Armistice Day blizzard.

If he had matches he could have set fire to the haystack and used it to keep warm, while the blaze would have attracted attention and brought help in time to save him from death. Nearby farmers were ready and waiting to rescue any hunters who might be lost in the storm.

A searching party comprised of E.V. Hanson, Bud Flynn, Earl Flynn, and Richard Johnson, all of Prairie Island, set out at 1 PM Thursday with the intention of locating the boat used by Kronberg since it was assumed at the time that the hunter had drowned attempting to cross North lake.

Melville Roberts, also of St. Paul, who survived the night only to die of exhaustion Tuesday morning before he could be taken to safety, told Hanson that a lone hunter had started for the Hanson place in a small boat. That was the last seen of Kronberg.

Kronberg was the best dressed of any of the dead hunters. He wore a heavy woolen shirt, a leather cap, canvas breeches, hip boots, a sheep-lined hunting vest, a canvas hunting jacket, and a University of Minnesota football parka. When his boat reached land sometime Monday night, Kronberg evidently threw off the wet parka, which was coated with nearly 30 pounds of ice. The parka lay in the boat with the ice-caked shotgun.

Kronberg evidently pulled the skiff ashore and made his way to one of three small hay stacks, several hundred feet inland. He had pulled some hay from one of the stacks, then he obviously collapsed, falling on his face 20 feet from the stack. Marks in the snow show he struggled to reach the haypile again. His knuckles were bleeding from his desperate struggle for life. Whether he had intended to build fire from the hay, or was trying to burrow in out of the icy wind, no one will ever know.

"Had Kronberg had dry matches, he could easily have set the pile afire and summoned help," E.V. Hanson said.

(Adapted from a story in the Red Wing, MN Daily Republican of November 15, 1940, by special permission of the editor.)

NORTHWEST MINNESOTA

The Red River Valley
The Lake of the Woods

BURNING EVERYTHING POSSIBLE FOR HEAT
by Lorraine Carlson
Roseau, MN

Yes, I do remember the Armistice Day storm of 1940. We were a young married couple with two daughters, aged one and two years, renting a farm about six miles northwest of Waseca. The house on this farm was large, without electricity or telephone, and we used just two rooms because our only source of heat was a cook stove.

Of course we had no warning of a storm coming, but when it started to snow my husband decided to go to Waseca for a sack of coal. Our wood supply wasn't as plentiful as it probably would have been if we had more experience in preparing for winter on our own.

As the day wore on and the storm got worse, I ran out of wood in the house. I went upstairs to the storage area and emptied all the cardboard boxes I could find, and burned them. I also burned newspapers and anything else I could find in the house. Night came and my husband was not home. The cows were bawling to be milked and fed, but I had no experience or know-how in that job. My husband had never before missed chore time.

Finally, after no more fuel was available to keep the fire going, I took the girls and crawled into bed, piling on all the quilts and blankets we had to keep warm. It was a sleepless night, wondering where my husband was and listening to the suffering cows in the barn.

Dawn came and the storm had somewhat eased, so I was able to find a little wood under the deep snow. After the house was warmed, I left my daughters alone and walked through the snowbanks, some over my waist, about a mile to the next farm to see if someone could come and milk the cows. We arrived back home about 11 AM to find the children were safe and, shortly afterward, my husband came riding home on a borrowed horse. He had run the car into a ditch just outside Waseca and had spent the night stranded with others in a nearby house.

All ended well, for us at least, after many worried hours.

A FISHERMAN'S LIFE ISN'T EASY
by Alvin Johnston
Warroad, MN

I have a very vivid memory of the 1940 Armistice day storm. I am a commercial fisherman on Lake of the Woods (ed.: on the Minnesota-Canada border). I am the third generation of my family to work as a commercial fisherman. My grandfather fished the lake with a sailboat called 'The Grizzly' in the late eighteen hundreds. I grew up in the business and learned my trade as a professional commercial fisherman. I needed all my training and experience on Armistice Day 1940 just to stay alive.

We carried on extensive fishing operations late into November each fall. Our boats were made of wood with metal sheeting to stand ice breaking. We had an enclosed cabin with a stove and we used hot water from the engine to clear the ice on the deck and windshield. On this particular day fishing had been good; we had some freezing days but they weren't too difficult. I added another man to our crew that day and so, with hopes of a good catch, we headed to our nets located about ten miles from Warroad harbor. We towed a small dory and did have some trouble with ice buildup in it. After dropping my two helpers in the dory to work the nets, I went below deck to work on a bilge pump that was giving us some trouble. When I came back on deck it was starting to blow and to snow. The snowflakes seemed as large as baseballs and, with the increasing wind, they came at us from all directions. Visibility was down to a minimum and I could barely make out the boys in the dory.

I decided then and there that this was not a simple snow flurry. By the time we had our nets pulled in the boat, large waves were smashing us around and we had zero visibility. I set my compass course for the entrance light at the harbor and we pounded into bigger and bigger waves.It was getting colder and colder and the boat, heavy with ice, could barely raise its bow for the next wave. We knew that if we were off course, or if the compass were wrong, or if my timing were off, we were in big trouble. Like magic the snow cleared for a second and there was the entrance light to the harbor.

The interesting end of this little story happened the next morning. I started up the boat to take it to the dry dock and, when I shifted into reverse to leave the dock, the propeller fell off without me moving one inch. If I had used reverse out in the lake during the storm, I would have lost the propeller and had no power. This story would not be told.

TWO FUTURE LEADERS BARELY MAKE IT
by Jarle Leirfallom
Star Prairie, WI

In 1940 I was a field representative for the Minnesota Welfare department. Since Armistice Day was just around the corner I called my long-time buddy, Paul Boe, a Lutheran minister in Fargo, and invited him to join me in a long hike into the huge wilderness area of Koochiching county. He was delighted because he too was enthusiastic about wilderness hiking.

After pouring over the Minnesota map I found an intriguing place lying in a circular area of fifty miles or more with a lake in the middle. We nicknamed it Round or Lost lake because it was so remote. We were to rendezvous at Bemidji; it was a mild fall day, so we wore light clothing, no jackets, caps, mitts or boots but took a couple of sandwiches to eat along the way.

Paul arrived and we started. A few light flakes of snow were falling but we didn't give it a thought. We drove many miles, finally found the abandoned railroad tracks we sought, and found the snow to be more worrisome. With no warning, the front wheels of the Chevrolet dropped into a hole which turned out to be the crosswise ditch of the old railroad track. We were really stuck and it was very late. The snow was coming down quite lively and it was a lot colder. We ate our sandwiches, curled up in the car as best we could and slept as well as possible until morning.

When we awakened, the wind had increased and so had the snow. Nevertheless, we decided to continue — to hike into the huge bog forest in search of our *lost* lake. Soon we were soaked; the going was very difficult but our enthusiasm didn't falter. By noon we broke out of the tangled brush, trees and heavy vegetation and stood in awe when we saw the lake. It could be likely that few people had ever found their way into this remote and treacherous spot.

But we now had to think of our long trek back to the car. It had gotten much colder and snow was coming down heavier. When we reached the car a couple of feet of snow surrounded it. We decided to investigate the nearby area. We walked on a trail that showed some old traffic, where the strong wind had blown the snow away. We realized that we were looking at a serious storm. Some distance from the car we found a rickety tractor shed with no roof or walls. Because our feet were so cold and beginning to freeze, we decided to stop for a breather but Paul insisted he had seen another shack, so we tried to find it. By now our hands, faces, ears, and, yes, even genitalia, began to turn white from the cold. We were getting very concerned and happy that this last suggestion of Paul's paid off — because we saw a cabin. Inside the cabin were many openings in the walls and floor with tongues of snow racing along the cabin floor and spewing into the room. Much to our surprise we saw what looked to be a person in an army sleeping bag lying on a wooden bunk. He did not reply or acknowledge our entrance, even though we tried to communicate. He would not talk or move. I thought about dragging him out of the bunk but Paul felt that could be dangerous. (A gun perhaps?) Rather than take any chances we started to patch up holes in the floor with old Minneapolis Star and Tribune newspapers we found there. We kept a few sheets of the paper to lie on and to cover us a bit and huddled close together to keep warm, back to back, and thus spent a miserable night trying to stay alive. After a long night, we woke up, alive and with everything hurting, but functioning reasonably well.

Very early a forest service truck came to rescue the young uncommunicative person. I might say that he slept better than he related to people. We had a very difficult time convincing them that we were not poachers. Still dubious about why we were there, they did consent to help us out of our predicament. They hauled our car back to camp, after finding it a block of ice, and apparently were convinced we weren't illegal hunters when they found no guns in the car. They fed us a breakfast which we devoured like starved animals and we finally started back to civilization.

Over the past 45 years, Paul and I have reminisced many times about our experience and realize we were very lucky.

(Editor: Mr. Leirfallom served in Minnesota government for 20 years as Commissioner of Social Welfare and later as Commissioner of the Department of Natural Resources.)

BLIZZARD HIKE NEARLY ENDS IN TRAGEDY
by Conrad Stai
Montevideo, MN

That Armistice day started like any other one as I drove my green 1931 Chevrolet sedan to the Northern Consolidated elementary school to put in another day teaching fifth and sixth grades. It was only my second year as a young teacher in the school affiliated with the Bemidji State Teachers college six miles north.

After a busy morning suddenly the three Northern buses pulled into the school yard with word to get the students ready to go home immediately. This was done hastily and the students were elated with the unexpected holiday. The other three teachers left for Bemidji and I headed for Earl Cronemiller's where I roomed and boarded.

After lunch I felt that a hike in a blizzard would be fun, something I hadn't done in a long time. Blizzards were familiar to me since as a child I had walked or skied from school district #57 near Pinewood to our rural home. I had done this many times through adverse weather and had no fear.

My gear of sheepskin coat, scarf, overshoes seemed adequate. I remember that I encountered no problems while I walked eastward. but when I turned north and was no longer protected by sheltered trees, I was greeted with a gust of wind that seemed very unusual. I tripped on a rock and flew across the road with my head down and my feet up on the road. As I lay there I wondered if I should turn back, but decided to continue.

It didn't seem that unbearable and I would turn my head occasionally to avoid the full brunt of the savage wind on my exposed face. Even though the snow was coming at me horizontally and stung my face, I still didn't realize that this was the beginning of such a major storm.

After struggling for some time I finally realized that this wasn't any place for me and that I needed to find shelter. It was now too far back over open country side to try returning and ahead only 300 yards was Jay Whiting's place;

they would surely let me inside. Now everything was white and the only way I could navigate was by zigzagging blindly backwards on that country road.

Once when I was zagging instead of zigging a car came out of the whiteness and brushed by me, making me jump and lose my balance. With the aid of the wind I sprawled once more head first into the ditch with my head buried in a snow drift. Then I decided if that car could make, so could I, so I struggled up. For a brief instance I saw Jay's house and knew it was close. I don't know how I ever made it except for the grace of God. As I came closer I could also see Ora and Ruth Whiting's driveway which was sheltered by some fir trees. Since I had acted in the Northern Community play with their daughter Dorothy, I decided to go to their place.

They took me in and warmed me with food and cups of hot coffee. We listened to the howling north wind that had stored up its anger and now hit the house so hard it shook and rattled the windows.

I think it was a week before everything came back to normal. The roads and streets of Bemidji had been blocked solidly. To add insult to injury I heard that the county plows were in the county garage for repairs.

After I heard the sad reports coming over the radio, I considered myself lucky.

NORTHEAST MINNESOTA
Voyageurs National Park
The North Shore
The Boundary Waters Canoe Area
The Mesabi and Vermilion Ranges

A LONG WEEKEND—NOV. 10-12,1940

by E. A. Anderson
Virginia, MN

We left Virginia early on Saturday morning for our usual hunting area at Vermilion river via Cusson and past Elephant Lake. *We* were the four of us who had hunted and fished together for several years. The accepted leader of our group was our high school swimming coach, L.L.Michels. *Mike* was a bear of a man, a great athlete, a man always in top physical shape and a veteran of World War I. Arthur J. Stock was our high school football and basketball coach, a big man in great physical shape. Walter Pike was an instructor in the business department of Virginia senior high school. Walt was not the physical education type and as a classroom teacher was not in top notch shape. I was a classroom teacher, the youngest of the group, and I thought I was in good condition. This trip proved me wrong and made me realize the importance of conditioning. I had a heart murmur from rheumatic fever as a teen-ager and my companions were aware of this.

Saturday was a beautiful warm day and we failed to dress as warmly as we would, had we received any warning of what lay ahead of us in the next couple of days. To my knowledge no weather people expected or reported the coming storm. I have a feeling that they studied their plummeting barometers and refused to believe what they saw. As far as I know no radio warning was given of this approaching storm which was to take 59 lives in Minnesota over the week-end. Certainly weather reporting was not the sophisticated science it is today.

We had a small two-man duck boat tied on top of Mike's Buick as we travelled north. We carried our packs, guns, sleeping bags, a large tent, a stove, cooking utensils, and food for two days. I can't resist a reflection on inflation and taxes. The four of us borrowed $20 from the Virginia Education Association Credit Union and with that bought four big game licenses for two dollars each (today that license is $16 each). We then bought most of the groceries for two week-ends with the remaining $12. We arrived at the south shore of Vermilion river, parked the car and unloaded everything. The river at this spot was about 75 feet across and the current almost non-existent. It took considerable time to cross and recross the dozen times necessary to convey four men and all the packs to the north shore. We pitched the 8 x 16 heavy canvas tent after cutting a long ridge pole. We then cut boughs for our beds, set up the air-tight stove in the tent, cut a lot of firewood and made everything comfortable for the night. Big game hunting season would start the following weekend and we planned to return to this camp. We did return two weeks later when the roads were open and we were able to travel. We then found the river frozen over and the camp in a shambles. Our ridge pole had broken under the weight of the snow and it took us a full day to get the tent, stove and supplies in usable shape again.

We arose early on November 11 to a quiet, heavy, ominous, solid grey sky with a few large snowflakes floating gently to earth. Art and I walked to the river where it plunges through a narrow gorge about a mile away. We began to feel uneasy as more snow began falling so we hurried back to camp. We arrived there about 11 AM and found Mike and Walt already starting to pack to leave. In the woods and at the camp, under the trees, we didn't realize that a heavy snowstorm was developing.

We went down to the river with our packs and guns and found several inches of slush on the surface of the quiet water. It took us several hours to make the many trips across the river. The heavy snow formed a slush which was freezing; it made it extremely difficult to move our small duck boat from shore to shore. Each time we crossed we had to cut a new channel because the pathway quickly closed behind us as we repeatedly negotiated that 75 feet of water. By the time we had completed this chore, we were already perspiring, tired, and wet. By this time snow was coming down so hard it was difficult to see and a wind was coming up with the temperature dropping rapidly. We packed our equipment in the car, left the boat, and started driving back the six miles to Elephant lake.

From there on we got in and out of the car repeatedly to push and run alongside as we busted through bigger and bigger drifts. When we reached the road around the south shore of Elephant lake we encountered real trouble. Here the wind had a sweep across several miles of the lake and as it slammed into the bluffs along that shore, the drifts were already two feet deep of hard-packed snow. At this point it was difficult to stand without holding on to the car. Fighting that damned wind while pushing that big car through the drifts helped to wear us out before our real problems began.

It took us several hours to pound our way around the bay to the regular Elephant lake road. It had already taken us five hours to traverse six miles and the storm was increasing in fury. We could and should have stayed at the small Melgeorge resort here on the lake. But we didn't do so for several reasons; we had promised to be home that evening, there was no telephone line open from here, and Walt's son had been killed in an automobile accident less than a year prior to this and we were afraid of the anxiety his wife would experience if she heard nothing from us. Also, we just didn't conceive of the developing fury of that mighty storm.

Up to this point we had the northeast wind at our backs and we decided we could walk the ten miles to Cusson. As a matter of fact, that wind was gusting to 50 mph and we expected it to help blow us forward. We even joked about putting up our coats as sails as kids do and getting help from the wind.

We left the car and packs and took only our hunting knives and a hatchet and started our trek. We hadn't gone a mile when the wind veered abruptly to the northwest and picked up intensity to gusts of 60 mph. With this change of wind direction the temperature took a nose dive into the mid teens. This put a new face on our problem.

The howling wind drove biting snow into our faces. Walking became extremely difficult because we were battling drifts waist deep interspersed with stretches of road blown clear by the fierce wind. The tendency then was to struggle through a drift with our heads down and then fall on our faces on the clear road when the drift was no longer there.

No one talked about *wind chill* in those days but it was bitterly cold.

We built six fires during that night, in hopes of getting warm and resting. We did neither. The whipping wind blew nearly all the heat away even when sitting down wind with the smoke and ashes blowing in our faces. Finding wood in the dark was also more tiring than restful.

If you would like to experience this part of our adventure I suggest you sit directly in front of a very large fan spinning at full speed. Sit close to the fan for at least ten hours, outside, when the temperature is near zero. Have someone throw snow, ice and water into the blast of air, interspersed with smoke and wood ashes. While doing this wear only light weight clothes like an old fashioned mackinaw and canvas gloves.

One fire that night I recall well. We climbed down the north bank of the old Virginia and Rainy lake railroad grade on which we were travelling to a great uprooted tree. The root network was eight feet tall and laced in all directions with great dead and dry roots. We got the fire going at the bottom and it roared up through the entire structure. Two things were wrong with it. First, the wind blew most of the heat away from us and, second, we were standing in eight inches of icy water in the large hole left by the upturned tree. I still kept thinking I was young and strong and I kept volunteering to break trail as we had to go in single file. At about 4 AM when we were two miles from Cusson and less than a mile from a shacker's cabin, I collapsed. My legs gave out and I simply crumpled flat on my face in the snow. Each time I got up and tried to walk, I caved in. Both Mike and Art slapped my face hard, intending to start my adrenalin flowing and I'm sure it was the right answer, but it didn't work. I was beyond resuscitation and even when angry and determined, my body refused to respond. I simply caved in again.

I had never heard the term *hypothermia* at that time but I expect much of our strength was draining away as that bitterly cold wind was taking its toll. In addition, the blowing snow was making us wet from head to foot as it blew down our necks and into our clothes, as we perspired and froze and struggled. Call it exposure for we had been travelling 18 hours without food or water. Up to this point there had been no buildings or shelter to protect us from the bitter 60 mph wind.

We then had to stop to build another fire and the good Lord must have been with us because we found a huge fallen tree with all of its brown leaves on it to give us a partial windbreak. This tree formed a dam for the fiercely driven snow and a huge drift formed among its branches and became a shield for us. That wild bitterly cold wind howled over our heads, forced up and over us by that tree and the drift.

Mike and Art dug a hole in the two feet of hard-packed snow and started a roaring fire. A number of dead trees in the area furnished wood. At this point I sat beside the fire, warmed up a bit, and fell fast asleep.

At this time, unknown to me, Art worried about my health and left alone and walked and crawled to the CCC camp two miles away at Cusson. On his way he stopped at a shacker's cabin and was given a cup of coffee, several eggs, and toast. That revived him enough to set out again for the last mile across the Duluth, Virginia and Rainy Lake loading yard. Bless that old shacker, long gone but not forgotten.

By this time the wind had subsided somewhat but because Art was worrying about me and my heart condition he left alone in hope of bringing help. This was an act of courage I have never seen equalled and I have always been deeply indebted to him — and now to his memory. God bless him. He made it. He struggled into the camp barely able to walk to report our situation. He went head-on into the teeth of a roaring blizzard in the black of night. The quality of this man was recognized by others. He was a member of the Virginia city council for many years and served as mayor of the city. Upon his retirement from school work the whole area honored him with a gala retirement party second to none ever held in our community. He deserved that and more.

In the meantime Walt had joined me at the fire and fell asleep. That left Mike all alone to keep bringing wood to keep the fire going. He, the oldest of our group, continued to gather wood from four to ten o'clock. That six hours must have been extremely difficult. But he did it. He kept that fire going while Walt and I slept. I'm convinced that had he not done so I would have quietly frozen to death.

I awoke about eight o'clock, feeling somewhat revived, weak but able to walk. I then began to help gather wood for the fire. By this time the wind had subsided.

At ten o'clock that morning we heard voices on the trail and we called to them. A number of boys from the CCC camp had struggled those two miles to us. Those boys were former athletes from Gilbert who knew both Art and Mike and volunteered to try to reach us. A group of southern boys had been assigned to the task of reaching us but they returned to their camp with the report that it was impossible to travel through those four-foot snowdrifts. Those northern boys were in their element and tough enough to reach us. They insisted I ride the stretcher back to camp but, with my resistance they gave up quickly. With the stretcher they could not go single file along the trail they had made to reach us. Besides, I weighed over 200 pounds. As I walked I felt better and the blood got flowing and the muscles got back into action.

When we were about four city blocks from the Duluth, Winnipeg and Pacific railroad tracks, with the camp just beyond, the doctor and several men met us. I told him I felt much better and at this point he brought out a pint bottle of gin mixed with hot water and some sugar. I took a large swig and I guarantee that I felt that drink course through my body, curl my toes, warm every inch of my body. I tingled all over and I swear I never had a better drink before or since.

We were taken to the mess hall and our frozen jackets were removed and stood up in the corner to thaw. We were brought hot coffee, bacon and eggs, and toast. In the warmth of that room, with the hot coffee, someone had to hold up my had because I kept sagging into my food. No one can imagine a fatigue so completely overwhelming. My six feet four inch body caved in like a rag doll. I ate the food and drank the hot coffee but actually fell asleep several times while eating. I had to look at the food and consciously order my hand to reach out and get it and direct it to my mouth. I had to think my muscles to do my bidding; they ceased to act on their own as is normal. When I walked across the floor of the camp, I needed help because I wasn't automatically placing one foot ahead of the other and because my knees rose high as they had all night in the deep snow.

Then they put me to bed, the doctor checked my heart, and I slept.

While I slept the camp people called our wives and told them we were fine. The next problem was getting home to Virginia. The highway was impassable, covered with drifts 10 feet deep. It took several days to open that road and rotary plows were brought in because the regular plows could not do the job.

My father-in-law was a close friend of the superintendent of this branch of the D.W. and P. railroad and learned that a train was coming south from Ranier and would go through Cusson. They stopped and took us aboard; I slept in the caboose all the way. Even the train had trouble breaking through the high drifts.

We were met by friends at the station and I was taken home where a doctor made a house call. My legs had been badly burned by my steaming wet socks by the fires, and my eyes were extremely painful from blowing wind, ashes and smoke. Eye drops helped my eyes and no ill effects remained. I slept 24 hours. I was back in school on Thursday of that week and, aside from scars on my legs, I survived in good shape.

Now 45 years later, I am the only survivor. Walter Pike died many years ago. Courage personified. Art Stock passed away several years ago. Mike passed away two days before Christmas 1984 at the age of 98 years and 11 months.

It is ironic that after all the concern these wonderful people had for me, that I should be the last surviving member. We met each year for 30 years on November 11 to relive that adventure. Now, alone, I drink a toast to all of them with a deep feeling of gratitude. Skoal! May the good Lord award each of you something very special.

ROASTED MALLARD SATISFIED OUR HUNGER
by Neil D. Beebe
Hibbing, MN

On Sunday, November 10, 1940, at 4 AM, an ordinary November day, my brother-in-law, Don, and I left for our duck hunting trip. We loaded our gear, a 17 foot rib and canvas canoe, and left from Kerr location for Deer river. It was snowing but we thought it would ease up toward daylight. By the time we reached Big Winnie near Bowens road the snow was heavier and visibility was poor. At about 5:30 AM we reached Blackduck lake, 30 miles north of Bemidji and parked near Erickson's farm road on the lake shore, put the canoe in the water, loaded our gear and shoved off for the large island, one-half mile away.

The wind was so strong by this time and the snow so heavy that the wave action rolled the snow into softball size pieces and piled these balls in layers on the water. As we neared the island we watched a canoe with two men simply blow over from the wind. They lost all their equipment but they were unharmed. By 7 AM we placed our decoys in a small sheltered bay and by 8 AM we had our limit of ducks.

By now we realized we could never get back to shore and to the car, so with my belt axe I downed a large balsam tree and constructed a leanto. We spent the better part of the day gathering firewood. The temperature kept dropping and the wind became gale force. Since it was out of the question to return, Don kept the fire going.

Hundreds of ducks tried to land on the slush and, with the spray from the waves and snow, their feathers froze dispelling any chance of flight again.

I cleaned and split a mallard duck, roasted it over the open fire and we had unseasoned duck for supper—but our hunger was satisfied. We kept warm with the backlog of birch, which kept the heat reflected into the leanto and we did get some sleep during the night.

Tuesday morning about 6:30 the temperature dropped to about 28 degrees below zero. We spotted open water in an easterly direction and decided our best chance to get off the island was to try the waves. As we paddled down the lake, huge flocks of geese and thousands of ducks flew overhead.

With the snow whiteout I thought I could see some lumber piles toward shore. We walked atop ice for 150 yards, pulled up the canoe and walked to the shore. The lumber piles turned out to be small cabins at Moose Point lodge operated by Martin Steen. A huge barking water spaniel welcomed us, so I knew people were nearby. We followed the dog through waist deep snow to the farmhouse where Martin was waiting with hot coffee and pancakes. We warmed our feet and hands by the oven door of the old wood range. Mr. Erickson, whose place we had parked nearby, called Martin to inquire about the two men on the island and to alert him of the geese heading his way. So the outside world knew that we were safe and sound.

About noontime we were able to help shovel a path to the barn to get the animals out to water. At this time there was nearly five feet of snow and some of the drifts were at least ten feet high.

After calling home to inform our families that we were okay, we settled in for the day. There was no transportation and the trains would not be running soon. The highway to Bemidji was partially open, so about 11 AM we began the mile and a half trek over the drifts to the highway. Our plan was to get to Blackduck and catch a train or bus to Bemidji. Luck was with us and we were picked up by a seed salesman from Faribault; we rode with him into Grand Rapids.

It was 6 PM and 28 degrees below zero in Grand Rapids. There was no bus transportation yet but we managed to hitch a ride to Hibbing and home. We arrived home at 6:30 PM Wednesday night where we found snow drifts as much as 14 feet deep.

The car, canoe, hunting supplies and ducks were stranded for 13 days before we could retrieve them. However, a mink had discovered our sack of ducks and had eaten the breast of a teal.

PLOW BEAT STORK IN RACE TO VIRGINIA
by Mrs. Carrie Kennedy
Erie, CO

By evening we had three feet of snow on the level and drifts many feet deep. Ray took care of the stock, carried in the wood and joked that I'd pick that night to go to the hospital to deliver. At 1 AM I had a little pain and soon the second one, so Ray went to the barn to hitch King to the sleigh. We started but King wouldn't move until a path was shovelled for him; he'd walk only as far as Ray shovelled. It was shovel and go, taking 3 1/2 hours to go one-half mile. At highway 53 we couldn't even see the road. At the neighbors, the Johnsons, I was put to bed to warm up while Ray tried to get the highway department to send out a plow. Then Ray called the doctor who told him what to do in case we couldn't make it to town. Ray argued with the doctor but a plow did come and a tavern owner three miles down the road said he would follow the plow to Johnsons and take us to town in his car. He did and we followed that plow to Virginia. Men shovelled ahead of us but I still had to walk quite a distance to the hospital. At 11 AM that morning I gave birth. Ray went home and slept the rest of that day and the next night.

WE WERE HAPPY TO GET OUT
OF THE MAHONING PIT
by Mel Philipich
Hibbing, MN

I was in the November 11, 1940 storm all day in the Mahoning pit.

It was a very bad situation and we didn't know if we were going to get out of the pit.

Finally a locomotive came down to pick up the eight of us. We were just wishing it wouldn't jump the track in all that snow. We got up to the yard and went to the parking lot to start our cars. We had five miles to go to Hibbing.

The mine provided a tractor to take us uptown. We were behind it in a line of cars. At one open spot we thought none of us would make it, but we did. It was snowing and blowing so hard the snow covered the other car tracks very fast. There were very high winds.

When we got to the edge of town we were on our own. We could get by on the main highways. Three men were stranded so we invited them to stay with us. They were coming home from the Calumet Interstate mine: they lived in Carson Lake and there was no way for them to get there.

After the storm was over, the mine sent the tractor to Hibbing so grocery stores could deliver groceries to Mahoning and to Carson Lake. In Carson Lake some women were home alone because their husbands couldn't get home, so there were few men around to shovel off the snow to the outhouse and the woodshed. No side roads were plowed in Carson Lake but we remember that the T.R. Hamre store there delivered groceries by horse and sled.

WEST CENTRAL MINNESOTA

Adams, E	Goose's Wings Two Broomhandles Wide
Arndt, WP	Found Them Locked Together Frozen
Beckers, WP	Steam Locomotives Collide Head-On
Bossenmaier, EF	How I Bagged A Canadian Snow Goose
Ellering, A	Watkins Head-On Train Wreck
Gorans, E	Saving The Poultry
Hoff, R	Only One "Blizzard Of The Century"
Lietzau, JM	The Horse And I Kept Our Cool
Luhman, BJ	We Snowplowed For 58 Hours Straight
Mitby, IL	I Made An 18-Hour House Call
Patri, AM	The Cows' Bags Had To Be Wrapped
Peterson, R	Broke Oar Trying To Finish Off Duck
Seffens, JM	Burn Anything To Keep The Baby Alive
Sellnow, R	Prisoner Of The Snow
Smith, H	You Start The Stove. I'll Milk
Tatge, M	Thanks For That Smelly Old Sheep Shed
Tatge, OL	Milking 49 Cows By Hand In Benson
Taylor, D	I Was In That Watkins Train Wreck
Waage, B	Seven Very Tough Blocks To Walk
Zaske, DW	Sheep Stuck To The Ground At Backus

GOOSE'S WINGS 2 BROOMHANDLES WIDE
by Mrs. Elmer Adams
Staples, MN

When Lee Swart arose at his farm near Staples he worried about the welfare
of a sow and her litter of three-week old pigs. The snow was then knee deep
and the sow and piglets were sheltered in a straw shack made with a pole frame
with straw blown over it. Lee wanted to put them in the barn so he made a
trail to the barn door by walking back and forth repeatedly through the snow.
However, the sow wouldn't leave her nest in the straw shed. Then Lee put a
rope around her and tried to pull her into the barn. He had previously taken
the piglets inside, carrying them one at a time, but he couldn't drag that sow
to the barn. At 225 to 250 pounds, she outweighed Lee; he finally made it with
him pulling the sow 10 feet forward and the sow backing up several feet at
a time.

During this time he was aware of multitude numbers of ducks and geese flying low through the air. They flew down to 10 feet above the ground and were
frighteningly noisy and nervous. He wanted to get his gun and shoot some of
the birds but the cattle needed to be cared for first. They were outside because
the weather had been so mild. The cows acted almost wild as they ran into the
barn, which wasn't at all normal for them.

Turtle lake was still open because it was 100 feet deep in places. This made
a good place for the birds to land which they needed to do because they
couldn't fly in that strong wind with heavy snow weighing them down. Lee got
his gun after the chores were done and crawled through the snow to get close
to the geese in the water. He emptied his gun and had one beautiful goose
wounded; Lee went to the house, got his 1/2 horsepower motor, put it on his
boat and went onto the lake to get that goose. Later he said the waves were
the highest he had ever seen on the lake where he had lived many years. He
was determined to get that bird which would be his first Canadian goose. As
he got closer he tried to put another shell into the gun but it froze so he had
to grab the goose and cut its throat with a pocketknife to finish it.

Many times Lee had chased geese for miles, sneaking through the brush to
get close. But geese, like crows, have a posted lookout to warn them. Now this
was to be his first and last goose. His hands, face and feet were almost frozen,
so much so that when he got to the house he laid on the floor and rolled in
pain, warming his hands in his hair and in water. But he had a beautiful bird
weighing 14 pounds with a wingspread two broom handles across. They ate the
goose eight days later with relatives who came for the funeral of Lee's youngest
brother who had been killed in an auto accident.

Later Lee remarked that he had never before, or since, seen a storm like that
one; never had he seen the lake black with ducks and geese. Later Lee got on
a horse, carried his gun, put a sheet over himself and tried to get close to the

geese and ducks in a slough. The horse waded to his belly in the snow but the geese got away. Lee tried making a depression in the snow and crawling along, but still couldn't get close. In a couple of days the birds gradually left.

FOUND THEM LOCKED TOGETHER, FROZEN AND OTHER STORIES

by W. P. Arndt, D.C.
Sauk Centre, MN

Early that morning my dad and I went six miles up Sauk lake to hunt ducks. The weather wasn't bad but as the day wore on the snow began falling at an alarming rate, so Dad said "Let's pull the decoys and go home."

Two flocks of snow geese had lighted on the lake so I headed the boat into the middle of the lake and the geese. Each flock was reluctant to fly and would simply swim out of the path of the boat. Each time I would raise my shotgun but Dad wouldn't let me shoot on open water. As we approached town we noticed that the lake was so saturated with snow it was just floating slush. When we got into the boat house Dad was sorry we hadn't taken those geese. We could have had a boatload.

When we were back at our house and warm, Dad became concerned about the anti-freeze in his '37 Buick. There was a garage only two blocks up Main street so we tried driving. We wound up with a small Allis Chalmers tractor pulling and several men pushing and shoveling to move that Buick just two blocks. Centre Jobbing is located at that spot today. Walking home was something else as we faced that northwest wind. We made it to the mill, out of the wind, and, after catching our breath, we walked backwards about halfway across the bridge to our point of land where the trees blocked enough wind we could stand walking face forward to our house.

After the storm we literally chopped that 16 foot boat out of the slush.

There were two ice houses within three blocks of the bridge. The ice men couldn't harvest and sell that frozen slush so they cut a five-foot wide channel to the dam and then cut two huge open fields and pushed the frozen slush slabs over the dam to get rid of them. The open water could then freeze into salable ice.

My brother in law, Dr. Lyle Johnson, was living in an apartment uptown and his next door neighbor, Ed Bartylla, wasn't home. Ed owned a big brown, shaggy Chesapeake dog who was about as ornery as they come. That dog wasn't friendly with anyone except Ed. That night, at the height of the storm, Lyle heard a noise at the back door of his apartment and there was that Chesapeake, so cold he could hardly wiggle. Lyle let him into the apartment and that dog was his friend for life. Two young brothers, driving a truck, stopped at the

Engle farm southwest of town. Mr. Engle urged them to stay at his place over-night because the storm was getting worse and they were lightly clad. They went only a short way and got stuck. They lost their way walking in the storm, following a fence line. The younger brother collapsed first; then the older brother carried him until he could go no further. My uncle, Nolan Gilbert, and some other firemen found them after the storm, locked together, frozen to death.

I've been in other blizzards but this one was the granddaddy of them all.

STEAM LOCOMOTIVES COLLIDE HEAD-ON
by Wendelin P. Beckers
Watkins, MN

This storm is etched in my memory indelibly, even to this day, because of its relative early onslaught. I can still recall vividly most of the things down to the last detail.

The day started like any typical early November morning with almost balmy breezes reaching well above freezing. Mother Nature gave no indication as to the onslaught she was about to unfurl. The serenity and calmness of the morning just caught everyone unprepared and unless you actually experienced it, it is almost impossible to relate factually. As the day wore on, though, the snowfall slowly worsened and eventually we were witnessing nature with ravag-ing fury unleashed, the likes of which I have never seen nor ever hope to see again.

Poultry, livestock and wild life succumbed by the thousands. One farmer just north of here, John Flaschenriem, had three thousand turkeys ready for Thanksgiving dinners and—you guessed it—between nine hundred and a thousand of them never made it to the table. The irony of it all was that they were supposed to have been picked up the previous day and for some reason the trucking fleet never arrived. Several farmers in this area actually lost their way from the house to the barn, seeking to tend their livestock.

The biggest tragedy in this area occured right in town in front of the Soo Line depot. The depot has long since gone but memories will always remain. Right during the height of the storm two steam locomotives ran head-on into each other. I was playing cards at the Mobil service station about a thousand yards away and the ground definitely shook when the two trains hit. The whistle on one of the locomotives partially jammed from the collision and for the rest of the day it let out the most eerie and mournful sound I have ever heard. Anyhow, as soon as we heard and felt the crash we immediately ran out-side to see what happened. We got about 50 feet away and had practically to crawl on our hands and knees to return to the service station. The force of the storm literally took your breath away. We then wrapped towels around our faces and went out to search again. Visibility wasn't more than ten feet but we finally reached the scene and saw the awful truth. In one of the engines, the engineer and fireman were dead. Some of the passengers were seriously hurt but, fortunately, all survived.

Evacuation then became our priority and as soon as enough local residents had felt their way to the scene, a human chain was formed to guide the passengers to safety. Most went to local business establishsments and some to private homes nearby. Several days after the storm subsided our weary but appreciative visitors slowly began to disperse.

Yes, I remember Armistice Day 1940. How could anyone old enough to have been there ever forget it?

HOW I BAGGED A CANADIAN SNOW GOOSE
by Eugene F. Bossenmaier
Winnipeg, Manitoba

I was with my mother and dad at our summer cabin on Lake Pulaski out of Buffalo, during the Armistice Day blizzard of 1940. We had travelled to the cabin from our St. Paul home on Friday evening, planning to return on Monday evening, the eleventh. My parents' intention was to spend a pleasant fall weekend at the lake; my sole interest was duck hunting and the possibility of encountering the northern flight that still had to pass through southern Minnesota that fall.

Sunday was a pleasant fall day at Lake Pulaski with a tremendous number of waterfowl moving through from the north. When I think back now I realize that this should have been viewed as a storm warning. At the time, however, I saw it as a potential opportunity for the hunt of my lifetime the next morning.

The wind was already strong out of the north and snow was falling when I got up in the dark on Monday morning. I was still thrilled with the prospect of an excellent hunt. My plan was to drive to Pelican lake about three miles northeast of Lake Pulaski and position myself on a duck pass. Those plans came to naught when the car stalled in a snowdrift only a quarter-mile from our cottage.

When I got back to the cottage, I woke my mother and dad, told them about the stalled car and advised them about the severity of the storm. They immediately became concerned because the cottage was not insulated and we had only a minimum quantity of food and firewood. It was obvious we were going to be there for a day or two longer than planned and also that severe winter conditions had suddenly replaced Indian Summer weather.

There were no other cottages in our subdivision occupied that weekend. The only people nearby were Mr. and Mrs. Frank Flynn, year-round residents. Mr.

Flynn knew that we two families would pull through okay, uncomfortable per-haps, but with enough food and fuel between us to avoid a real crisis. His immediate concern was for several hundred turkeys he was looking after that were penned in an open field about a quarter-mile past where I had stalled the car earlier that morning. Mr. Flynn, my dad and I decided we'd better inspect the turkey flock. What we discovered will remain etched forever in my memory. The turkeys had all drifted downwind into a corner of the pen where they had piled up several deep. It was obvious that we had a disaster on our hands and there was not much we could do about it. The turkeys were mature and heavy, and nearly dead from suffocation and exposure. Even those we managed to carry through the blizzard to a small, unheated building nearby had little chance of survival. As I recall, we finally gave up the rescue attempt and most, if not all, of the flock had to be written off. To make matters worse, insurance on the birds had ended on October 31, only a couple of weeks before they were going to be processed for Thanksgiving.

When the storm finally abated and the air cleared, Lake Pulaski was still open and had more waterfowl on it than I had ever seen before. I was able to shoot several ducks and was talked into trading two ducks for a *Canadian snow goose* that another hunter had shot in the lake. At the time I thought he was one of the finest sportsmen I had ever met. And perhaps he was. After all he did give a 16-year-old boy an opportunity to thrill his parents with a large Canadian snow goose at a modest exchange rate of only two ducks. On the other hand, did he know that the bird was actually a whistling swan? I was both saddened and embarrassed when the truth was revealed to me later by an exper-ienced friend who viewed a photograph that my proud parents had taken of the bird and me.

My experience during this blizzard left only interesting memories. Other duck hunters from our district out West Seventh street in St. Paul suffered much worse.

WATKINS HEAD-ON TRAIN WRECK
by Amanda Ellering
Minneapolis, MN

We were living in the small town of Watkins, MN, population 350, where my husband was manager of the Farmer's Coop creamery.

We had been having very mild weather and it began to rain the night before the eleventh. Farmers had their cattle out in pastures where many froze to death.

About 11:30 that Monday morning the wind changed to the north and it began to snow. By noon electricity was off, telephones were out and one couldn't see across the street.

We lived a short block from the depot, the Soo Line. John had closed the creamery and we were home.

At about 2 PM we heard the most awful crash. The house shook and we couldn't imagine what it was until the train whistles started blowing. A passenger train was heading for Minneapolis. They had called the dispatcher to say that they wanted to stop because they couldn't even see the towns. They were told to come on in as there were no other trains out. But there *was* a freight train going out. They hit head-on, right in front of the depot. Both engineers were killed. The passenger train heading for Minneapolis was carrying 22 duck hunters coming back. A few had received back injuries but most had broken noses.

The men of the town formed a chain brigade to take them to the doctor's office where, by lamp and lantern, the doctor tried to patch them up as best he could. People took blankets to the city hall and many of us took in as many people as we could handle.

By morning all we could see of our garage was the roof and it was still snowing and blowing. It was to be three days before any roads opened.

We had six children, four were home from the local school while the two oldest were being bused to a high school in Kimball. It was a trying time, just hoping they were being cared for, which they were.

I now live in a high rise in Minneapolis but every once in a while I reminisce of this event with my children all of whom live in this area.

Although my husband has passed away and I am 80 years old, I can still hear those train whistles, blowing in that storm until all the steam was exhausted.

SAVING THE POULTRY
by Esther Gorans
Glenwood, MN

I well remember the blizzard of November 11, 1940.

The first thing my husband did that morning was to move our hogs. We had about 20 hogs that were still on summer pasture with only a small straw pile for protection. This was along a creek that ran through our farm. He opened a gate and was able to chase them out to a straw shed he'd built for a temporary winter shelter. One would not follow the rest and we figured that one was lost.

A few days after the blizzard subsided, a neighbor had walked over to see if my husband, Art, would take him to town. We had horses and a sled with a double box. These neighbors were in need of fuel and other supplies. As he was walking back he found our lost hog, called my husband and together they were going to lift it over the fence. The neighbor had the tail, Art the head. As they were heaving him over the fence, the tail same off. It was frozen! The neighbor's mouth flew open when he came up with only the tail. The pig lived.

After doing the milking and feeding we had a small flock of turkeys that we saw would not survive. We were able to chase them to an open-front chicken shed but, as the day progressed, and the storm worsened, we saw the turkeys would not survive there. The snow was sticking on their heads as it swirled in through the open front. We were depending on those turkeys to pay bills, so we couldn't let them perish if we could help it.

We had laying hens in two small houses. We caught and carried those hens into the one house and then started transferring the turkeys into the one we had emptied. It was some distance between the two sheds so it was a big task. I caught them and Art carried four or five at a time against that awful wind. It took a long time and we were exhausted. There were about a hundred of them.

All this time our ten-month old son was in the house alone. We had a play-pen and an old-time baby carriage with a safety harness on it. Every couple of trips we would check on him. Once he had maneuvered himself out of the carriage and was hanging by the strap around the waist. It was a scary situation and a constant worry.

My husband had to change his clothes from the skin out three times that day, walking against that wind, with the snow blowing up his arms and into any crack or opening of his clothing.

We survived better than some, as many lost their poultry, hogs and cattle which were still out on pasture. The weather had been so nice until that weekend when the storm came up so fast.

ONLY ONE "BLIZZARD OF THE CENTURY"
by Robert Hoff
Farwell, MN.

I will try to give my recollection of the Armistice Day blizzard of 1940. I was 32 years old at that time and farming in Pope county. I am 76 years old now but anyone who lived through that storm and had to tend to full chores— cattle, pigs, chickens and horses—can truly say it was the most terrific storm of their lifetime. The old timers of those days agreed that it was without a doubt the worst storm of the century.

I remember that the day before (the 10th of November, 1940) we went about our chores as usual and it was a mild day with no portent of what was to come. Toward evening the wind turned to the northwest and it became very still. Then about evening big flakes of snow started to fall. We had about ten horses which were grazing in our pasture about a mile from home and I became concerned about them and went to get them home. By that time it was snowing very heavily but still no wind and the temperature was quite mild.

But soon the wind started to come up. This was the beginning of this terrible storm. At about one o'clock our neighbor started calling on our party line asking for help to round up his turkeys. But it was impossible for people to try and help. They would surely have perished if they had even ventured from home. He lost nearly all of his turkeys. About 2,000 birds died in that storm.

The eleventh of November dawned with a howling blizzard the likes of which we had never seen before or since. It was so intense that it felt like we wanted to smother to walk to the barn and back. There had not been any radio warning of the impending storm and many hunters perished, mostly around the Minnesota river bottoms.

I remember seeing pictures in the Minneapolis papers, pictures of ranch cattle in the Dakotas frozen standing up and huddled together. I don't remember the number of persons in our three state area who perished but it caught people not prepared for a storm of this intensity and many human lives were lost.

I recall reading a meteorologist's explanation of how a storm like this was spawned. There were three separate storm systems, one from the northeast, another system from the north and still another from the west. All these systems converged in the western states and roared across the Dakotas and Minnesota. They called it a combination that was entirely unforseeable.

The third day, November 12th, dawned bitterly cold with all the roads blocked for the next two weeks. This snow storm got its name from the date, November 11, 1940, which was called *Armistice Day*. We call that date *Veterans Day* now. It was on November 11, 1918 that World War I ended — the eleventh hour, the eleventh day, of the eleventh month, 1918.

I have heard and read during our present era from 1960 on people mentioning recent snowstorms as blizzards of the century. Well *I know* that there was only one blizzard of the century. It was November 11, 1940. So there!

THE HORSE AND I KEPT OUR COOL
by J. M. Lietzau
Cosmos, MN

Cosmos is a small town about 70 miles west of Minneapolis on state highways #7 and #4. I am 81 years old now and my wife and I still live in our own home, retired but very active.

The weather forecast for that Monday was for warm and rainy weather turning into snow and sleet. I owned and operated a local business and a farm three miles north of Cosmos. I realized after hearing the forecast that I should go to the farm to help the tenants, Mr. and Mrs. Robert Dallman, to get the 80 head of cattle, plus hogs, into shelter before the storm hit. If the weather were to be as bad as reported, we needed to get them inside for protection.

I drove there in my pickup truck and parked it about 50 feet from the dairy barn. Rob, his son, and I went to work right away, making room for the cattle in one of the barns while sheltering the hogs in a pole frame with straw piled over the top for protection.

After we had all of this done I told Rob I must start for home but he said that the weather was too bad. He suggested I might take the riding horse, particularly since my pickup was now covered and blocked in with four feet of snow. Rob insisted that if the going were too rough I should come back.

At first I went through the neighbors place, that of Erwin Nelson; it had a wooded farmstead which broke the storm and the weather didn't seem too bad. When I got to highway #4 heading south the horse and I were soon out in the open in the full blast of the storm. There was much ice mixed with the snow and when that hit it didn't feel too good. The horse would turn so her back was against the wind, refusing to face the storm. We had gone about a mile and it seemed impossible to go either ahead or backward. I had tied a scarf over my face for protection from the ice and now that it was dark decided I should lead the horse. The horse was willing to be lead.

I thought to myself, don't panic. I'll take my sweet time, keep moving and follow the hum of the telephone lines, which I could hear easily. It was rough going. Visibility was now zero with high winds and the full blast of the storm. Also I wasn't dressed very warmly. There were many drifts over the road so the horse and I had to walk slowly. I would hit a drift, stumble and fall down with my hands in the snow. I would get up and do the same thing over. The horse was very careful not to step on me as I lay in the snow. I tried to stay cool, which I did. Of course I thought many times "Are we going to make it?" Then "Yes." We walked for several hours with the constant hum of the telephone lines my guide.

The first time I had my bearings was when we were in front of the First State Bank building. There was a large snowdrift along Cosmos' main street. It was great to know we were in town. Our little town was very small at that time, 45 years ago, with open spaces between the buildings and few trees for guides.

I went on south through town to a line fence going east a quarter mile from the bank corner and followed the fence to my brother Rob's place. It was 8 PM and he and Pearle were just finishing their evening chores as I came into the barn with the horse. I asked him to care for the horse while I went back about three city blocks to my house to see how my wife and four children were. When I had left in the morning, it had been so mild I hadn't thought of fuel for the furnace, so I had been concerned about them keeping warm. When I arrived home I found them huddled around a cook stove in the basement and I asked about coal. My wife said "Yes, Levi (our oldest son of 16 years) took the sled and got some coal from your folks' place." I was greatly relieved.

In the next few days after the storm we begin to hear all of the terrible things that had happened. A number of hunters had died in the fields because they couldn't find their way back to safety. Many farmers didn't get their stock to safety and, as the storm became worse, the cattle had gone with the wind until they came against a fence. They were overcome by the snow and sleet and died right there. Many were standing frozen solidly.

A local farmer told me he was missing a few fully grown pigs. It turned out that they had made their bed against a straw stack and had become buried beneath the snow. They finally found their way out in about two weeks. They had lost a lot of weight but were okay.

I often thought about what could have happened to the horse and me if I had panicked and gotten lost. I had made up my mind on this venture to stay cool and not to plan any other route than the one I knew so well. It was obviously the thing to do.

WE SNOWPLOWED FOR 58 HOURS STRAIGHT
by Bernard J. Luhman
Howard Lake, MN

I'll never forget that storm—because I was there. I live in Wright county, Middleville township, to give you the exact location.

On the tenth the weather was heavily overcast and rather warm. A buddy wanted me to go on a duck pass on Lake Sylvia just northwest of here 25 miles but I turned him down because it looked like it would rain. I don't like duck hunting in the rain. Besides, I had all my chores to do and duck hunting started too early for me. He went ahead with some other fellows because the big flight was on.

The next morning, November 11, it was still very dark and dreary and by about 9 AM it began to snow very gently but with big flakes. Very soon it started snowing much heavier and the flakes were as big as half dollars. I remember standing in the barn door watching it fall and I could see how rapidly the ground began to be white. Within an half-hour we had two or three inches of the stuff on the ground. Then the wind started, coming from the southwest, and that caused the huge snowflakes to break up. By this time I couldn't even see my house which was 300 feet away. So I did all of my outside work for that day, knowing we were in for a very heavy snowfall.

By noon it seemed we had nearly a foot of snow, the wind was really blowing and travel would have been impossible. It got worse constantly and continued all through that night. (We had no electric lights on the farm then, which situation didn't help during a bad storm like this.)

At nine o'clock I got my flashlight and opened my front door, but it was so bad it felt as if someone threw a shovelful of snow through the partially opened door—right in my face. Actually, I was covered with snow in just the couple of seconds I stood there. I went to bed and did sleep well because I knew by morning I would have my work cut out for me just to get to the barn to do my chores.

You bet that when daylight came it was impossible to see anything but snow. I had an awful time getting out of the door of my house; I could see only the top of my scoop shovel handle. So I did a lot of shoveling just to free my door and stoop from what appeared to be four feet of snow.

Then I waded through the snow and storm up to my barns, which were very close together.

After feeding my cattle, horses and chickens and doing the milking, it was midday and I was worn out with much still to be done. But the storm raged on. It continued all day and through the night again. By the next noon there was only the blowing snow flying through the air. The wind let up a little but the temperature was falling fast too. Once again, I finally got the major chores done.

I had been expecting to be called to plow the roads, since I was one of the county plowmen. That call came about noon on this day. The plow and caterpillar tractor were located only a mile as the crow flies from my place, so I decided I'd have to walk it. I put on my storm coat and boots and started at one o'clock. That trip to the plowshed was awful; I thought I would never get there. When I did arrive I knew I wouldn't get back home that day, so my wife with three small children had to do the chores by herself.

My plowing partner, Walter Priggie, was living on the farm where the snowplow was kept, so we worked there all night through and until 3 PM the next day to get the plow attached to the cat and ready to go. We started after a quick cup of coffee and a little lunch and plowed until 3 PM the next day, nearly 24 hours. The storm was over but the snow was very deep and so wet it would freeze to the plow. At 3 PM we met the next plowing team who took over so we could back track to Walter's place to get some sleep. We had worked for 58 hours without sleep. This might be a good time to mention that we were paid 35 cents an hour in those days.

Thereafter, all three teams worked eight hour shifts for nearly two weeks to clear the roads for good winter driving. The snow depth was hard to measure but I know positively that after the snow had settled, we had at least three feet of the stuff on the ground. As I remember, we got very little snow the rest of the winter—but nobody wanted any more either.

We had another bad seige of weather in 1936 when in January and February the thermometer never got above zero for 41 consecutive days. My father kept a record of each day's temperature. I am almost sure that the average temperature would be about ten below zero—with a lot of snow too. I remember when it finally begin to warm up and the temperature reached twenty degrees (above zero, of course). Almost everyone was working in shirt sleeves so don't tell me you can't get used to very cold weather, if it stays cold.

I MADE AN 18-HOUR HOUSE CALL
by I. L. Mitby, M.D.
Minneapolis, MN

I received a telephone call at about 5 AM at my home in Aitkin; a patient of mine had started labor pains and would I come. Being half asleep and not knowing the weather conditions, I replied affirmatively.

Upon going outside I found the snow piled up about three-fourths of the way up my garage door. There was no way I could get my car out of that garage so I called my partner, Dr. Carlson, who told me I could take his car. He had chains as well as a driver for me.

We had a good 25 miles of highway going north of Aitkin on highway #169 and another seven on a county road. The arrangements were for me to drive to a small store, a distance of 25 miles north. The husband would meet me there with a team of horses and travel another six or seven miles on the county road to their home.

After I picked up my equipment at my office, we started. Travel was very difficult to say the least, driving the car in second or low gear most of the time. I was certainly glad to have a good driver. Snow was still coming down, visibility was poor and there was no other traffic. We did get to the store and the husband of the patient was there with the team hooked to a wagon with rubber tires. I put my equipment in the wagon but I started walking behind the wagon.

The horses were plowing through snow up to their abdomens and it was slow travel for those six or seven long miles. I had finished medical school and my internship a few years before this so I was young and active.

Upon arriving at their home I went into the house and there was a newly born baby to greet me. Fortunately, everything was okay. I completed the delivery and in due time was on my way home. I think the return trip was somewhat easier in spite of the continual snow.

It was 11 PM when I got home. The episode had taken from 5 AM to 11 PM but it was an experience I won't forget. Best of all, a live, healthy baby girl, plus I did something I always instruct my patients to do—get exercise.

THE COWS' BAGS HAD TO BE WRAPPED
by Aletia M. Patri
Staples, MN

I recall stories my mother-in-law had told us of the blizzard of about 1880, maybe 1888, in South Dakota. They had some terrible ones then, too.

On this particular Armistice Day we had a house full of company on our farm 8 1/2 miles southwest of Staples. On Saturday night we had gone to a dance and the next Monday my husband was plowing in the field. But, after this storm, for a week we went no place. Milk trucks, school buses and gasoline delivery trucks had not come in yet. It took the big rotary plow with a truck load of men behind it to open some places on our road.

We had no drinking cups (for cattle) in our barn. In fact, we had no REA (rural electrification) yet. We let the cows out of the barn two at a time to drink but had to put burlap bags around them so their bags (teats) wouldn't freeze. We had many laughs and giggles over that situation.

It was cold. Believe me. I remember seven guineas which froze to death roosting on the limb of a tree. My aunt and mother dressed one each day for our daily dinner. Potatoes froze in the basement. Drops of water froze on the kitchen floor. We wore boots in the kitchen all day to keep our feet warm. Thankfully, no one got sick but I'll never forget how cold it was.

To me the blizzard of March 1941 was worse because it arrived with a bang in just moments. People were caught at house parties for days, cows were unmilked, barns uncleaned. Eight people perished in the Randall-Cushing area north of Little Falls, stranded in cars and trucks. Some walked and died; two were brothers.

As an aside, speaking of weather, I must say that my most delightful Christmas gift last year was the book *Bring Warm Clothes*. I believe Dowling School for Crippled Children in Minneapolis used to be called that. My father, who was a doctor, told me that Michael Dowling, perhaps in those same 1880's, was caught in a blizzard in Dakota and took refuge in a haystack. His legs froze and were amputated. He survived to start this hospital.

Editor's note: Ms. Patri's thoughts led us to contact officials at the Michael Dowling School in Minneapolis. Part of that school's official release reads that "Dowling School is a Minneapolis public school. It is a special facility for the physically and multiply-handicapped elementary age children who cannot be accommodated in their own regular schools.

"This school is named after and in honor of Michael Dowling, a physically handicapped person himself who overcame his handicap in a very able way — (At age 14) he wanted to go into the country to say good-bye to a pony he owned (and was overtaken) by the blizzard of 1880. He fell from the wagon and his two male companions couldn't hear his cries for help in the storm. He searched for shelter; finally coming upon a woodpile, he threw sticks in various directons hoping to locate a house. He failed. A straw stack provided his shelter for the night. When morning came, he was able to reach a farm house. He was badly frozen and the doctor attending him despaired of saving his life. It was necessary to amputate both legs below the knees, the left arm below the elbow, and the fingers and part of the thumb on his right hand. The story continues to show how determined a man he was and how he overcame that severe handicap.

"Dowling received financial help for a year at Carlton college, then taught school, did odd summer jobs and became principal at Granite Falls and superintendent in Renville. He was very active in helping rehabilitate wounded soldiers returning from World War I and was instrumental in helping the Rotarians in 1919 to pass a state bill providing aid for the education of crippled children.

"When Dowling died in 1921 at age 55, the community raised $100,000 as a memorial to him. That money was put into the school that now bears his name, which was erected in 1924 on land donated by William Henry Eustis, a former mayor of Minneapolis, who was handicapped himself."

So Michael Dowling and William Eustis, two handicapped men, provided this special school for handicapped children.

BROKE OAR TRYING TO FINISH OFF DUCK
by Roger Peterson
Marshall, MN

On Armistice Day 1940 my home was in Willmar. One week before this date Charlie Remer and I were hunting pheasants about four miles south of Kandiyohi and were surprised to see hundreds of ducks at Swan lake in that area. We made up our minds then and there to keep this a secret.

Charlie worked in a grocery store with about ten other people and the secret was too much for him to keep so he let his friends know of it. Well, four of those guys wanted to come along.

On Armistice Day Charlie came to get me in his 1929 Model A Ford coupe while his friends were riding in a new Lincoln. The weather was mild and mist was falling.

We drove to Swan lake, put out our duck decoys in the bay and a few off the point. We sat there for six hours and all that showed up was one duck. Charlie's four friends couldn't stand that kind of hunting so they went home.

My thoughts were that if I got the decoys from the point and put them in the bay, to make a larger spread, we would do better. I went to get them, stepped in a run and sat down in the water up to my armpits. I got up damned fast so I didn't get too wet, other than my hip boots were full and my arms wet to the shoulders.

By the time I got back to the bay a single redhead came in and Charlie dropped it. We took the boat out to get the bird and it dived. When it came up Charlie tried to club it with his oar but broke the oar and the duck got away.

We decided to quit so we picked up the decoys and went back to shore. We sacked the decoys and put them in the trunk—and about this time it started to snow big heavy flakes. That was no time to stop hunting so we walked southeast to get to a duck pass. The ducks started coming and we started shooting. When we dropped a duck, we had to go pick it up right away or it would be covered with snow and we'd lose it. The weather was getting bad and it was harder to hit a target; we couldn't see the duck until it was right on us. Anyway, we did get our limit and went back to the car.

We loaded the gear in the trunk and tried to drive to the road. The heavy, wet snow had us nearly socked in. We didn't have tire chains but when you're nineteen years old you don't worry about that. Charlie put the car in second gear, pulled down the throttle and both of us pushed until we got to the road. We got back to Willmar about dark, not knowing how lucky we were.

BURN ANYTHING TO KEEP THE BABY ALIVE
by Mrs. J. M. Seffens
Willmar, MN

I was about 20 years old and I will never forget that storm. Many hunters were out and were caught by surprise. Many lost their lives and a lot were stranded in Willmar. It had started raining and before the day was over it was blowing and snowing so you couldn't see anything.

We were living with my folks on the farm about three miles from Willmar. We had two children, one 17 months old and the other 5 weeks. My folks had only a wood and coal space heater to heat an eight room house. The weather had been so nice that they hadn't prepared for winter—or this storm. It was a very big job to keep enough fuel inside, fuel like wood and corn cobs and even paper, to keep tha stove burning so the children would keep warm. We kept the baby in a little basket beside the stove.

My brothers and husband had to go outside in that storm to find wood, digging in the snowdrifts. We had no modern conveniences so we had to carry water about 200 feet from the well house.

The men had a lot of chores to do. They had to do them in the morning but gave them up in the evening because it was storming so bad they couldn't see.

The next day it was still storming so my husband and brothers were going to try to go to town to get some coal and other things we needed. They hitched the horses to the sleigh; they went about one mile before they had to turn around and return. Then they tried the next day, made it to town and back, but it was still bad.

When the storm was over, we had a bank of snow on the north side of our house that was about 10 feet high. You could walk up on it, it was so packed.

Some of the highways were so full of snow that when they were cleaned they had high banks and were so narrow that only one car at a time could get through.

PRISONER OF THE SNOW

by Ruth Sellnow
Staples, MN

The alarm went off at 7 AM the day after that Armistice Day. I crawled out of bed and started a fire in our Round Oak heater. My husband, Edward, had not come home from work the day before because of the raging snowstorm. I assumed he had spent the night with his folks in Staples. We lived on a farm nine miles north of this little railroad town.

I knew it was up to me to go out and milk Georgia, our one milk cow. I also had to feed and water Barney and King, our two plow horses. Knowing the storm would be deep, I bundled up well and opened the door. My God! What a shock! I couldn't get out of the door and could see only a mountain of snow. I was a prisoner of snow.

After a few moments of panic, I collected my thoughts and decided to check the windows. One window on the east side was clear at the top so, after opening it and clearing the snow, I crawled out the top. I made my way to the pump house to get a shovel after which I dug a tunnel to the door so I could get back inside.

I grabbed a pail and headed for the barn. I was a city girl and had never milked a cow in my life. I guess Georgia knew it so, to add to my frustration, she put her foot in the bucket and completely destroyed the first half of her generous gift. After that she put up with me. For the next four days the animals and I became friends.

Because the house was covered with a blanket of snow, it kept fairly warm, but also was very dark causing me to keep the Aladdin lamp burning during the day. We had no radio and no telephone so I had no means of being in touch with the outside world. I just waited — for four long days.

Toward evening of the fourth day two men with a sleigh and horses came into the yard. I was sure it was my husband who had come to rescue me. My joy was short-lived when my brother LeRoy and a neighbor climbed down from the sleigh. I was happy to be rescued but a bride of only two months and nine days wanted her husband. I cried myself to sleep that night because Edward had not come. He was working ten hours a day on the coal docks at 50 cents an hour and had decided we had to have the money. My brother, who was not working, could take care of the farm chores until the road was opened.

I returned to town the next day. Being with child at the time of the storm, I turned the tables that same winter. On March 17, 1941 we had a St. Patrick's day blizzard which was almost as bad as the Armistice Day one. I had come to my folks' home in Staples two weeks before and on St. Patrick's day gave birth to our first son, Gerald. As soon as he heard about it, Edward rode horseback the nine miles to town to be with us.

I guess the Lord was watching over us. Separated, we had survived two of the country's worst blizzards and now together with our son we realized it was all worth while.

YOU START THE STOVE. I'LL MILK
by Helen Smith
Clara City, MN

The day before the storm it rained hard where we lived. When we awoke the next morning we were having a bad snowstorm. It was very cold in the house because we didn't have our hard coal stove set up yet.

We had a three year old girl in the house and our cows had to be milked. Not thinking it was as bad as it actually was, I told my husband to stay in the house and get the stove going and I'd do the milking. But before I left the house, I told him as a joke that if I got lost "I am going to holler like hell."

When I got done milking I picked up the pails of milk and wondered if I should go from building to building or straight across the yard to the house. After walking a while I realized I didn't know where I was so I started yelling. My husband heard me. He never took time to put on his jacket or cap but yelled "Where are you?" When I answered the wind let up just enough so he heard me and came running. He took the pails from me and went too fast for me, so he had to come back for me. I was standing in front of the hen house. If I would have reached out I could have opened the door. I was that close.

THANKS FOR THAT SMELLY OLD SHEEP SHED
by Mary Tatge
Benson, MN

The evening of November 9 was very nice for Minnesota in winter time although I had to use my umbrella as I met a friend getting off the train. It was raining but we enjoyed it on a warmish night. We went to a show.

To our surprise, Sunday the 10th was white and big lazy flakes of snow were drifting down as we walked to church. This too was a beautiful sight in our Minnesota winter because it wasn't cold; we did a lot of walking after our noon meal.

Later in the day I had to go to work as the nurse for the night shift at our local hospital. By morning the weather was so bad other nurses couldn't come. The night aide and I couldn't leave so we just stayed and took care of the sick.

The day after the blizzard a young honeymooning couple from Canada was brought to the hospital. Their car had stopped in the storm and they weren't dressed for that kind of weather, but felt their only chance was to leave the car and look for help. They had walked a short distance and hit a wall. They said they were unable to breathe in that very strong wind. Holding to each other, they followed the wall and came to a door. They discovered it was a shed full of sheep. That's where they stayed until the farmer found them. Warmth from the sheep had saved them although the woman's legs were frozen quite badly. I well remember the big blisters that hung down while she was our patient. They looked like burn blisters. In a few days, they were transferred to Minneapolis where they had relatives.

They sent us a Christmas card that year to tell us they were well in Canada. They also stated they would always have a soft spot for a smelly old sheep shed, saying they thanked the Lord for providing it when they needed it most.

MILKING 49 COWS BY HAND IN BENSON
by Orville L. Tatge
Benson, MN

My father and we three sons were running a dairy farm in 1940 at two farm sites, one within Benson city limits and the other three-fourths of a mile south of town. We milked 35 cows in town and 14 at the south farm. I lived on the farm south of town with my folks, while my two brothers lived on the farm in town. However, we did the work together.

We did the milking by hand so we were up early in the morning. On the morning of the storm I was up even earlier than usual, saw that the weather was bad and awoke my father. We decided to go into town to get those cows milked first so we could get started delivering milk. We finished there at 5:30 AM and headed for the south farm to milk and do chores there.

It was bad traveling on the highway but we made it. When we turned into our own driveway it was terrible and we could see only a few feet. My father was not too well so I let him drive while I pushed and shoveled. I have been in some tough weather since but never anything quite that bad. I could hardly breathe and my eyes froze shut. My brothers did get some milk delivered but had to quit. We were so close to town that they took a sled and walked to get milk to a bakery-cafe, as well as to those families who had babies. Milk was delivered daily then and people didn't keep a supply on hand.

Besides cattle we had about 110 hogs on feed at the south farm and I had been using a wheelbarrow to haul ear corn to them about 300 feet away. After a day of blizzard weather, there was about five feet of snow where I usually went with the wheelbarrow. At first I carried the corn in five-gallon pails—but what a job! Then I put some boards on top of the snow so I could use the wheelbarrow.

We didn't lose any livestock but the storm just about tripled the work needed to take care of them. The rest of that winter was very tough on the farm. The haystacks, corn cribs, granaries, were all snowed in so it was much more work caring for the livestock.

Some farmers in this area suffered heavy losses. Many flocks of turkeys (500 to 1,500) were lost. One flock of nearly 10,000 was lost. One farmer had 96 head of fat cattle stray in the storm and 24 of them died; the others were frostbitten and in bad shape. We had an older bachelor neighbor who had Hereford cattle. On the third day of the storm we walked our driveway to look it over and there at the end of our driveway was a dead Hereford cow.

I went to the neighbor's place to tell him one of his cows was dead. He got excited and counted his herd only to find they were all there. That cow had strayed in the storm about three miles!

We had 18 horses on fall grazing but they found shelter next to some trees and were okay. Horses are tough in a storm.

My wife was a nurse at the hospital here in Benson; I did not know her at the time of the storm. Our farm adjoined the hospital and we had horses in that field. My wife and the one aide, both caught at the hospital and hence forced to continue working, heard something walking in the snow outside the building and had visions of who or what could be caught out there. They climbed on a stool to look out and there were our horses. Later, when we were first introduced, the person introducing us told her that we were the people that owned the land adjoining the hospital. The first thing she said was to tell me of that experience to which I replied "I'll bet those horses gave you the horse laugh." Anyhow, it hasn't stopped us from having 42 years of happily married life.

I WAS IN THAT WATKINS TRAIN WRECK
by Dorothy Taylor
St. Louis Park, MN

As a student at the University of Minnesota I was returning that day from my home town of Belgrade. Because of the severe cold and high winds, a friend of my father's literally picked me up and carried me the last two blocks to the Soo line depot.

The train was very late arriving but finally I was on my way back to school. There were many students and hunters on the train, with their dogs being in the baggage compartment. We could feel the train hitting something very often—which turned out to be the drifts of snow across the tracks.

However, the moment came when the *something* was not a drift but a freight train coming from the opposite direction on the same track. Needless to say there was much confusion and excitement and injuries. I was thrown from my seat and a piece of luggage from the overhead rack hit me on the head.

We were told to leave the train because of loss of heat; I was shocked to see the wreckage of the train and the injured lying on the ground. We were in the town of Watkins and people came and formed a line to guide us to the business district. The 10 rooms in the hotel were immediately taken and I was given a room in a bar-restaurant. Three of us were *guests* there for three days until the tracks were cleared and we could return to Minneapolis.

I remember learning to play pinochle at the bar and I've disliked the game ever since. Upon arriving in Minneapolis I experienced an eerie feeling when I saw how quiet the city was. So cold, so much snow, nothing moving, no street cars, no people on the street, no traffic. I still don't know where this lone taxi came from but there he was to take me back to the campus and the safety and warmth of my room.

SEVEN VERY TOUGH BLOCKS TO WALK
by Betty Waage
Morris, MN

We lived on the outskirts of town and, as the oldest of six children, I was out with my father. I was 13 and we needed to get groceries and coal for our cook-stove, which also provided heat for the kitchen and entry. It was not too unusual for dad and me to be together in cold weather; we always carried supplies and water, wood, cobs, and cared for the chickens and sometimes a hog.

But this storm was different. With the bitter cold, the wind was swirling so fast it came into our faces so we could hardly breathe; even with scarves around our faces it was difficult.

We lived about seven blocks from Main street so it wasn't too bad getting to the grocery store and the lumber yard for coal, which we carried in a gunny sack between us. We were protected by buildings for the first blocks going homeward but the full force of the wind hit us and we couldn't even tell if we were following the road. It was so terrible that we hadn't gone one-half block when my father said we had to turn back; we could see no buildings and felt lost. Then I saw a clump of lilac bushes where we had played and I knew where we were, so we pushed ahead. My father was having a hard time breathing with the wind and snow coming up into his face. Somehow we had to make it.

We had only one-half block to go and were wondering if we would ever make it when we heard a car. It was right in front of us. It was our neighbor, who asked us to get in. What a relief to be out of that awful cold. We were really worn out. He gave us a lift to our door and probably saved us. I can still remember how happy my mother was to see us. She was left at home with small children and with supplies running low. You couldn't see out the windows because snow had blown between the storms and the windows. We had no telephone and a radio that worked only some of the time.

We decided we should try to get to the chicken shed when the winds had gone down. When dad and I got there and opened the door, the snow was packed tight to the roof and there was no sign of life. Father decided to take off the side of the shed so we could at least remove the dead chickens. He took the shovel and proceeded to remove the snow when he heard a loud squawk. We cleared away snow with our hands and, believe it or not, the chickens were alive, even though packed in snow. I don't remember how many we dug out of the snow that day but we were thankful for every one that was alive.

We were thankful also that we were all alive and survived that storm. For me, it was an experience that I will never forget.

SHEEP STUCK TO THE GROUND AT BACKUS
By Dorian W. Zaske
Minneapolis, MN

It was a school holiday for me, a student in the tenth grade at Backus high school. I was living with my parents, Harry E. and Ellen R. Zaske and my sister, Jean E. Hachfeld. We were living on the south shore of Lake Wabedo in Cass county.

I was awakened that holiday morning by my dog wanting out of the house at 6 AM. When I opened the door there was approximately a yard of snow drifted in front of the door. It didn't seem very cold but I awakened the whole household because of our farm animals, which were all outside. It had been unusually warm in northern Minnesota for that time of the year. The cows and horses had no problem getting into the barn when the doors were opened for them but it was our 15 sheep that caused some problems. They were all laying on the ground, stuck to the ground and had to be broken loose to get them into the barn.

It still wasn't particularly cold but soon the wind became strong and it did turn bitterly cold. I doubt seriously that Lake Wabedo even had ice around the edge and I know positively it was not frozen yet. After it turned so cold, it snowed enormous quantities of snow. I have no recollection of the number of inches or the temperature recorded, but it was much colder than in the Twin Cities, which we thought were semi-tropical by our standards. We had electricity but the REA had only gone in the previous year and we weren't too accustomed to it so when it went out it really didn't seem such an inconvenience to us. We heated with wood and had an ample wood pile, so were not cold in the house. The lake soon froze over but it was probably a good thing it had been open at the beginning of the storm because many tons of snow went into the lake that otherwise would have been on our road.

My father was disturbed because the deer hunters would not be able to get there with the roads all blocked. He always guided deer hunters and the season started on the 15th of November in those days—regardless of the day of the week.

Our neighbor, Ralph Fenton, who lived at the intersection of our road and what is now known as county road #47, plowed for Cass county on a contract basis with a big truck he owned. He got both my dad and me to go with him and he literally used his truck as a battering ram to open the roads. He would get up speed, sail into the snow as far as he could go before being grounded to a halt, then back up, sometimes with considerable shoveling, and then repeat the whole process. We worked for days clearing the road.

As I said, I don't remember the number of inches of snow or the temperature, but I do remember that the figures for the Twin Cities seemed insignificant to us at the time.

EAST CENTRAL MINNESOTA

The St. Croix River
Mille Lacs Lake

THE GOOD PEOPLE OF MILACA
by Howard and Sophie Albright
South St. Paul, MN

We left South St. Paul Friday the 8th of November about 6 PM during a heavy rain. We were planning to do some fishing and duck hunting on Round lake, 30 miles north of Deer River.

We tried fishing but it was so cold the water froze on our lines and reels, so the men decided to hunt. The ducks were very heavy on the lake and wouldn't fly. Even when I took the boat and motor and tried to flush them, they would get up and land right behind me; they just didn't want to fly. We should have known that something was wrong but being young and inexperienced we just returned to our cabin at Martin's resort and sat around the wood-burning stove to keep warm.

We got up the next day to find snow on the ground but, sitting in a grove of jack pine, we didn't realize how bad was this storm. . .until we had started home.

As we came around Mille Lacs lake the highway was a mass of frozen ice and the left side of our car was the same. We drove mostly on the shoulder for traction. It was still snowing and we didn't know where we were until we got to the outskirts of Milaca where the road was blocked. Nobody could move. The guys took off their clothes to put on hunting clothes. The snow whipped right through their pants and was coming through the doors and windows of the car.

Just in front of us was the Peabody filling station but we couldn't see it. Two trucks were moving as many vehicles as they could. Finally they wore out, just as our car was the last to be towed in. We were put into a Chevrolet garage where we slept in cars all night. Every place in town was filled. They stopped all traffic at Milaca. Those who couldn't make it into town, walked in with the help of the townspeople who went from car to car to see that no women or children were left stranded. There wasn't any food left in town. What we had with us, we shared with others in the garage. When the town plowed itself out, the local people baked bread and brought food for us. The newspaper took a lot of pictures.

We stayed from Monday until Wednesday, awaiting the rotary plows. The road to Princeton was drifted so badly that we had to detour to St. Cloud to get home.

From this experience we learned never to travel without enough funds to keep us on top. We had to wire for money. When the lines were restored we called home to tell them we were alive.

BENEDICTINE TEACHERS AT SOBIESKI GET CHILDREN SAFELY HOME IN TIME

by Sister Elvan Drayna, O.S.B.
Saint Joseph, MN

I was missioned at a very lovely Polish community four miles southwest of Little Falls. We were three Benedictine teaching Sisters at St. Stanislaus school, Sobieski. The total St. Stanislaus parochial school enrollment averaged approximately 100 students, for which the per month teaching Sister's salary was $35. During the school year, on Saturdays for two hours, the Sisters also taught large religion classes to public school children attending surrounding district schools. The average total enrollment annually was about 125 students. For this extra service to the parish the Sisters received no stipend.

Needless to say, we were never short of work; sometimes the convent funds were low; at times we were physically very tired; but we never suffered hunger. The generous Sobieski parishioners supplied us with eggs, dressed poultry, cream, milk, butter,and sometimes sausage and meat cuts. For transportation to Little Falls and elsewhere we depended on the people's generosity.

The 1940 autumn weather was unusually mild. Monday, November 11 saw sunny skies, a mild temperature, no snow cover and a chance for the students to enjoy their paper bag or syrup lunches outside, which they did, until the school handbell summoned them for 1 PM classes.

About 2 PM a few snowflakes fell from a slight cloud cover. There were no signs of apparent danger. At 2:30 parents were knocking on my classroom door relating the radio forecast of an approaching blizzard. Acting fast, I alerted the teachers to prepare the children for a prompt dismissal, and by 3 PM all students were homeward bound, an hour early. Children whose parents weren't listening to the radio were car pooled by fine Samaritan neighbors and everyone reached home safely. We had no school buses in those days.

As time passed the rapidly approaching blizzard increased in ferocity. At 3:30 we locked the school doors and rushed homeward to the convent, bucking a heavy snowfall and strong, gusting winds. After arriving safely we listened to radio weather reports. Of course there was no television then. Later, in the evening hours, we learned that many school children had been stranded at school, particularly in the Sauk Centre area. Apparently no one had listened to the weather report in time to warn the school administrators regarding the approaching storm. We were so thankful that our parents had heard the forecasts. For three consecutive days and nights the blizzard raged and howled, creating high, hard drifts, stranding farmers trying to get to dairy barns and leaving travelers in their cars stalled on highways. On highway #10 a number of people froze to death in stalled vehicles. One must remember that in 1940 there was no interstate system and that highway #10 was a main route for northbound traffic from the Twin Cities to St. Cloud, Little Falls and Brainerd.

After the storm it took highway crews at least a week to open the main roads. At Sobieski, for a week we had no school until the roads were opened. Instead of shoveling a path to the church and school, we walked on top of the four-foot hard snowdrifts.

After the Little Falls and St. Cloud newspaper employees could return to work, those papers carried many interesting blizzard episodes and photos of stalled vehicles. I recall one of a farm family who were fine Samaritans to many stranded travelers. For three days a large group of stranded travelers survived on food (canned and otherwise) which this family provided from kitchen and basement storage shelves.

Though I am a 1984 Golden Jubilarian, I hope I'm around to read this completed book.

BIG 1924 BUICK BECAME A GOLD MINE

by Bob Duncan
Hackensack, MN

I got up at 2 AM and my buddy Rud Smith picked me up at 3 AM to go duck hunting at Coon lake near Soderville on highway #65. It was dark but nothing unusual for that time of the morning. We were both 23 years old and single. Rud drove his 1923 four-door Buick and we had a duck boat on top. Two great hunters going approximately 25 miles on a great hunt.

We arrived at the lake at approximately 4 AM and put the small duck boat in the water. We had parked in a field next to the lake: then we got our gear and guns and started for the weeds in the lake, to be ready for the dawn flights.

We got out to prepare a small blind and settled down to await daylight. It was cloudy and cold, a late fall morning.

It started to drizzle and then to freeze on the guns and the boat, the wind came up and we decided it was time to get to the car to stay dry until the rain let up. Or so we thought.

As we retreated across the open water, it was getting rough. Rud pulled and I pushed on the oars and as we looked around at the waves, we saw they were getting higher and higher. We got to the shore and realized we should leave. We were having trouble walking and getting the slippery boat onto the car. Everything was covered with ice, even the high weeds, the grass, even the ground was starting to freeze. Walking was very bad.

The next job was to get that big, heavy car up to the road. Back and forth we moved it, working down to the sand, then go some more and finally onto the sandy, icy road. It wasn't bad from the lake to highway #65 but from there on it was glazed.

We rode the right shoulder with the two right wheels at from one to ten miles per hour, taking three hours to get to Columbia Heights, where we ran out of gas a block from a staion. On the way into the cities there were many cars stalled in the ditches and even on the hills of the highway where they couldn't get traction. Finally we got to Goldner's drug on 19th and Central. We were almost home since we lived in the 18 1/2 and Jackson street area. By the time we got to Columbia Heights it had started to snow, amounting to a foot or more of the stuff by the time we reached 19th. There was ice under the snow so traction was about nil.

The storm had come up so quickly that no one was prepared. At that time, 1940, we used chains in winter. There were no snow tires or studs.

Ice on the tracks made it almost impossible for street cars to run. My girl friend had called from a dime store at 8th and Nicollet to ask if I could come down and pick up a few girls and take them home to *Nordeast* Minneapolis. Of course I had to go. Damsels in distress, you know.

All downtown stores were closing so people could go home, if they could get out of town. I had a new 1940 Plymouth so I was sure I could get through, so went downtown. It took about an hour, using side streets, alleys, round about ways to get there, then almost two hours to get back to 19th after taking a few girls home. Cars were crossways on side streets, especially on Jackson street northeast and 18 1/2 avenue because many people working at Northern Pump company on 18th avenue tried to get home. Cars were just left as people walked home or got rides with others.

The main streets were blocked by stalled vehicles. When I returned I couldn't get close to my home so I drove the car into a big drift behind the drug store where it stayed for two days before we dug it out. A delivery truck had backed into it and dented it.

Also that day there was a pileup of cars, a bus and a highway patrol car on highway #8 near New Brighton. There must have been twenty cars in that accident but luckily no serious injuries. All of those people were taken to New Brighton where they stayed a couple of days at taverns, churches and homes. We went to the accident scene about three days later. There were cars in the ditches and men were using 12 foot poles to go through drifts to locate cars. Then they'd dig to see if someone was in them. Luckily, they found no one. The cars were dug and towed, many being badly damaged, and were hauled to garages for repair.

Friends were hunting on another part of Coon lake but they (three men) stayed at an uninsulated cabin. When they couldn't free their car they walked through Soderville to the railroad tracks north of town and flagged the train as it came from Duluth. They got to Minnepolis but I don't know how they got home from downtown.

Some other friends, Art and Ralph Carlson, worked at Stephens Buick and Ralph had a 1925 four-door Buick, the largest made at that time. It had large wheels and tires and set high off the ground. They put on two sets of chains, one over the other, and went to the Nicollet hotel.They told people in the lobby they'd make a trip or two to the Lake Calhoun area and take as many as they could. For a price, of course. I believe people paid from $5 to $25 to get home. They made a couple of hundred dollars each that night and the next morning.

The people were stranded downtown, nothing running, all hotels were full and people just sat in lobbies hoping to get home somehow. Art and Ralph would make trip after trip, up sidewalks, around cars, even pushing some out of drifts so some people could get going, for which they received anything people wanted to pay. They had no set price. "Pay what you want to pay" was their motto. And people did pay. The cars in front of our house on 18 1/2 avenue NE between Jackson and Central were stacked every way imaginable. I drew a sketch of them and know there were at least 12 in that one block.

The next day some traffic started to move and the plows tried to get through the main streets. Then they worked on side streets a few days later and alleys much later. People worked together and shoveled whole alleys so they could get in and out. Neighbors were all outside helping each other. We walked around helping push many a car. Made a few bucks but not much. People weren't making much money before World War II.

TWO HUNDRED PEOPLE PACKED FOUR ROOMS
by Bernice Elwell
Hill City, MN

Six of us had come to Minnesota from North Dakota, two stopping at St. John's university, one going on to Morris. After a pleasant weekend we were assembling to return Monday in order to be at work Tuesday morning. The one at Morris decided to return by train because of weather conditions and the rest of us started for home. The Minneapolis weather bureau had taken a weekend vacation and we had no more weather information.

We left Minneapolis in a slight mist and soon were driving in icy road conditions and in snow. Ten miles from St. Cloud cars had gone off the road, were stuck crosswise in the road; travel lanes were no longer open and we had to join the stalled traffic jam. We were only a few rods from a farmhouse and able to get our car into the farm yard. There were only a few people there but by the time we left the next day about 200 people had sought refuge in that farm house.

Have you ever thought what you would do if 200 people suddenly forced themselves into your house? Some rang the telephone off the hook until it no longer worked—trying to get help or to get messages to their family. Food became a pressing need. Toilet facilities were non-existent. There was a little house outside but some people apparently didn't know about such things. They went upstairs, used jars or whatever was available, even spilling so that urine soaked the ceiling of at least one room.

The owner of the house was apparently a single male. There was not a lot of food in the house, but enough that at one point pancakes were made and everyone had a taste. Also the owner killed chickens and everyone had a taste of chicken. It was thought by some of us that he was paid for this food but an article in a St. Cloud paper stated that he received very little from the collection.

Among the crowd was a Maxwell House coffee salesman who had some candy bars which were quickly devoured. Also, he supplied coffee. A truck driver who had some fruit in his truck brought that in and offered it to the crowd. It was my understanding that people paid for each item taken. As time passed and the crowd increased, the urgent need for cigarettes caused some to say "I would pay 50 cents for a pack of cigarettes." The driver of our car had purchased some cartons in Minnesota, at a better price than he paid in North Dakota but they were in the iced-in car trunk. After tearing the insulating material around the door, he got them out and put them on a table where men were playing cards. He didn't set a price but most people put down 50 cents and said nothing. However a rumor developed that a cigarette salesman was taking advantage of the situation and charging the outrageous price of 50 cents a package. The women with whom I worked in the kitchen complained and wanted to know who he was. I wasn't very informative but told him of the furor and he set the price at 15 cents. So the rumor was countered by women who said "Oh, no, the price is fifteen not fifty cents."

Increasingly the air in the three rooms became quite foul. Although the owner lived in one room, he opened three others in order to accommodate the crowd. By 5 AM on Tuesday morning I went outside to a car which the driver kept warming up and slept. At least the air was fresh.

It was interesting that the world is so small. In addition to a car from my home town in North Dakota, there was a car of people from a town in which I had once been employed. There may have been others I didn't recognize.

Before noon on November 12 the highway department had cleared the road, but all cars wouldn't start. Two of us rode into St. Cloud and took a train to get home, missing only one day of work. The driver of our car was delayed at least another day. The two at St. Johns enjoyed the extra day of vacation, saying, "Hurrah," when they learned they wouldn't be picked up that day.

I've thought very much about what should have been done at that farmhouse. Probably a cover charge should have been set as people came to the house.

DUCKS KNOCKED HATS OFF ON LAKE MOLLY
by Walt Hepokoski
Wadena, MN

With Armistice day falling on a Monday, the double holiday made it possible for my hunting buddy, Sherm, and me to make a last effort to hunt ducks. Sunday was lackluster hunting so Monday we left Brainerd to go north to Lake Molly, a shallow lake of floating bogs which make ideal blinds.

Having just registered with Selective Service three weeks earlier, and with the duck season coming to an end, it was to be a last hurrah for a war-interruped six years. The morning hunt was excellent with bluebills and a few redheads. In early afternoon the ducks were swarming in, at times almost knocking off our caps as they whirled to our decoys. By mid-afternoon we had approached our possession limit and the high winds and whirling snow made an early exodus desirable.

A tavern stop on the way back into Brainerd was shortened as word of the intensity of the storm farther south reached us. The protection of the forested Brainerd area made the trip back relatively simple.

One of the large turkey producers north of Brainerd was the Ostenso Turkey ranch. Pete Ostenso managed the farms owned by authoress Martha Ostenso. The big turkey market in 1940 was for Thanksgiving. Pete marketed his birds before November 7 and recommended to a cousin that he do likewise. However, the cousin opted to hold, hoping for a further jump in prices. More than seventy-five percent of his flock ended frozen in drifts from this storm. The cousin had been born in Norway, spent several years as a New York City butler and had opted to try the turkey business.

The next March 15 a blizzard rivaled the Armistice day storm in our part of the state. This storm hit on a Saturday evening, in those days the night out. There were a lot of stranded people at that time too.

HOW I GOT RICH FROM THE STORM
by Al Kuehl
Minneapolis, MN

I was spending a few days at my cabin at Leech lake, Walker, and radio reports of the weather were not good. It was snowing hard on Shingabee bay but among the pine trees, the cozy cabin and fireplace, I was so comfortable I found the intensity of the storm hard to accept.

Something told me to head for home, which was at Inver Grove, 15 miles south of the Twin Cities. The going was not too bad even though it was snowing hard, but traffic was moving. As I came to open country near Little Falls, the wind and snow really hit, visibility became nearly zero and traffic slowed down. Cars were stopped on the shoulder and cars were in ditches.

I stopped to assist a car in a ditch and pulled out a couple who lived in south Minneapolis. I loaded them into my car and we headed for shelter. We found it in a railroad section house at Rice, where we stayed for two days. Highway #10 then was opened and we could proceed. I delivered the couple safely to their home in Minneapolis. The gentleman asked what he owed me and I replied something like whatever he thought was fair, since I considered it a privilege to help. He thanked me very much and gave me fifty cents. I thought "Well, whatever you put your values on."

So that's how I got rich from the blizzard. Fifty cents rich, that is.

CIGARETTE ALMOST BROKE UP FRIENDSHIP
by Phyllis LaVigne
Hopkins, MN

Albert J. LaVigne, my father-in-law, lived to be 94 years old. Each year with the approach of November 11, Grandpa told us of his experiences in the big storm of 1940.

Amid sunshsine and a warm breeze Grandpa and his good friend, Harry Cook, went for a weekend of deer hunting at Effie, Minnesota.

As they drove northward they talked and smoked their hand-rolled cigarettes; neither could abide tailor-made ones.

After a time the sun disappeared, light flakes of snow began to fall and, in a short period of time, the snow fell very rapidly and the wind blew so hard it was difficult to see.

At Milaca they decided to go no farther. The small cafe they entered was rapidly filling with other travelers, truck drivers, other hunters, and families, some with children. The worried cafe owner called the mayor asking where he could put all these guests. The mayor set up cots in the armory while women of Milaca prepared sandwiches and coffee.

By now that *beautiful day* was long gone and the snow fell heavily while the wind blew strongly.

About 10 PM both men decided to retire and at that time discovered they were out of tobacco. They finally laid down, wishing to end the day with one last cigarette.

Grandpa had been resting for about an hour when he remembered all the tobacco that had spilled in his jacket pocket. So he got his jacket and carefully scraped the tobacco and lint out of the pocket, rolled the cigarette and lit up. It was a little strange with all the debris mixed with the tobacco. He was really enjoying the smoke when Harry bounded out of bed and began calling him a no good so-and-so for holding out on him. Grandpa was able to restore order when he explained the source of the tobacco. Harry then rolled a cigarette out of his own jacket pocket leavings. He smoked it with great pleasure and both men then went happily to sleep.

They remained at Milaca for two days before roads were cleared. At last they were able to return home to St. Louis Park.

DAD'S HORN WAS LIFE-SAVING BEACON
by Gladys Muncil
Blaine, MN

That year I was a 14-year old schoolgirl still living at home on the farm, thirty miles northeast of Blaine. Our buildings were a mile from the main road with our house perched atop a rather steep hill overlooking a lake. This lake had good fishing and sometimes good duck hunting.

I don't recall what the weather was early that morning but when my dad came in from his chores for breakfast, he remarked to my mother that we were going to have some bad weather. In those days we didn't have sophisticated weather forecasting systems like today. Farmers and other outdoor people forecast weather by natural signs: cloud formations, direction of wind, sun dogs, how well sound carried, whether chimney smoke went straight up or curled toward the ground, whether there was dew on the grass in the morning, whether fog rose or settled — and they were often amazingly accurate. After breakfast dad went outside to his chores and we all went about our usual routines.

About 10:30 a car drove into our yard and out stepped two of dad's deer hunting buddies, one from each of the Twin Cities. After back-slapping greetings and some conversation they told dad they were going duck hunting on *our* lake. Dad tried to talk them out of it, pointing out the bad weather signs and the danger to them if they got caught in a snowstorm on the lake. They replied that they had come up from the Twin Cities to hunt and that they were not just going to turn around and go back, that they had hunted in bad weather before. I can still see the two of them, jolly men sitting on the front seat of the car putting on waders and telling dad he worried too much.

When my dad saw he could not dissuade them, he gave them a sturdy pair of oars and they set out to try their luck. Being good friends and having hunted at the farm before, they knew where everything was kept and would have helped themselves anyway. Dad came into the house, very unhappy over what they were doing and saying that they'd probably be up in a half hour or so. It was then about 11 AM.

At 11:30 my dad came into the house again after first going to the top of the hill to listen for their voices or the sound of the oarlocks squeaking, but heard nothing. He asked my mother if she had heard anything from them and then went about his chores again. It was now snowing heavily and the wind had picked up.

At 12 before coming in for dinner, dad again went to the top of the hill and listened. Again he heard nothing. He was visibly worried, but ate, then listened to the noon news and the farm report. He left the house again at 12:30 telling my mother if the two men hadn't come up by 1 PM he was going to try to get them up. In the thirty minutes he had been inside, the wind velocity had increased and it was snowing harder.

Dad left the house, but came back quickly saying they wouldn't be able to see shore unless they were very near it — and he was going to call them. He went to the top of the hill and started shouting their names. Then waited a bit to see if he could hear their voices or any sound from their boat. He came in almost right away, saying he didn't think they could hear him. Then he took one of his guns and a handful of cartridges and went back to the top of the hill. He fired a distress signal, a pre-arranged signal his deer hunting group used, then waited a bit to listen. He fired twice more, listening between each time. Then he brought the gun inside, saying he wasn't sure they could hear the shots or would be able to tell the direction from which they were fired, because the wind was so strong.

Next he picked up one of his musical instruments, a cornet; he played in a community band and his friends knew that. He went again to the top of the hill and played a march he often whistled which the men would associate with him. He returned almost right away saying the pitch of the wind was such that they wouldn't be able to hear the cornet. He then took another instrument, a circular alto, and returned to the hill. He played the march three times, pausing between lines to listen. After he had played it the third time, he heard their voices and the sounds of their unloading the boat. He brought the horn into the house, very relieved, and said he was going down to help them.

He met them halfway down the hill, two cold, wet, scared and very grateful men. They told dad that when they realized they should get to shore they could no longer see any shoreline. After a quick discussion they started rowing toward the direction they thought the dock would be. They didn't hear dad call, nor did they hear the shots nor the cornet. However, they did hear the horn right away and the sound was at their backs. They were rowing out toward the middle of the lake. They were very appreciative that dad had continued playing the horn, because its sound was the only guide they had to find the shore.

When they reached the top of the hill dad asked them to come in and warm up before starting back, but they declined, saying they were going back right now and hoped they'd make it. We too were concerned about this but they did reach their homes and from then on whenever they came hunting, there was much reminiscing about the Armistice day blizzard.

THE QUESTION WAS—WHERE TO DIE?
by Joyce C. Nelson
Onamia, MN

Milaca is located on highway #169—the gateway to Mille Lacs lake.

Many people from the Twin Cities had travelled north to spend the three-day weekend in their lake homes, at resorts, perhaps duck hunting. Ducks were flying and duck hunters were excited. They and their families travelled without proper winter clothing or equipment because there was no snow on the ground.

On Monday morning heavy wet snow began to fall and people decided to head back to their homes in the cities. Among them were friends who were duck hunting on Onamia lake. They started to row to shore and the slush was so thick they barely made it to shore.

Many people got as far as Milaca and could go no further. Hotels and motels were soon full.

My father, Oscar A. Dahl, was a deputy sheriff and town constable. He worked with village officials setting up cots in the Milaca armory. Cars became stuck north of Milaca on highway #169 and were backed up for five miles north of town. Dad and other men from town helped people walk into town for shelter. One lady said her husband would have to stay in the car because he had heart trouble. My father said no—that he couldn't do that—so they helped him—with eighty mile winds at their backs and heavy snow falling. They made it to the first aid station where the man had a heart attack and expired. This was the only fatality.

By morning all stalled cars north of Milaca were entirely covered with snow drifts.

Meanwhile every available place in Milaca was filled with people who could go no further. Stores were sold out of overshoes. Telephone lines were jammed with people trying to locate missing relatives. School buses were stalled at a farm home southeast of town; the children stayed all night and the next day. The lady of the house ran out of food and began to bake bread to feed them.

When I awoke the next morning snow had drifted over the top of our front door.

I'LL NEVER FORGET WHAT MY FATHER DID
by Gerald T. Nordstrom
Minneapolis, MN

I was only seven years old and in the second grade but the day stands out clearly in my memory. It began unusually—I got a ride to school. I nearly always walked the two miles by road or one mile across the fields and pastures to the Mille Lacs county school. My father had attended before me. It had always been assumed that if dad had walked to and from school every day, I could do the same. It seemed logical enough.

But now it was 1940, not 1914, and things were different. Not only did the family own a car, we also had new neighbors who didn't acquiesce to my father's assumption. They didn't want to send their eight-year old into the cold, stopping in, as I often did, at Aarseth's to warm himself after that half-mile into the northwest wind. So, unwillingly, but to be neighborly, my father agreed to take turns, interrupting his chores every other morning, to take us to school. After school we were on our own to get home.

On this morning, as we rode along the narrow gravel road toward school, it was unusually dark with heavy clouds hanging low over the empty fields. It wasn't particularly cold and there wasn't any wind, but the air had a sort of heaviness. Something was brewing. Rain? Snow? At this time of the year there was no telling and in 1940 no predictions to be trusted.

Some families must have foreseen the worst and kept their children home because the school was emptier than usual. There were never more than a couple of dozen kids present.

With windows on one side only, and no electricity, much of the room was still rather dark at 9 AM when Miss Selma Olson rang the *dinner* bell on her desk.

But then it began to snow and as the schoolyard became white it reflected light through the large windows onto the ceiling, giving the room a kind of brightness not seen since the previous winter. And, as on any day of the first snow, everyone found it necessary to use the pencil sharpener frequently — it being on a window sill.

Soon the wind began to increase and everything outside the window became obscured in a blur of white.

Lunch time came and we opened our dinner buckets as usual but we were easily convinced to play indoors afterwards. The wind, whistling around the corners, excited and subdued us. The teacher's glances toward the window became more frequent. Not long after Miss Olson's bell called us back to our studies, there was a stamping on the porch and the door opened. It was Ed Hansen, the school's nearest neighbor, standing there covered with snow. He was apologetic about interrupting school but he thought we should call off school and, because the storm was getting so bad, no one should try to get home but should come to his place for the night. He had telephoned whomever he could so the families wouldn't worry. He particularly told me that my dad had called, asking if we might stay with the Hansens because he couldn't come get us.

This latter message mystified me because neither we nor our new neighbors had a telephone. Later I learned that Dad had walked to Aarseth's, the closest farm having a phone. It had to have been the longest half-mile he had ever traveled, staggering into a blinding wind wo strong that he couln't face it. If he walked backwards he stumbled over the drifts,; the wind sucked his very breath away as if to suffocate him in a vacuum. There were times, he said, that he wondered if he would ever make it. He hold it only as phenomenon of the storm but we know that he had risked his life for us.

Miss Olson told Ed that she had considered dismissing school but was concerned about sending us home in such a storm: his invitation was no doubt the best solution. Perhaps, she said, we should finish the school day and then take him up on his generous offer. No, he said, it would be better if we came with him now.

Before she could disagree we were heading for the cloak room and, as soon as the dampers on the stove were closed, the drinking fountain drained and buckets emptied, we were out the door.

Two of the bigger boys insisted on going home.One lived only a third of a mile away but the other was a good mile away. Because he couldn't telephone his parents and he didn't want them to worry or to try coming after him, there was no dissuading him. We watched nervously as they disappeared in the haze. Miraculously, they both made it home safely.

The rest of us started to cross the small field between the school and the Hansen farmhouse. The snow wasn't particularly deep but the ground appeared to be moving before us as the wind-whipped drifts formed behind every weed and straggling corn stalk. I recall vividly how nonplussed I was that the simple act of walking across a field should be so difficult. Why was it so hard? I glanced behind to see the others struggling also. Miss Olson said something encouraging but her words were lost in the wind.

When at last we arrived, we were welcomed by Mrs. Hansen and her parents who shared the house. One could see they were relieved that we had made it safely but detectable also was a feeling of uncertainty. Now what? While the adults worked out the logistics of feeding and bedding us, Jeanne and Warren Hansen, our schoolmates and now junior hosts for the night, proceeded to entertain us. They enthusiastically brought out their favorite games and soon a party atmosphere took over.

As daylight disappeared, however, reality again began to intrude. The Hansens were among those fortunate enough to have electricity on their farm — but not tonight — and their reserve supply of kerosene lamps was small, not enough to provide light for the various activities throughout the house. After supper there was little for us to do and lamps were carried from room to room as makeshift beds were prepared.

The house was difficult to keep warm but, once between the blankets in that bed made of chairs I was warm and comfortable physically. The angry wind rumbled loudly overhead, roaring ominously, thwarted by the creaking walls that kept us safe. But were we safe? Were my mom and dad safe? Was my dog, Browney, safe atop the straw stack where he chose to sleep, regardless of the weather?

I wasn't the only one for whom this was the first night spent away from home. Mixed with the wind's howling and hissing were the sounds of muffled sniffling from across the room. Mrs. Hansen and Miss Olson made rounds, comforting frightened and homesick children caught in this storm of the century.

In the morning we awoke to a day of dazzling brightness. The world was white and the sun beamed through the air, cold, crisp and clean. The wind was down and the house was warm. There was the smell of bacon and eggs in the air—and there was no school! Games and storybooks took up the morning until Mrs. Hansen reported that someone was coming down the road. We all dashed to the window to see who was challenging roads so drifted. Through the deep snow came two not quite matching dappled grays, Jack and Dick, and behind them my father's old bobsled with him bundled up almost beyond recognition.

Mittens, coats, caps and buckle overshoes were quickly sorted out and everyone living in our direction made a dash for the sled, hurrying to find a good place among the blankets and straw. I aimed for my grandfather's ancient buffalo robe.

My father headed the team toward home but it wasn't the same country we had seen yesterday. The way couldn't have appeared more changed. Where the road had been open yesterday and the fields brown and bare, there were now wildly-sculpted, wind-hardened drifts of ridged snow. It was beautiful but other-worldly. The horses had to work hard to pull us along the tracks they had already struggled to make.

I don't remember how many days went by before the roads were plowed and school resumed but I do recall feeling very fortunate when stories reached us of the many people and animals that had lost their lives. And I'll never forget the ends to which my father went to provide for my safety—and transportation.

FLICKERING LIGHT IN WALL OF GRAY HELPED HIM TO SURVIVE
by Linda Norlander*
Mora, MN

Wally and Vera have treated me like a daughter since I married their son. They have a very special relationship that has held them together for over 45 years.

On that Monday morning, 28-year old Wally watched the early morning drizzle before he drove to Bock to pick up supplies. Back home he did some

*Adapted from a story by Linda Norlander, as it appeared in the November 12, 1983 edition of the Minneapolis Star and Tribune.

chores and worried about finishing the plowing. He worried about his young cattle which were pastured at his folks' farm, two miles away — down impassable roads. Assuring Vera that he could make it, he started for the other farm, reaching it and herding the cattle into the barn. He was wet, tired and concerned about getting back to his wife and son. The cold wind had turned into a steady blast and the temperature was near zero.

After a quick cup of coffee with his parents, he donned his heavy sheepskin coat and started home. When he looked back at the farm lights all he saw was a wall of white and gray. Soon he could no longer see the road, only the fence posts telling him he was on course. He gradually lost his bearings, looked for landmarks but saw nothing but snow.

Losing track of time, he plunged through the wet, sticky snow up to his knees, then up to his thighs. He strained to see farmhouse lights through the darkness, but saw nothing. He cursed the burden of his heavy coat weighing him down. He was overwhelmed with a need to stop and lie down, if only momentarily; perhaps a little sleep would help him regain his strength. Then he remembered hearing of people doing that and never waking up; picturing his warm house, his wife and son waiting, he redoubled his efforts and trudged on. Dimly at first he saw the light flickering through the snow. He closed his eyes, opened them, and it was gone. Then, as the wind died for a second, it returned. He stumbled on. He was home.

Vera stood at the door shaking with relief. He stepped into the bright warmth of the kitchen, took off his hat and mittens and sank to the floor, still wearing the sheepskin coat.

Wally lived to tell his story to his children and grandchildren.

MAROONED 30 HOURS WATCHING CATTLE DIE
by Evelyn M. Olson
Ogilvie, MN

The alarm was ringing at 6:30 AM that Armistice Day, 1940, and my first reaction was why did I set it? As a teacher in a rural school that observed this holiday, why had I set the alarm? Then I remembered.

My brother, who was attending St. Cloud State teacher's college, had been home for the weekend. He usually returned on the train but because of my having the day off, had persuaded me to drive him back to school. St. Cloud is 40 miles west of Ogilvie and Ogilvie is 60 miles north of Minneapolis.

The day was gray and gloomy but, although it had been raining Sunday evening, it was still quite warm. There was no indication of what was to come. Because of our hurry to get started, we didn't take the time to listen to the radio weather forecast.

Our mother wanted to go with us and our trip to St. Cloud was uneventful, arriving during a little snowfall. My brother learned of the impending bad weather from a professor who advised him to accompany us home and to leave immediately. We started homeward but, even in that short time, it had become increasingly bad. We decided to take the chance and left for Ogilvie.

We had gone only about three miles when we got stuck in a snowdrift, at which time we decided to walk to a farmhouse we believed to be nearby. Because of the blowing snow and difficulty in walking, my mother soon collapsed and we retraced our steps to the car. We had barely climbed in the car when a larger car stopped. In it were three men, one of whom was a doctor from Foley trying to return home from the St. Cloud hospital. Since there was no chance of getting my car from the snow they encouraged us to get in their car, which was newer and warmer.

We had gone about a mile when we were stuck again; the storm showed no signs of abating; in fact, the wind was increasing and it was getting colder. Luckily, we were all dressed warmly and the doctor had a tank full of gasoline. At one time he tried to get a heavy robe from the trunk but the lock was frozen. He decided to run the motor 15 minutes and shut it off 45 minutes of each hour.

Before starting home from St. Cloud, my brother had hurriedly put a razor blade in his pocket to help clean the windshield. Just before the doctor arrived, he had put his hand into that pocket and cut off a fingertip, so we were most fortunate to have a physician to attend to it.

By noon we realized we were going to be snowbound for some time. All traffic had ceased. We talked and got acquainted but never felt any need for food or water. We just sat talking, or staring out the window at the blowing snow. We felt as if we were in an isolated part of the world, especially when we heard over the radio that people were concerned as to the whereabouts of the doctor — and he had no way of informing them.

It grew dark early because of the storm. We were able to keep fairly warm with the heater running as discussed plus the body heat of six people We dozed a bit, listened to the monotonous howling of the wind, tried to keep up our spirits.

Finally morning came with its dull gray light. There was some gasoline left but we were beginning to wonder how long the storm would last. Beside the road was a fence behind which stood cattle with their eyes frozen shut. Blood was streaming from some of their throats as they tried blindly to get through the wires. We had to sit there helplessly and watch some of them collapse and die. It was so very pitiful!

Time went slowly. The wind and snow's intensity had decreased somewhat but the cold was worse.

Noon came but only the restless, bawling cattle disturbed our lonely world. We continued dozing or making small talk. Strangers a few hours ago, we now felt a bond of friendship — and a desire to survive.

We waited and waited. The fuel supply was getting low. Then we heard a noise like a machine of some sort. Maybe help was on the way. But then the sound disappeared until about five o'clock when a snowplow finally reached us. When they had reached my car, they found another one which contained a young couple in such serious condition that they had rushed them to the hospital.

The drivers recognized the physician and got word to his family. They also arranged for the three of us to return to St. Cloud where we stayed with friends; the others went ahead to Foley.

After a wrecker had towed my car to a garage, it took two days to chisel out the snow and to get it running. I'm sure we wouldn't have lived had we remained in my car.

Every Armistice Day for a few years my mother would write a thank-you note to that wonderful doctor. In his first reply he wrote that after an experience like that he would never spend another winter in Minnesota.

It's hard to realize we had spent 30 hours out of touch with the world and at the mercy of the elements. Never once did anyone show signs of panic. There were prayers being said and they must have been heard and answered. We were a fortunate group of six who made it. Many were not as lucky as we were.

I am now retired, having spent 35 years as a rural teacher and 10 in the Ogilvie school system. My brother, Ronald, is also retired; he spent 37 years as a teacher.

WILDEST MINNESOTA BLIZZARD EVER SEEN
by William Patenaude
Elk River, MN

My memories go back to a warm Sunday afternoon of November 10, 1940, the day before that bad Monday, which brought the worst snowstorm I have ever seen in all my 69 years. I was a young man of 26, living in Elk River. I had seen some bad snowstorms and a lot of bad winter roads, but none were ever so bad, or came with such devastation. This nice afternoon my brother and I had cut up a lot of wood. I had my sleeves rolled up and received a slight sunburn. The grass was still green with temperature in the forties. There had been no snow yet that fall.

I had taken a temporary job in Big Lake, ten miles from my home, to help an electrical contractor who needed someone with a Minnesota master electrician license, which I had. Monday was a holiday but they had lots of work so I decided to go to Big Lake.

The weather was still nice when I left a 7:30 AM that Monday morning. It was about 35 degrees, with no ice or snow on the grass. It looked a little like it might rain. Three of us were rewiring a large older house and were all work-

ing in the basement. We couldn't see outside but did hear lots of wind. At 11
AM one of the others went outside for something from the truck, returning to
say we had about a foot of snow on the ground and he thought we should go
back to the electric shop. When we tried we found that a V-8 Ford with snow
tires couldn't get us out of the yard, because the snow was so wet and heavy.
We wrapped the tires and wheels with some large wire to act as chains to get
us a half block to highway #10 and three more blocks to the electric shop.
Streets were already almost impassable and cars were stuck everywhere.

Two of us went into the shop to eat our lunches while the third, the man
with the truck, started for home a mile away. When he hadn't come back by
2:30 I decided to leave for home at Elk River. When I went to my car it was
completely covered with snow, including the roof. I began shovelling it out
which took about an hour because it was still snowing and blowing. My almost
new 1938 Pontiac with new Goodyear snow tires couldn't get me out into the
street, but a young farmer with a new Chevrolet with snow tires and chains
helped me do so. I then put on my chains and headed toward Elk River. I was
driving through a foot of snow on the level and lots of drifts of three feet on
the highway.

I had gone about a mile and a half from Big Lake when I plowed into a drift
so deep I couldn't even open the doors; I had to crawl out the window. I was
a strong man at age 26 but that wind was so strong I could barely stand
and walk.

I headed back toward Big Lake walking and sometimes crawling on all fours.
I didn't have overshoes but luck was with me because the wind was mostly at
my back, coming from the east and north. As I walked, I could see cars, trucks,
semi-trucks and oil semis everywhere in the ditches and some out in the fields
where they had been blown by that fierce wind. Several vehicles had people
in them; there was no way I could help them, nor they me. Some people were
crowding into a small house and the Elk River bakery truck was stalled nearby.
People were carrying in bread and rolls to eat. The house was full with no room
even to stand so I kept going. When I did get to the shop I was too weak to
open the big door. Someone opened it and helped me in. It was 4:30 PM,
getting dark, and people were walking around all over town talking about the
storm and their cars being stuck somewhere.

At 5 PM the electricity went off all over town, just as I was trying to call my
folks in Elk River. I succeeded, a good thing because within an hour every
phone out of Big Lake was down. To keep my family safe my father went to
my house and took my wife and young son back home with them. He then
went back and forth to my house to keep the coal furnace going.

That wind was so strong at our place that it blew fine snow through new windows. There was an inch of snow on the floor as far as three feet from the windows. My wife had taped paper over some windows to keep out the snow.

That evening I was still in Big Lake and three of us went to a grocery store for some food, which they had begun to ration. I remember we did get a half pound of butter, one half loaf of bread and a few canned goods. The stores were short of food because they were overrun by about 200 people who were gathered in the railroad depot plus another 300 in the schoolhouse, which you could say had no food at all.

At about 6 PM we heard that a school bus loaded with children was lost in the storm a mile or more from Big Lake. Local men put together two teams of horses and four men who hooked up a big bobsled with a large box filled with hay. They went looking for the bus. Later they came walking back into town, having left the bobsled in a huge drift somewhere. However, they had heard that the children had walked to a nearby farmhouse and were safe. These men could barely walk from exhaustion. They were holding to the horses reins and harnesses to keep from falling. Had the horses been unable to find their way back, they would surely have perished. Several of us slept in the funeral parlor for two nights. It was a brick building with good heat, but no beds.

The next morning it was eight degrees below zero, there was lots of snow and the big V-plows on road maintainers were trying to clear the roads. These maintainers plowed out from town until they came to a vehicle blocking their way. They would hook to the vehicle and back up into Big Lake pulling the vehicle along. My car came into town that way the next day. There was a solid block of ice in the air-breather intake and snow everywhere.

After some warming up it finally did start but didn't run too well. I then started for Elk River on highway #10. It was slow going, only a single track road with only a very few places where I could pass an oncoming car. I passed dozens of stalled vehicles. The streets of Elk River were just big drifts, not yet plowed. People were shovelling everywhere. I finally got to my family and we moved back home.

I know that we were some of the luckier ones because we suffered no great losses or lasting effects. We saw probably the wildest blizzard ever seen in central Minnesota this century. It will stay in our memories as a storm that was unbelievable—but it did happen.

DAD COULDN'T SEE BUT
THE HORSE BROUGHT HIM HOME

by James Rocheford
Willmar, MN

My dad was a dairy farmer eight miles west of Princeton; I was nine years old.

The day the storm started, we were in town getting our weekly supplies of groceries. On the way home when we were still two miles from the farm, we got stuck in a drift. It was near the farm of a Mr. Crossman. He hitched up his team of horses and sat on the fender of our '34 Chevrolet and pulled us the two miles home. Then he rode one of his horses home.

It was very cold already and getting worse as the night wore on.

The next day in the height of the storm we could barely see from the house to the barn or to the other farm buildings. My father was very concerned about some young stock that was not in the barn — or even in the yard. He decided to ride one of his plow horses and to go looking for these young heifers. He put on a lot of clothes with a scarf over his face so only his eyes were showing. My mother didn't want him to go because it was so bad outside but he insisted and went anyway.

We stayed in the barn and watched through the window. It was blowing so hard we sometimes could not see more than ten feet. We couldn't see where the lane fence started. He was gone for so long that we thought for certain that he had fallen from the horse and could not get home, but after two hours we saw the horse coming with him on it. We opened the barn door and the horse came in. My dad just fell off the horse and the scarf on his face was solid ice up to his cap. He could see nothing, couldn't see where he was going, but the horse was good enough to bring him home. He never did get the calves home but they were in the brush, mostly covered with snow. Three days later he did get them home safely.

One of our neighbors was not so lucky. He went out to locate his prize team of horses and three days later they found his body draped over a fence. The horses survived but he did not.

The day after the storm we dug out the snow in the farm yard where it was almost four feet deep everywhere. It took quite a few days of shoveling by hand since we didn't have plows like we have today.

We lived through this storm, including my dad who is now 84 years old.

WORKING ON THE HIGHLINE CREW
by Warren Sylvester
Amery, WI

At one time there was a contracting firm in St. Paul named L. A. Bumgardner
& Company who built railroads and highways. In the late thirties, when the
Rural Electrification Act (REA) came into being, this firm converted their operations to constructing power lines. Since I had worked for them on construction, I worked for them on four different high line jobs.

They had a job in Elk River with their equipment in the fairground barns
on the west side of town, down by the river. They moved in two of their camps,
one for an office and the other for a bunkhouse for any of the crew who would
like to use it. It was on wheels and could be moved easily. It was equipped with
a stove, upper and lower bunks and lots of good blankets. Cris Larson, their
shovel operator, and I stayed there and boarded with a Mrs. George Hamlet
about two blocks away.

Sunday morning two lads from Sleepy Eye, Whitey Huvensburger and Rod
Gentz, asked me to take them five miles in the country to get some hazel nuts.
We got two sacks of nuts and came back to put the pickup away. It was a mild
but rainy day.

The next morning when we went to breakfast it was snowing pretty hard.
After breakfast it became worse; we were ready to go to work but Sidney Bumgardner felt we should not. It got worse all day. Harold Gush and Gordon
Johnson came down from Zimmerman to go to work but I suggested they call
their folks to tell them they were going to stay in camp that night. It was
getting too bad to travel.

We didn't have any fuel so we took a broken cedar power line pole into the
camp, used a frameing jack and a trimming saw to make wood we could burn.
Louie and Sidney stayed the night with relatives in Elk River.

The next morning there was a huge snowdrift in the camp. The snow had
blown under the door. I got up and built a fire. We got the snow shovelled
out and were quite comfortable after a while. However, the door to the office
had blown open and it was packed with snow. I never saw such a mess. The
wind let up a little in the afternoon so I had a chance to get to the lumberyard
and bring back two packages of coal.

The next day the snow had gone down so the whole crew, armed with shovels
of all kind, shovelled for two blocks to get up to the street. The next day I went
to town to get a new pair of boots. One of the crew was there grumbling because the roads weren't open. He didn't like paying for board and not working.

About that time a man with four horses hitched to a sled came down the
street with about a half ton of coal. I asked him how the road was and he
replied "What road?" He said he went right over the top of the roads, over

fields and fences. The horses never break through. He said the snow is so hard you can hardly break it with a shovel.

Lots of bad events were occurring. A highway crew plowing with a big 60 Cat between Elk River and Big Lake hit something hard. They shovelled out a new Chevrolet coupe with a school teacher frozen to death inside.

Lawrence Olmsted from Cornell, Wisonsin, hauled poles and had gone to Hayward to haul logs for the winter. After the blizzard we couldn't find the poles and Sidney drove to Hayward to bring him back to help locate the poles. Lawrence would drive a ground rod into the snow and hit the pole every time. They would mark the spot with a lath and a piece of red cloth. He located all of those poles in two days.

Harold Giesh and I were frameing poles. We had to dig where the mark was, get a chain hooked on, and pull out the pole.That was one of the worst jobs I ever had.

Although it's been 45 years, I can still make a list of those men with whom I worked on that job. They were good hard-working men.

7-COUNTY METRO AREA
The Twin Cities And Suburbs

Anderson, BG	The Women Canned 200 Jars of Turkey
Aubrecht, J	The Paper Boy And His Pony
Bartlet, M	His Clothing Just Stood There On Its Own
Berge, J	Alone, Pregnant And No Fire
Bernier, L	Old Herman And The AR-MIS-TIK Day Blizzard
Bren, RJ	Needed 8-Foot Probe To Find Pickup
Burton, NS	Captives At The King Kole Hotel
Carlson, KA	I Laid Down To Sleep — In The Street
Cates, E	They Couldn't Get The Body To Town
Caverly, L	Our Duck Blind On The Mississippi
Creapo, PS	Cocky-Leeky Soup At The Ryan Hotel
Culbert, E	Nasturtiums Unharmed By Snowdrift
Daniel, GL	Free Pepsi-Cola
DeHaven, B	Bob De Haven On Weather Reporting
DeMaster, JW	I Worried About Vern And Mitch
Dittmar, A	Cream of Sauerkraut Soup! Ugh!
Earley, OO	No Hanky-Panky!
Enersen, B	Crawling Home From Work
Fenlason, MA	You Can't Go Out — You'll Get Lost
Foss, ME	Lady Bunked Overnight In Hennepin County Jail
Fretag, M	Red Hot Stove Danced Around
Fritz, S	I Started To Cry, Thinking I'd Never Make It
Gregg, MJ	Flying Cloud To Shakopee Packed Cars
Groess, C & V	Young Charles Jr. Help De-ice Cattle
Hanson, D	Gaiety Theater Free Burlesque Show
Hayes, RW	A Fraternity Man's Point Of View
Hegg, J	Jimmy Hegg's Famous Snow Removal Sign
Henkel, DF	Waves of Millions Of Waterfowl
Heryla, J	I'm 78 — No Storm Like That One
Hoeft, LH	Didn't Find The Pail Until Spring
Hull, WS	Bourbon For Half-Frozen Accountant
Jacobsen, L	My Husband And I Were Duck Hunters
Johnson, B	One-Eyed Man Drove 20 Miles At Height Of Storm
Johnson, ZA	Was I Freezing To Death?
Jorgensen, HM	Pounding And Screaming At The Door
Keller, R	Brought Baby Home In Thirty Below Temperature

THE WOMEN CANNED 200 JARS OF TURKEY
by Benjamin G. Anderson
Chaska, MN

At that time our family lived on a farm about 30 miles west of Minneapolis. It looked rather blustery so we felt the men should go to Waconia for supplies. We didn't dally because the wind was whipping across the lake and the road. We just made it back home.

Our family was raising about 60 turkeys which were in the northwest corner of the woods about three-quarters of a mile from the house. There were roosts for them and we also nailed boards on the north and west sides for their protection. To protect ourselves we took along scoop shovels to hold before our faces.

As the day wore on, the weather got worse. We were glad to get the chores done and to get a good night's sleep. The next morning, after milking chores, we went to see how, or if, the turkeys were faring. A couple had flown into some trees 25 feet high. My brother saw the tail of one bird sticking out of the snow and said "Well, there's one gone". He grabbed it by the tail and it flapped its wings; to our surprise, it was okay. It had been insulated by the snow! On the roost, all we could see was snow instead of turkeys. We poked around in the snow, and heads popped uip like jack-in-the-boxes. All but a few were saved.

How to get them home? An old Ford truck with a cattle box did the trick. We followed a dead furrow to the turkey area, loaded them in without too much trouble, then to our chicken house which was 40 feet long and divided. The chickens were moved to the far section and the turkeys put in the near part.

It was time for chores again which we finished about 11 PM. Then it was time to try to help our neighbors, the Selby Petersons. Their turkey roosts were exposed to the northwest wind. We arrived about midnight and they had gone to bed, tired from working with 1500 birds. However, they got up and we did help them. We put the turkeys in the cow barn, above the hog barn in the horse barn, in the hay barn. Back home and to bed about 3 AM.

Petersons had lots of birds frozen solid. The women canned 200 jars of breasts and thighs in two-quart jars. There were lots of parts for creamed turkey, stew, soups, etc. I don't recall that they did it, but there were many turkeys sold frozen to city people for 25 cents each.

The next day one old turkey gobbler was spotted strutting around and Mr. Peterson butchered him. He weghed 27 pounds dressed. He was then sent to the governor of the state as a gift. I believe it was Governor Stassen.

THE PAPER BOY AND HIS PONY
by Jim Aubrecht
Richfield, MN

I was Little Jimmy Aubrecht, a seven year old lad living in Richfield back in 1940—and I had the world by the tail. Literally, because I had a pony which I kept in the back yard barn and for which I was the envy of all the other lads. After all, it was then, and is today, a big thrill to have a pony all your own. I not only had a saddle so I could ride the pony, I had both a cart and a sleigh so I could use that pony three ways.

We were lucky to be able to keep that pony, even though Richfield wasn't built up as it is today. Anyhow, I supplied horse manure to the gardeners on each side of us and they didn't seem to have any problem with a nearby horse. They really liked that manure in their gardens too. I always thought that my folks knew they might be on thin ice by keeping a pony in town, but no one ever seemed to care. Maybe parents were all glad to see us kids enjoy the pony.

When it came time to run the evening paper route, I would hitch the pony to either the cart or the sleigh, depending on road conditions, and off we'd go to pick up and distribute the paper, accompanied by as many kids as could get on the vehicle. I had just one rule: "Anyone who rode had to run to the houses with the papers." It was a little like Tom Sawyer and painting the fence. I wasn't stupid. Of course, the kids were pleased to do it because we were having so much fun.

Came the day of the storm, I went out to hitch up the pony to the sleigh but, you know what? I couldn't get that pony out of the small barn. He wouldn't budge. He sniffed that howling wind and that blowing snow and said "No way. I'm not going out." Well, you know kids. We have no fear and no knowledge of how dangerous the situation is sometimes. So I trudged through those huge snowdrifts and delivered the papers without horsepower. I well remember slipping and sliding all over that end of town. I can still see in my memory how difficult it was to get from house to house—much less across those snow covered streets. I'll never forget how high those drifts were and how that wind blew. I've never seen anything comparable to it since then.

(Ed: Jim runs a barber shop in Minneapolis on Nicollet Avenue.)

HIS CLOTHING JUST STOOD THERE ON ITS OWN
by Margaret Bartlet
Roseville, MN

I was a housewife with a one-year old daughter and watched the storm develop during the day. I was anxiously awaiting my husband's arrival from downtown Minneapolis. After many hours, he (Stan) appeared at the back door. His car had gone off the road about a mile away and he had walked home. He was completely covered with snow and ice, literally looking like a frozen giant. That sight has remained stamped into my memory to this day. I don't know how we got his frozen clothes off but they just stood there on their own. He is dead now but I know that he too never forgot that day. If you didn't live through it you have no idea of the magnitude of that storm and what effect it had on so many people.

ALONE, PREGNANT AND NO FIRE
by Jess Berge
Elk River, MN

The day of the storm I was working at Honeywell, 2713 Fourth avenue south, Minneapolis, and was 24 years old. We lived in Spring Lake Park in a one bedroom bungalow with a coal furnace, a small quantity of coal in the basement and no garage. My wife was seven months pregnant with our first child and she didn't know how to fire the furnace yet.

As usual, that morning I picked up Louis Nesby, a neighbor, and dropped him off at his job on 16th avenue and Central NE, then went on to my parking space at my job. I walked to the plant through the sprinkles; it was cloudy and quite warm.

About 11 AM rain and sleet were getting pretty heavy. By noon snow and wind were causing problems for the cars and street cars on 4th avenue. At 3 PM we were told we could go home but many stayed all night after being unable to start their cars or after hearing radio reports of the severe driving problems. Like others, I walked to the parking lot but couldn't even get into my car. Not only was the keyhole frozen shut but rain had frozen around the door, making it impossible to open even when the lock was turned. I returned to the plant, got two milk bottles full of warm water, poured the water in the crack around the door and finally got it open.

I had a thin coat, no hat, cap, gloves or rubbers, much less overshoes. By now I was miserably cold and wet.However, I had little choice. My wife was expecting, Louie was waiting for me outside in the cold . . . I had to go. I had a good car with a standard shift, I was a better than average driver in snow, having been raised on a farm where there were no snowplows or tractors. So I started for home, twelve miles away, narrow roads, deep snow, cars, street cars and trucks stalled in every block.

In order to keep from getting stuck I didn't dare stop, just kept moving as fast as I could in second gear, regulating the speed with the accelerator. I passed on the right, went over curbs, passed street cars on the left and only slowed for stop signs.

I picked Louie up at about 6:30 and went on to Johnson Drug on Lowry and Central, which was the only store open. I talked the manager into selling me his cap by showing him that my hair was frozen into a cake of ice. While there I also called my neighbor and asked him to go over to my house and build a fire for my wife and to tell her I wasn't coming home. That way she wouldn't worry that I was stuck or in the ditch. There was no place, or time, to get any food. We stopped at the Heights Liquor bar but all the peanuts and such food had already been sold. We had a shot of bourbon and took off for home, both of us with our heads out a window to see the ditches.

Driving was a little better when we got onto the two lane highway. No one else was out and I could keep the car at about thirty-five or forty in second gear.

I then turned off onto the local streets of Spring Lake Park. No tracks. Nothing. Just step on the gas and keep it in second gear. When we got to Louie's to let him out, we couldn't open the door. It was frozen solidly. He had to crawl out the window as we sat there cutting a deep channel in the snow.

Now I was alone with about three-fourths of a mile to my home and I really felt a little scared. That car was wonderful. It kept going without a hitch.

Then I spotted my home. It was without a light. I knew it might be easy to get stuck turning into the driveway and the car might stay dangerously out in the street. I stepped on the accelerator, still in second gear, turned, and felt sick as I drove deeply into the ditch. The snow had blown level and I had turned in between the wrong trees along the front of our lot. I couldn't open the door, climbed out the window and went into the house.

I was really welcomed but my wife reminded me that her mother had no coal nor wood. Knowing it was dangerous, but I knew every tree and bush by heart, I filled a gunny sack with about fifty pounds of coal and walked over to her house across the fields. I started her fire, returned home, very cold and tired, hungry but very grateful. It was about 9:30 PM.

Two days later my neighbor and I walked to highway #10 only to find that it still had not been plowed. The roads weren't open for three or four days. Even then it was easier to drive in the country than in the Minneapolis city limits . . . but we were glad to be able to move at all.

OLD HERMAN AND THE AR-MIS-TIK DAY BLIZZARD

by Lou Bernier
Burnsville, MN

We didn't have a holiday that day in Rosemount. School buses arrived from Mendota and Eagan, from South St. Paul, from Lakeville and Farmington. Shortly after mid-afternoon the superintendent dismissed school and sent the buses to take us home, but it was too late and they were lucky to return to the school. We lived three blocks away so I went home happily, dressed in my boots and sheep-lined coat and walked two blocks to my dad's garage. I was put to work on the tow truck with Herman Menzhuber. Old Herman was glad to have me to do the hooking up of cars in the ditch. That 1936 Chevy with rear wheel chains could pull almost anything out of a ditch. However, the highway was getting glazed and dangerous. We could hardly stand up on it, the windshield wipers couldn't keep the window clear and the driver could see only a few yards ahead. We made three trips when we had to stop. Conditions were impossible. I walked back home where my Irish mother made me take a hot bath or "I would catch my death."

To get back into action, I returned to the garage. The showroom and shop were wall-to-wall with stranded people. My father sent me home to tell my mother that he was sending two stranded couples, one with a small baby, to stay with us. In the old-fashioned way, my mother moved out of their bedroom for one couple. The other had my sister's bed and I kept my single bed.

Not only was our garage full of people but the cafe and two bars down the street were also full. The cafe was soon serving whatever food was on hand. Our village hall (for dances and church socials) was over the drug and the grocery store and it was opened for people, especially the younger ones. A local dance band made up of the depot agent on drums, the bank teller on the trombone and the church organist on the piano, came to play.

Lots of little things happened. Two of my dad's employees were overcome with the gaiety of the situation and instead of watching things, got roaring drunk and then joined the travelers sleeping in the shop and show-room. My dad fired them on the spot. I learned to play Solitaire from one of the wives and my sister learned Hearts from another. And she loved having the baby around.

By the third morning farmers were coming into town with farm sleds pulled by their sturdiest horses. They came through the fields because the roads were too deep with snow. They came by our house with milk and cream cans covered with blankets, and went home with sacks of feed.

I'll always remember Old Herman telling people forever about the *Ar-mis-tik* day blizzard. In fact, to this day I still call it Ar-mis-tik in his honor.

NEEDED 8-FOOT PROBE TO FIND PICKUP
by Richard J. Bren Sr.
Eden Prairie, MN

I was employed by Minneapolis Moline in Hopkins but living on a farm in Eden Prairie. It was so mild that November 11 morning that I went to work in my shirt sleeves— but about 3:30 PM we were dismissed to go home because of the extreme change.

I was driving to my farm and got as far as county road #4 past the Glen Lake state hospital where there is a very deep cut in the road. I couldn't see where I was going because it was snowing and blowing so hard and then I was stuck and could go no further. Ahead of me about ten feet was a car, also stuck, with no one in or around it. I left my truck and started to walk home with much difficulty. I had to walk two more miles in that deep snow.

About four days after the storm, when the wind and snow had quietened enough so I could walk those two miles back to the truck, I did so, again with much difficulty in walking.

The car ahead of me belonged to a cow tester from the state; he had been coming from the state farm school at Glen Lake when he got stuck. As I arrived at the scene he was on top of the snow bank with an eight foot rod trying to locate his car. He struck the top of what he thought was his car and began to dig down about five feet until he came across my pickup. He saw the yellow color of my truck, knew it wasn't his and kept poking around until he found his own car.

See photograph on page 127.

CAPTIVES AT THE KING KOLE HOTEL
by Norma Schroder Burton
Minneapolis, MN

How well I remember the *Great Storm*. My mother, my brother (9), and I (16) had gone downtown to have lunch and go to the movies. We left our car at the Hudson dealer's garage on Harmon and about 13th for repairs and walked downtown.

By the time we came out of the movies the storm was in full force. We took a bus to the garage with my mother intent upon driving home. At that time we lived on Webster avenue near Excelsior boulevard. The garage owner persuaded mother that it was not safe to drive because he had made the journey to that area with a tow truck and had been forced to return. We found some of the last available accomodations at the old King Kole hotel across from Loring park.

We battled our way through the drifts to the hotel to find that we were the only children there. It proved to be a real bonus! Those stranded business men were delighted to have young people for whom they could buy treats. Bathing suits were found and my brother and I enjoyed the pool all by ourselves.

Meanwhile, my mother tried to locate my father who had already left work at the National Lead company plant in St. Louis Park, but who had not arrived at home. There was much calling among relatives to let each know where we were—until finally my father was able to call us from a small plumbing shop about a mile from his plant. He was ensconced with about twelve people, men, women and children. The latter two groups were sent up to a loft to bed eventually and the men played poker all evening. My father lost ten dollars.

Meanwhile the three of us were captive at the hotel until my father could arrive with money to pay the bill. Needless to say, my brother and I enjoyed the attention we were receiving.

When my father came to get us and we made the journey home, we travelled west on Excelsior boulevard, under the bridge that is the walkover for Mini-kahda country club. We were awed by the depth of the drifts. It was there that one of the storm victims lost his life. When we arrived at our home, which was a dutch colonial style, we were taken aback to find that snow at the back of the house was drifted to the level of the low roof. The front door was also drifted shut and it took some time before we could even get into the house.

A small side story we remember: an aunt and uncle owned a store in Lebanon, Missouri, and we sent them the newspaper stories and pictures, which they posted in the window. They were the town entertainment for a number of days.

I LAID DOWN TO SLEEP—IN THE STREET
by Kermit A. Carlson
Minneapolis, MN

The November 11 storm almost ended my life.

I was a young apprentice screw machine operator at Minneapolis Honeywell and worked on the second shift in the basement.

The weather was getting bad when I left for work that afternoon but I didn't think much about it; I was 26 years old and had a lot of vim and vigor. Toward evening we began to hear reports that street cars were stalled on Fourth avenue so we went upstairs to look. It was pretty bad. So bad that our cafeteria people took coffee and sandwiches to people out there in the street cars.

I worked until the end of my shift at midnight and was going to ride part way with a fellow worker. We pushed his car onto 28th street and that was it.

We could go no farther. Although the pushing made me tired, I decided to walk home, which was approximately two miles. I got to Lake street and headed east to Cedar, finding it necessary to plow through drifts and to zigzag into doorways of closed stores. At Chicago avenue I was feeling exhausted and rested for a while in a doorway. There was no one around — only the blowing wind and snow.

Again I started and when I reached Cedar there was a drift so high it seemed to be only four or five feet from the trolley wires.

Finally, reaching Longfellow avenue, where I lived between 33rd. and 34th. streets, something didn't seem right with me. My heart pounded and when I had pushed through more drifts for about 1 1/2 blocks, I became very warm and disoriented and laid down in the middle of the street and wanted to sleep.

Just then I became aware of a familiar looking house and struggled to the porch. I rang the bell, pounded on the door and immediately passed out.

The next I knew I was being pulled into the porch. The people were the folks of a neighborhood pal. They took me into the kitchen and gave me hot coffee and called my family. After 20 minutes or so I started for my own house 1 1/2 blocks away. My mother and brother, plus a neighbor, met me half way. Even though I had a lot of stamina, having been a gymnast some years before, I frosted my lungs and I contracted pneumonia. People didn't go to the hospital in those days for such minor things. A mustard plaster broke up the congestion and I was okay in a few days.

If I had not been heard by those people that night, it might have been the end for me.

I am now 70 years old and thank the Good Lord for that.

THEY COULDN'T GET THE BODY TO TOWN
by Earl Cates
Prior Lake, MN

One of our neighbors died at about the beginning of the storm. The snow was so deep the hearse couldn't get to her place in Prior Lake from Shakopee. The family left her in the room where she died for three days. A relative from Shakopee tried to come out there by team to get the body, but his horses played out and he had to return home. Next, the family decided to take the long way around through Savage, then by #101 to Shakopee and on to Marys-town, the place of interment. They put the body in the sled and five neighbors armed with scoop shovels went along to shovel the drifts. A team and men from Shakopee were waiting to complete the trip to Marystown. This was about a 25 mile trip, which should have been only six.

They made it.

OUR DUCK BLIND ON THE MISSISSIPPI

by Len Caverly
Rochester, MN

I was employed as a ticket clerk in the Minneapolis office of the C.& N.W. Railway and my hunting buddy, George MacCarthy, recently deceased, had the same job in our St.Paul office.

We went hunting every chance we could get but were hampered by our work schedule. Working until 3 PM on Saturdays meant the best we could do was to go duck hunting on Sunday mornings. This we did on Sunday, November 10, 1940 down at Hastings on the Mississippi where we rented a boat from a nice old lady, pushed it into the backwater rushes, built a nice blind, set out the decoys and awaited the sunrise. When the sun came up, it was with a vengeance; it was so hot and muggy that the mosquitoes nearly drove us crazy. We had to pull our earflaps down and put our collars up to keep them off. Needless to say we saw very few ducks and had only a few desperation shots.

It was clear and warm on Monday morning but George and I couldn't go that day either because it wasn't a railroad holiday at that time. We called and talked about it, agreeing that it was going to be another bluebird day and it was probably just as well that we couldn't get away. Then about 10 AM it started to snow and it was coming down so heavily that George and I then wished we were in that blind we had built.

As the storm intensified people started making hotel reservations to stay downtown but those of us who couldn't afford that luxury made plans to get home. I bought a set of chains for my 1940 Plymouth (practically new then) and awaited the chance to start for home. We stuck around until 5:30 PM because our boss had a hotel reservation and it mattered not to him. With eight of us in the car, and the tire chains, we had good traction. By going down back alleys and through filling station driveways we were able to bypass a lot of traffic and all bodies were delivered to their front doors.

The next Sunday, November 17, George and I hightailed it down to Hastings again and rented a boat from the same nice old lady. We asked her how the hunting had been on Armistice Day. She told us that four hunters had frozen to death in the very same blind George and I had built the day before. That's how fast the blizzard came in, she said, the wind being so strong that the men couldn't or didn't dare move — and, of course, they were not properly dressed for the big drop in temperature.

Incidentally, I still have that set of tire chains.

COCKY-LEEKY SOUP AT THE RYAN HOTEL
by Priscilla S. Creapo
River Falls, WI

My home was the small town of New Richmond, Wisconsin. It was an hour's drive into St. Paul because my father never exceeded his self-imposed speed limit of 50 mph. I was excited with anticipation of an all day shopping trip into St. Paul on this Armistice day. My father worked at the local bank and this day was always a holiday for him. The four of us (I have a brother) got up early, enthusiastic over our visit to the big city. After breakfast we climbed into our shiny black 1935 Ford sedan and headed west.

We stopped at a small store where my brother bought equipment for his ham radio station; I believe it was called Hall Electric. Mother and I left to walk to the Golden Rule and Emporium department stores on Seventh street and agreed to meet dad and brother at 12:30 at the Ryan hotel for lunch.

Mom sewed like a professional so we spent time looking at yard goods. I had many hand-smocked dresses, some of them with matching bloomers my mother made. What child today even heard of bloomers? Although I would fully appreciate mom's sewing years later, at that time I wanted the currently fashionable Shirley Temple dresses.

We met my father and brother at the Ryan hotel and were seated at a table covered with a white linen cloth and even a menu! Choosing just the right food was such fun. I saw an item that caught my eye; it was called *Cocky-Leeky Soup* so that was my instant choice for lunch. The waiter brought a lovely bowl of a creamy soup with green pieces of leeks in it. Delicious! After finishing our leisurely lunch we stepped out into the fresh air again.

Instantly I saw the look of alarm on my father's face and the worried tone in his voice scared me. Snow was falling heavily. We all wore rubber overshoes, but weatherwise ill-prepared for a heavy snowfall. From the look of the sky it was more than just a snowfall; it was fast becoming a blizzard. As quickly as we could we walked to the parking lot because snow was already becoming deep in the streets. I don't recall the exact time of day we left St. Paul but I remember cars being stuck along the road when we reached the eastern edge of town.

The atmosphere was heavy and formidable and the world was just a big white blanket. Nothing was visible for more than a foot in front of the car. Our Ford crawled along the road and inside we were not speaking. The silence in our car and the cold force of the driving snow was bone-chilling. My father was a good driver and the car was kept in top condition by the local garage. I'm sure that dad knew this might not be enough to get us through the frightening storm but we kept up our hopes. Before reaching Lake Elmo I remember seeing cars that had gone off the road, or at least I thought they were cars—the visibility was so bad. Dad couldn't stop to help them because other cars would smash into us. We just kept going at a snail's pace, passing more cars of stranded motorists. It must have been a heart-rending decision for dad to pass them by, but it was our only chance of survival.

In three or four hours we arrived in New Richmond. No roads had been plowed but somehow we reached home. It must have been the most wondeful looking house my folks had ever seen. What a miracle to be there.

God had truly been guiding us and caring for us that day. The newspapers and radio stations carried terrifying stories about the storm. Pictures were printed of the stranded cars we had passed. People froze to death. Such sadness. Such tragic deaths. Such unspeakable sorrow. The storm had come with frightening speed, and with no forewarning, and with untamed fury. Our trip home had been successful. We were a happy family, forever grateful that we had made it home.

NASTURTIUMS UNHARMED BY SNOWDRIFT
by Ed Culbert
Minneapolis, MN

I remember that day well. I was busy weatherstripping north dormer windows because we were making some rooms in our unfinished attic. Wind and rain turning into snow stopped me.

Our six-year-old Eddie was watching cars on Portland avenue out of the front window. One car turned around; others ran up on the curb as the street became icy. Traffic ground to a halt. By nightfall a string of cars lined the curb across the street, all stalled by the snow. The drivers deserted them but even wallowing in the ever-deepening snow was increasingly difficult. Two couples came to our door for shelter after dark. My wife, Barbara, thinks they were both from one car; my memory is that they were from different cars and didn't know each other. One of the men set out to walk to a relative's house on Nicollet but returned because of the snow depth and lack of adequate clothing.

We bunked them for the night on cots and a partially finished bunk in the one habitable area in the attic. The men departed early the next morning and came back for the women about midday.

The next day there was a great bank of snow along Pearl park (then mostly a swamp) between 53rd and 52nd streets on Portland. Not visible but underneath that huge snowbank were a number of cars. Cars in front of our house were partly visible.

I had heard on the radio that street cars were not running but decided I'd try to get to my teaching job at school. There were big drifts on 53rd street, hard and compact. I found tht I could walk on them — or so I thought. Unfortunately, every so often I broke through the crust. If you have ever gone down to your hips on one leg, then broken through with the other (or rather with your knee) as you strive to climb out, you know my predicament. After about a block and a half, I returned home.

The rapid change from mild rain to heavy snow to sub-zero temperatures produced some interesting results. At that time I had grown old-fashioned vining type nasturtiums on the northeast corner of our house foundation. A couple of days after the snowfall I dug down and found the nasturtiums— leaves, flowers, buds and all—looking just as I had seen them before the blizzard. They were fresh and untouched by frost.

FREE PEPSI-COLA
by Gigi Luccaro Daniel
St. Paul, MN

I love the memories of the Armistice Day Blizzard.

I was a mere seven years old and already knew the joy of being snowed out of school. We put on our winter gear and trudged through the snow, one half block to the boulevard, now highway #55. Cars were stranded one after another and, as we looked around, we discovered a Pepsi-Cola truck, half turned over in the drifts with bottles tilted every which way. Some were frozen with caps popped off.

To any child not accustomed to treats of this nature, it was a sheer delight. For some strange reason we thought it was ours to take. The driver had abandoned the truck to seek refuge and we wasted no time in descending upon it. We carried home as many as our little arms could bear. The next day a rap on the door brought the city police. We thought the worst but they came only to collect the empty bottles and to deliver a short reprimand. We never dreamed it would be classified as *stolen merchandise* and that our innocent *neighborhood gang* would be thieves.

It seems like such a small event now, but what a dent that event has left in my memory—of happy childhood days, of lots of snow, of no school—of free pop—and of my wonderful mother's birthday.

BOB DE HAVEN ON WEATHER REPORTING
by Bob De Haven
Minneapolis,MN

I was program director of WTCN Radio in the Wesley Temple building and had been driven to work by our sales manager, Lee Whiting, now deceased. Storm warnings were broadcast as they were obtained from the U.S.

Weather Bureau in those days. They were inadequate and not intense or extensive. We didn't tell listeners what to do such as saying "Get the hell home and
stay there."

The pressure to close up and go home mounted and, although the station
did not shut down, Lee and I started home. We made it to the street going
west past the Walker Art Gallery, that street being blocked by stalled cars. Lee
wheeled across the open lot, still there opposite the Guthrie theatre and up
Kenwood Hill to my house at 3343 Ivy lane.

My brother and his wife were in town and we had been invited to Dick
Sawyer's home for dinner. Dick was the well known amateur golfer. Leah, his
wife, was worried about the dessert which had not been delivered by Chapman-
Graham, a caterer located near Hennepin and Lake. We marched down Ivy
lane to dinner to find the caterer's truck stalled at the Sawyer house. Later in
the early evening, the four of us walked down the street with locked arms to
hold us against the mighty wind. The next day, from a sense of that silly attitude that the show must go on, I started to drive to town. The caterer's truck
was still there. I picked up Doc Stanwood of the downtown YMCA and we did
reach work, heroes of a small kind.

Readers may remember that famous photo of cars (only the tops showing)
stalled on Excelsior avenue, also showing the footbridge from one side of Mini-
kahda golf club showing? Five days after the storm I drove through the single
car path between those cars, with the Reverend George Mecklenberg of the
Wesley Methodist church. We were en route to testify at a hearing of Henry
Soltau, a crime-busting preacher, at Shakopee.I was a witness as program director of the station on which Soltau made some charges about gambling. I believe
those charges were made on air time given the church as part of the station's
lease of space in the church's building. This is a digression but it pinpoints the
five days that passed between November 11 and the cars remaining unmoved
on Excelsior avenue.

I WORRIED ABOUT VERN AND MITCH
by John W. DeMaster
White Bear Lake, MN

As I recall that day it was the type you would pick for late season duck hunting.
At noon my friends Vern and Mitch and I decided to leave White Bear
Lake and go to Otter lake to hunt. By the time we got there the wind seemed
stronger; so we discussed the best place to hunt where we could return fairly
easily if the weather got worse. I suggested going into the wind, hoping to
get to open water east and north of the pump house, from which we would
be starting.

We had two boats. I got into the one-man boat and Vern and Mitch into the two-man boat. We paddled and pushed our way to open water and set out our decoys. By this time it was sleeting and snowing and the ducks were flying low and seemed tired. They would drop into the decoys without any circling. We had good shooting but had trouble picking up the downed ducks and several floated away from us.

We stayed on, enjoying the hunt until my gun — a Winchester Model 12 — froze at the pump action. The three of us discussed this situation and decided to call it a day. They suggested I lead the way back, so we picked up what decoys we could find and I turned to paddle and push back.

The storm was getting bad by this time. As I paddled I saw animals, musk-rats I think, trying to swim through what appeared to be slush. It was happening so fast that I could almost see the slush and water coming together and freezing.

I was getting tired and had lost my sense of direction when I ran aground. I wasn't sure where I was so I tested the shoreline to see if it would support my weight. It did, so I tried to look for Vern and Mitch. They were not around, so I wondered what to do. I heard someone shout and followed the sound until I came to a stranger. He wondered where the two of us were and I said I thought near the pump house, so he decided to try to find it. So we set out and eventually found his car, almost drifted over by the snow.

During this time we talked and he asked who I was, who I was with and whether I intended to go home before I found my friends. I realized it was a must situation that we stay together if we expected to survive so I looked some more for my friends until I came across their car. I shouted several times but received no reply. The stranger, in the meantime, was getting sort of impatient and asked if I wanted to come with him. I said I would go with him if I could leave something to let my friends know that I had been there. He suggested I leave my outside overcoat, so I did, placing it over the steering wheel of Vern's car. We then started home. It was hard to see the road but we hung our heads out the side windows and managed that way. At a few places we weren't sure of the road so we'd get out and walk and look until we knew which way to go. We made it home finally. Of course my parents had been worried and my oldest brother had organized a search party and was not home when I got there.

By this time I had more time to think about what had happened to Vern and Mitch. We had no news from them and I hadn't seen them since I turned my back to paddle ashore. Later that evening my brother returned home, but no news. We all felt helpless because we didn't know what to do. It was another day before we learned what happened.

As they had tried to follow me off the lake they couldn't handle the two-man boat in the storm and heavy wind. Vern, who was older and more experienced than Mitch, turned the boat with the wind to drift across the open water part of the lake. They hit the shore in the vicinity of a farm home and made their way to the house. They were fed, warmed and treated very kindly by the people at the farm. They had no way of letting us know where they were since telephone lines were down and roads were shut.

About two days after the storm we returned to Otter lake to pick up our boats, decoys, etc. You wouldn't believe it but there were ducks frozen alive in the lake. Some were frozen by the wings, some were all the way in, with just a little water near their necks and heads. I'm not sure how they were able to stay alive. With ice chisels we chopped some out of the ice.

The storm really didn't cause the three of us any physical problems except I was frostbitten on my face and neck, so I lost all that skin a few days later. Such an experience has often reminded me to be ready for the worst in winter.

CREAM OF SAUERKRAUT SOUP! UGH!
by Alice Dittmar
Hopkins, MN

I was in high school and on that day had a piano lesson. My teacher lived eight long blocks away from my home and I always had to walk. After school I walked to her house and the lesson went all right but after it was over I was told about the weather and that it would be better to stay the night—so my parents were notified.

My teacher was married to a well known professional man and had a son and daughter whom I considered quite homely. The problem was that her son thought I was made to order for him. My teacher was crippled and *made to order for him* meant that since she was confined, he could catch me in the hallway or any place where she wasn't. I stood my ground all right but it was an awful experience I can't forget. Also I couldn't sleep all night, being afraid he'd come into my room.

At mealtime my stomach was ready for a good meal. I was hungry. They served for me, their guest, their favorite meal. It was cream of sauerkraut soup. To me it was gross and I had a hard time keeping it down,trying politely to say it was good but no,thanks, to seconds. They were much wealthier than my family but my stomach was still waiting for some good food.

I couldn't wait for the all clear to leave the next day and the eight blocks were a breeze walking for good old home.

NO HANKY-PANKY!

by Olive Olsen Earley
Minneapolis, MN

I boarded the streetcar with neighbors at 33rd and Nicollet avenue south, taking my seat and opening my suit jacket because it was so warm. When I arrived at the John W. Thomas & Company store, where I worked, the guard greeted me with a big smile and said "Beautiful day for the parade but not good for business."

I took the elevator to the fourth floor to my small office. I was personnel director, assistant to C.J. Allert, the store superintendent. I went about my normal routine: morning papers, sorted mail and memos on C.J.'s desk. I recall that the paper headlined "Perfect day for a parade."

Exactly on schedule at 7 AM Carl J. Allert, now deceased, arrived. Customers would be waiting at the door when the store opened at 8:15 because we were having an Armistice Day sale. I had 45 minutes to be ready for job applicants which we always expected on parade days. Many people also applied for jobs on those days to kill two birds with one stone and have only one carfare expense. I distributed memos to executive offices, the last one being the advertising office where I had enjoyed eight years working under Leila Bon *Bonnie*; she was at her desk so we enjoyed a few minutes watching the view from the spacious windows. She commented on how unusual it was to have the window open in November. Young girls in blouses, light sweaters, skirts and bobby sox. Young women carrying their suit coats or sweaters or light weight coats. Men in suits, no topcoats. All were on their way to work, to school, or to await the parade later. It was a treat to have such a beautiful day.

At 9:45 C.J. came in with a concerned look. "Dayton's just called to alert us that unpredictable weather is ahead and we should prepare for an emergency condition." He turned on his small radio and we watched the crowds out the window as we listened to reports of coming bad weather. Yet the view of tranquility contraindicated what we were hearing over the radio.

Dayton's called again in 15 minutes. Situation serious. A blizzard coming our way. The weather station doesn't know when but it's coming fast. During that 15 minutes it became a lot cooler and we had to shut the window because of the strong wind. By 10:15 we noticed snowflakes and at 10:20 Dayton's called again. This is going to be bad. You should canvass your employees and make arrangements for them getting home. We are reserving a whole floor at the Radisson hotel just in case we need it.

I must intercede to tell you more about superintendent Carl J. Allert who was in charge of employee relations and building maintenance. I don't think anyone could top him in understanding and fulfilling his responsibilities. I have never known an executive officer who was better able to size up a situation, see the potential problems and mentally work out a plan before the solution was necessary. From the first alert from Dayton's (obviously a friend) he was mentally making lists: customers, employees, transportation, whether to close the store, food supplies, blankets, how many cots, lounges, lavatory supplies, 24-hour maintenance if necessary for extra people, weight on the roof of the building, wind velocity affecting windows, protection for store windows from breaking and damage to pedestrians. I knew his mind was in a whirl but he was as calm as the proverbial cucumber. We started into action.

At 10:30 I called the Radisson hotel and reserved as many rooms as I could get. Believe me, they were in a dither. I gathered that their lobby was full and demand for rooms was great. C. J. and I worked out a procedure.

We had a complement of about 500 clerks and executives. Lists were prepared for all offices, departments and sections, requesting names of all employees at work that day, the transportation they depended on, whether they drove, details about where they parked, capacity of their vehicle, condition of gas supply, where they lived, how many persons rode with them, etc. Employees were to be told of the weather but cautioned to be calm and not panic. Since the street cars were still operating, our instructions were that any employee who knew he had a way home safely was to be excused. Customers were to be advised of the difficulty and recommended to return home.

Some executives were asked to volunteer to stay the night; we would need them as sentries throughout the store. Maintenance people were asked to stay if they could, with pay of course. A practical nurse on duty volunteered to stay and C. J. managed to get a doctor to come in, just in case.

By 11 AM we checked and found few taxis were available, the snow was getting thick, snowplows couldn't get going because they couldn't assemble their crews that quickly. By noon the street cars were almost completely stopped, snowed in, and the radio was announcing the cancellation of the parade. Many of our employees had left the store by 10:45 and caravans of cars had left from our inside parking places with loads of people. Some adventurous drivers made repeat trips, saying it was exciting and a challenge. Remember, in 1940 we didn't have front wheel drive, nor radial nor snow tires, although a few people had chains. They were told to refill their tanks when necessary, at store expense.

There was a tremendous feeling of togetherness, which we don't often experience. There was magic in the air. Those that could—did. Those that could not—were helped. I wish I could remember the stories related by those who shuttled fellow employees and customers to their homes. They enjoyed it. Many of them finally got stuck and had to walk home themselves, but we heard no complaints.

By one o'clock things were falling in place. Mr.Langford, manager of the coffee shop, a leased business, had graciously offered to stay the night and remain available, along with some of his staff. They would do what they could with present supplies and, if possible, obtain more. They would keep the coffee urns going. Employees would not have to pay and customers could pay if they wished. No one would be refused because of lack of money.

By this time Mr. Allert had guards at the doors; anyone coming in was told he could do no shopping; they could use certain designated telephones for emergency use if desired. If they wanted to wait out the storm and could not get home, or in a hotel, they could stay in guarded security areas. We set up lounges on the second and fourth floors with new blankets from the linen department and pillows with cases if needed. Those used were later laundered and sent to the Little Sisters of the Poor.

By 1:30 PM I had completed my assignment list of stranded employees who were to stay at the Radisson. We had 12 rooms which would be adequate. Four rooms for men and eight for women. It was time for me to get to the Radisson to be ready when employees arrived at 2 PM. So I left the store at 1:45 and, in walking past the 7th street side, I noticed that all the wooden braces had been installed on the windows. When did they do that? With my precious list of people and a few things I had purchased for the overnight stay, I was ready for our people. I was to be the monitor for the women and a male supervisor was to monitor the men's rooms. Mr. Allert wanted no hanky-panky. He told us both that the reputation of the store would be at stake and we must insist on decorum.

It was quite a struggle walking the 1 1/2 blocks to the Radisson. The snow was piled so high in the streets it made them almost impassable even by foot. And the wind was fierce. I had to lean into it to keep from being blown over.

I reached the lobby which was jammed with people. Complete chaos. Everything available on which someone could sit or lean was in use. I had never been involved in such confusion. I notified the hotel people I was there, signed the reservation form and received the room keys. I posted myself by the door to await my chickens and, as they arrived, checked lists, issued keys, etc. The first one checked got the key and was told to keep his/her group in line. No hanky panky! When the keys were all issued, I could give a sigh of relief. We supervisors had our own single rooms as a precaution for any problems that might develop.

At 2:30 when I had gone to my room to freshen up, I called C.J. and reported that all the waifs had been accounted for and were assigned to rooms. He told me that many customers were stranded in the store and appreciated the accommodations. A few diehard shoppers wanted to shop as long as they were there and were disgruntled because they couldn't. With all the service they were being given, this sounded unconscionable to me. C.J.'s parting words were "You have to keep your eyes open; we want no scandals." I told him that he'd have to do the same and no sleep for him tonight.

At the window I could see snow coming down so thickly I couldn't see across the street. This was at 3 PM. Street lights were on but nothing was moving. The street was like a crazy quilt of cars turned in every direction, stalled. I thought that this wasn't going to let up soon. It didn't either; it snowed all night.

I went looking for my charges. Knocking at doors got no response. They weren't in the lobby. Aha! The Viking Room. There I found them. Singing, dancing, drinking, eating. The Viking Room had such good food. It was a glorious, hilarious night for everyone. I didn't feel I could participate and at age 27 that's a tough limitation. But I enjoyed the festivities by observation. I kept watch until about 4 AM, then went to my room after having a well-earned breakfast in the coffee shop. I checked all my rooms and was assured that nothing unusual had happened. Everyone would report back to the store at the regular time or I could excuse them if they wished to find their own way home. I put in a call request for 6:30, settled the hotel bill in the morning and made it to work by 7:10. When I stepped out of the Radisson the sun was shining but snow was piled high in drifts.

The only staff in the store were those who had been there all night. C.J. was still alert but tired from his vigilance, saying "As soon as we can get the customers on their way, we'll close shop. I think we've done enough. Let's tell everyone they can go home any way they can."

A friend called to say he had a car and would come get me. I could leave without walking home without boots and with only a suit and tiny hat. Little did I know that I would spend that afternoon in borrowed clothes, shoveling out one car after another, but it was fun. I had gone from the sublime to the ridiculous.

I haven't mentioned Mr. Yolostein, the owner of the store, who graciously extended the expense charges and payment for services granted. Also Mr. Benson, president, who sanctioned what Mr. Allert had ordered. Without their support we would not have been able to accomplish the things we felt were necessary.

CRAWLING HOME FROM WORK
by Bob Enersen
Clearwater, FL

I was working from 4 PM to 12:30 AM as an inspector on the second shift of the plastic molding department of Minneapolis Honeywell. The job was very important to me because we were just pulling out of the depression and during it I had been laid off three or four times from the Honeywell factory.

We lived in a small house on the back of the lot at 5524 Kellogg avenue in Edina, one block east of the golf couse. During the day we heard radio reports of the developing storm so I dug out the four-buckle oversoes, stocking cap, scarf, leather gloves, large mittens and a long sheepskin coat with a high colar. I also let some of the air out of the U.S. Royal tires (snow tires had not yet been invented and I never used chains) on the 1935 Terraplane (small Hudson or big Essex). The Terraplane was a good snow car.

I recall passing many cars and even a streetcar on the wrong side of the street to reach the top of a hill. I picked up four fellows who paid me to drive them to and from work, so we soon had plenty of manpower to push us through snow banks and ice, a normal part of Minnesota storm driving.

Towards the end of the shift word came from Deke Foster, Honeywell superintendent, that the company would allow anyone who wished to do so to sleep in the plant that night. However, the fellows and I decided to go home. We had no real trouble until I had dropped off the last rider. Then I was driving on 50th street approaching Wooddale avenue—which runs alongside the Edina golf course and parallel to my street, Kellogg. A policeman pulled up, flashed me to stop and asked where in the world I thought I was going. I told him to 55th and Kellogg and he said I would never make it because of high drifts on Wooddale. I said that I would ram the car into a snow bank and walk from there; he gave me a reluctant okay.

He was right. I had no sooner turned onto Wooddale than I had to plow the car into a huge snow bank. I stuffed my pant legs into the overshoes and wrapped the scarf around my head, leaving only a small slit for my eyes and an opening between turns for my nose. It was to be the toughest walk of my life. In fact, it wasn't exactly a walk.

The wind was screaming across the gold course with such velocity that I had to lean into it at about a 45 degree angle to stay on my feet. Even then, on bare spots it would slide me sideways and I would have to get on my hands and knees to crawl back. I also had to crawl or slither over the large snow banks and in some way barge through the ones only a foot or two high. Each step consisted of pulling the foot up, sliding the leg as far as possible over the snow and pushing it down. My legs felt like lead. There was ice around my nose and mouth and my breath came in gasps. I was a battle between the storm and me.

I became so exhausted after three or four blocks that I actually thought how nice it would be to lie down in the soft snow and go to sleep. However, the thought of my beautiful wife and my two-year old son depending on me, kept me from ever considering it. In some way I made the six and a half blocks, pulled the door open far enough to fall into the arms of my waiting wonderful warm wife. It was then about 3 AM.

YOU CAN'T GO OUT—YOU'LL GET LOST
by Mary Ann Fenlason
Edina, MN

My dad, who lives in Edina but winters in the sun belt, speaking of this storm, said "I missed it all. I had a good idea of what was in store for us, so I came home early."

Indeed I do remember him arriving home at an earlier hour than normal with comic books, coloring books and candles! What a surprise for my brother and me. I was very young in 1940 but that memory lingers on.

Dad grew up in Cloquet and in Duluth. He was on the last train to leave Cloquet on October 11, 1918, his eighteenth birthday, as the town was being consumed by fire. His early years must have given him weather knowledge long before the present meteorologists and their up to the minute weather weather reports came along. I do recall how dad still mentions that November 11 day as starting being warm, almost balmy; then the rain started and that changed to a cold rain and finally snow.

I had a best friend who lived next door and I wanted to go visit her. Those coloring books were best when shared. I dressed and got as far as the back door before my mother stopped me saying "You cannot go out. You'll get lost!" Of all the ridiculous things, I thought, it wasn't dark and I had been going to her house for at least a year. It really was most confusing to a child. Mother had grown up in Cokato, MN and told of having to tunnel out of the house some winters. She, too, must have known winter weather that we have only heard about.

LADY BUNKED OVERNIGHT
IN HENNEPIN COUNTY JAIL
by Mildred E. Foss
Minneapolis, MN

This was to be a very pleasant day.

I worked for the County of Hennepin so it was a holiday; I had a dental appointment in the afternoon and had met a friend for dinner downtown.

We separated and I went toward my street car line to go home. Yes, street cars were still running on tracks with a trolley overhead. It didn't take long to realize that every street car downtown was stalled on the track. Ice had formed on the cowcatcher on front and this pushed the snow and ice along the tracks until it coated the track with hard-packed ice.

Fortunately I had a key for our office in the court house so I walked in the biting cold wind, intending to spend the night in the office. The office was cold and it wasn't too comfortable to be alone there. I knew Mrs. Tollefson who was the city jailer and took an elevator to the city jail and asked for space. She gave it to me and I slept in the hospital room of the jail, not seeing any of the persons in the cells. After coffee and a sweet roll in the jail kitchen the next day, I went back to the office to answer the phone calls. No one else could get downtown except Judge James G. Kehoe, now deceased, the probate court judge, who had walked downtown from south Minneapolis.

By late afternoon Tuesday the street cars were back in order and we left the office as usual.

Virginia Blythe, a rare female attorney for that time, was the only one, together with her female client, who came in for a court hearing that day.

RED HOT STOVE DANCED AROUND
by Mary Fretag
Minneapolis,MN

I was just shy of my twentieth birthday and living in a three-room house on a dead end street with my husband and baby boy, Dennis, born just two years previously.

The beautiful day suddenly changed as wind and snow appeared, coming on heavier quickly and the wind began whistling. The severity became alarming so my husband brought stovewood to the house. He found it impossible to open the kitchen door and came in through the front door, piling the wood in the kitchen. We had a cookstove and an *Air Tight* stove on an asbestos pad in the living room. No other heat. Never thinking these conditions would last, my husband left for work at 3:30. Besides, times were tough and we needed the money, so he had to go to work.

Within a couple of hours I was unable to keep the kitchen warm, so I hung an army blanket over the door between the kitchen and living room, using nails pounded onto the door frame. The wood was burning so fast I wondered what I would do if it were all burned up. Would my baby and I freeze to death?

I was able to telephone for wood delivery but they called back to say they couldn't travel—the snow was too heavy and the temperature too dangerous to venture outside.

The *Air Tight* stove began to dance. It was solid red and I feared it would melt apart. What should I do? I held my baby close and prayed that the Lord would not let us burn up. "Please stop snowing and blowing so hard." I couldn't see out at all. I tried the telephone. No service.

Sparingly, I put another log in the *Air Tight* even though the pipe in the ceiling was red hot and the stove was dancing. The draft, caused by the wind, was too strong but I couldn't reduce it. I had a hard time keeping the blanket in place as the strong wind blew right through the house.

I wrapped my baby in a big wool afghan my mother had made and stayed close to a window. I planned to break it and try to escape should the house catch fire.

Almost as fast as all of this started, it quit. The wind subsided and the snow stopped. The stove quit dancing and lost its glow. "Thanks be to God", I said, knowing that someone would be able to save us now. I was so happy when my husband got home and dug us out.

I STARTED TO CRY THINKING I'D NEVER MAKE IT
by Stella Fritz
Richfield, MN

They let us out of work at 3:30 PM that day at Warner Brothers Pictures on 11th and Currie avenue.

I had to walk in that storm four short blocks to Hennepin avenue and took a street car at Fifth street. The car went very slowly the last five miles or so and finally stopped at 38th street and 23rd avenue. We were in front of the Nile theatre. The motorman told us we could either stay in the street car or, if we lived nearby, might want to try to make it home. My aunt and uncle lived three blocks from there so I thought I could make three blocks with no trouble.

Little did I realize until I had gone several steps just how rough it was going to be. When I walked I was in snow over my knees, so it was very, very hard going. When I was a half-block from their house I started to cry because I thought I would never make it. When I did get to the door and they opened it, I fell right on the floor, sobbing, now from relief. I HAD MADE IT.

They were just in the middle of their dinner so I ate with them and stayed the night. My folks lived only a mile away so my boy friend came to get me that afternoon. The blizzard had then stopped and main thoroughfares were cleared.

Boy-oh-boy, I'll never forget that lost feeling I had during that last block, plowing through knee-deep snow with the icy snow pellets being blown into my face by that terrific wind.

FLYING CLOUD TO SHAKOPEE: PACKED CARS
by Mary Jane Gregg
Richfield, MN

I was in my second year of teaching in Wessington Springs, South Dakota, and with my boy friend, and two other teachers had come to St. Paul for the holiday week-end. My parents lived in St. Paul.

That morning we had been shopping downtown. The weather was rather snowy by noon but it didn't seem too bad and we agreed to start for South Dakota that afternoon.

We picked up the other two teachers and were driving west on Lake street behind a street car. The storm was increasing. Our plan was to go as far on our way as possible but the storm kept getting worse as we headed south on highway #169.

When we were at the top of the hill approaching the Minnesota river into Shakopee, near the present Flying Cloud airport, we were really only creeping along, barely able to see the road on either side. Suddenly a young man tried to come to our car from the left ditch but the wind was so strong he could hardly get to us. He held up his hands for us to stop, which we did.

He said to go no further because there were many cars stalled in the snow down that hill along the highway. We had hoped to get to Shakopee. He said there was a filling station to our left (which we couldn't even see) and he would guide us to it. It was only a few yards away. Of course we went into the station to join others standed there. I tried to call my parents in St.Paul but the lines were already down.

We stayed there a couple of hours while the storm kept getting worse. The station operator suggested we try to get to a farmhouse a few yards to the east. The snow was drifting by this time. The wind was unbelievably strong. We couldn't see the house but he showed us exactly where to go, so we joined hands and forced our way through the wind and drifts.

When we arrived at the porch door a young woman greeted us, looking very distraught. She said we could stay with her. Her husband worked in Minneapolis and couldn't make it home that night so she and her little one-year old girl were alone. She pointed out that she was low on groceries but we had supper. She gave her bedroom to the two fellows. It was cold in there and the snow was piling up around the windows. She opened the couch for she and I and the baby between us. The other teacher insisted on sleeping in a big rocking chair with a footstool.

It snowed all night with so much strong wind that the windows were almost covered in the morning and snow had come into the bedroom under the windows. They must not have been very tight.

We were concerned for the animals in the barn east of the house so the two fellows tried to get there; the wind and deep snow made it impossible. We were comfortable inside and thankful for our safe haven, wondering when we would be able to take to the road again.

I think it was sometime that afternoon when we looked from the front windows and saw the plow going south slowly. Evidently the gas station had shoveled, so we got onto the highway. Other cars were in back of the plow so we followed. We had paid for our stay and had expressed our gratitude. I'm wondering today if we truly realized at that time how fortunate we were. Later we learned that people had lost their lives in that very area, even some along that very highway into Shakopee. It could have been us!

YOUNG CHARLES JR. HELPED DE-ICE CATTLE
by Charles & Virginia Groess
Pequot Lakes, MN

We lived on a small farm five miles southeast of Forest Lake with our two small children, Charles Jr — 29 months and Karen — six weeks.

The men had poured a new cement floor in the barn the day before and planned to haul hay on the eleventh. There were 20 head of young cattle and a team of horses in the pasture. We were going to winter them in our barn for a neighbor.

November 11 began as a typical November morning, grey, cloudy and rainy but mild. The wind soon switched to the northwest and it began to turn colder; the rain turned to ice, sleet and then snow as it quickly became a full scale blizzard.

My husband went to the pasture to check the animals and came hurrying back saying the cattle were freezing to death, totally encased in ice — and the horses were almost as bad. He quickly asked for my help because he knew he couldn't move them alone. I fed the baby and sat our son in a window to watch his daddy and me.

Charles took a halter to the pasture with us; after quite a struggle I got it on the blind mare while he worked with the horses. I managed to knock the ice off the noses of the cattle and he started to lead the blind mare. Other horses decided to follow and with my slapping, yelling and switching them, the cattle followed the horses to the corral.

Again they were encased in ice from head to toe. We had to work hard and fast or all of them would be lost. I hurried to the house, checked the baby, dressed our son warmly and took him to the barn with me. While I was gone my husband had gotten the team inside. Now he started the cattle singly into the barn. Our young son and I used burlap bags to knock the sheets of ice off the animals one at a time as they came through the door. The cattle were frightened; to keep Charles Jr. from harm, we had to stand him behind the stanchions. I was knee-deep in ice and it was very slippery when the last one was deiced. We had no feed, not a bit, but we could water them.

Early the next morning the snow had stopped, the wind was still, my husband hitched the team to a bobsled to go six miles round trip for hay for the livestock. The snowdrifts were very deep with hard icy crusts over them and it was extremely cold. He made it to the hay but the return trip was a nightmare. The sled kept tipping and the wind whipped the hay away. After many hours spent loading and reloading he finally reached home but had only enough hay left for that one night. He was exhausted. It was a long, trying day for me too. The cattle were crying and I was very concerned for my husband. God was merciful. The cattle survived and my husband was tired out but spared. We shall never, never forget that blizzard.

GAIETY THEATRE FREE BURLESQUE SHOW
by Mrs. Don Hanson
Minneapolis

I was on my way through Minneapolis to visit my parents in Milaca, taking a bus scheduled to leave at 1:15 PM. Since there was so much rain and snow, I went to the bus depot about 12:30. By departure time so much heavy snow had started with strong winds whipping everything around that they announced all departing buses had been cancelled. Another girl and I decided to get something to eat before the coffee shop closed and had a hamburger and a Coke. It was to be our last meal until the next afternoon.

I had no boots, hat nor scarf so made no attempt to walk to the nearby Radisson hotel. I heard later that all the rooms had been taken anyway and that there were crowds of people in the lobby looking for a place to stay because they could go no further.

By late afternoon the storm was so bad we couldn't see across the street and no one was leaving the depot. It was packed not only with travelers but people off the street.

In the evening the bus people announced over the speakers that the Gaiety burlesque theatre, directly across the street from the depot, would put on a free show for anyone who could get there. The wind was so strong that it took several men to open the depot doors and we formed a human chain to get across the street. This was very exciting to me as I had never been to a burlesque show. We waded in snow up to our hips and could hardly make it because of the high wind.

When we got back to the depot every chair and bench was taken. People were sound asleep and snoring all over the place. I went up to the balcony and got a Christian Science Monitor newspaper out of the reading rack and spread it on the floor. That's where I spent the night. The wind howled all night and the glass panes rattled as if they were going to come crashing in.

When morning finally came, nothing was moving outside and there was an abandoned fire truck stuck in the middle of the street. Later in the morning, four of us were able to get a cab to take us to the Great Northern train depot. We got a train which took us as far as Elk River. Our breakfast consisted of another Coke and candy bar.

After waiting all day in a restaurant, we learned that no buses would be through until the following day. Another girl and I were able to get a room for the night. I froze two toes just walking three blocks because it was still fifteen degrees below zero. Finally, the next evening, a bus for Milaca came through.The ride all the way was like going through a tunnel, as the snow banks on either side of the highway were higher than the bus.

I have lived in Minneapolis since 1943 and have never seen anything that could compare to this 1940 blizzard.

A FRATERNITY MAN'S POINT OF VIEW
by Robert W. Hayes
Eden Prairie, MN

I was a student at the University of Minnesota, working part time as a promotions man for Dayton's university store on campus. Also I worked in the store three or four hours daily.

As I recall, the day started with rain that got heavier as the day progressed until by noon it had turned into heavy snow. That snow was rapidly filling the streets and by 1 PM some of the Dinkytown stores were closing. So did we.

I walked the four or five blocks to my fraternity house to find a very convivial scene. Classes had been let out and the brothers were congregating. There was music, card games, laughter and a big fire in the fireplace. What did we care?

Later in the afternoon my father, who worked downtown, decided he should head for home on a street car. I had dropped him off in the morning and I had the family auto parked at the fraternity house. By that time no street cars were running and the town was closing down. Dad went to the Dyckman hotel and tried to finagle a room for himself for the night. Apparently everyone else in town was doing the same thing and, luckily, he wound up sharing a single room with a Dayton's manager whom he knew slightly. After a call to my mother, who was getting nervous, he proceeded to the Dyckman bar, joining a cast of hundreds.

Meanwhile, back at the fraternity house, the party was revving up in a big way. Beer and booze had magically come out of the woodwork and there was plenty of food in the kitchen. Fortunately, the house mother, who had her own private quarters in the house, was still there, and cooked.

Later in the evening one of the brothers who owned a business coupe (no back seat) had the brilliant idea of driving to the East Hennepin bar. He had a set of chains, which we installed, and six of us piled into the coupe for extra weight — or so we said.

We had no trouble getting there. The coupe moved like a Sherman tank. The cityscape was like a scene from a distant planet. Nothing seemed to be moving except us. It was genuinely eerie.

When we got there we were amazed to find people all over the place. We eventually closed the bar and beat our way back to the fraternity house. No sweat. It had been a truly great time. Finding a place to sleep at the overcrowded house was another matter. None of the city brothers had gone home and space was at a premium. Brothers were piled every which way, some even sleeping in the holiest of holy chapter room, where we held our meetings.

This went on for three nights and if you will imagine a bunch of young animals partying for three days, most without a change of underwear, you might get a whiff of the ambience at the house.

It was one of the best times I ever had!

My father finally beat his way home on the street car to meet the dark looks of my mother who no doubt considered herself the real victim of the storm.

JIMMY HEGG'S FAMOUS SNOW REMOVAL SIGN

by Jimmy Hegg
Minneapolis,MN

At that time I was working as a singer and master of ceremonies at Curly's Theatre cafe located at 20 S. 5th street in downtown Minneapolis.

Somehow, that night at closing time, with five assorted waitresses, cooks and bartenders packed in my 1937 Pontiac, plus my good friend, Alan Cameron, a baker on his way to his night job at a northern Minneapolis bakery, we plowed our halting way.

Somtimes we had to push our way through the deepest drifts but I managed to deliver all the occupants to their destinations. With the deepening snow and the reduced load, the car's traction became less effective and I got stuck firmly one block from my home in the middle of the street. My car stayed there for three days undisturbed by tow trucks or car thieves or anybody else.

Another snow storm later on provided a bit of humor to an otherwise grim situation. My wife, Jeanette, and I erected a sign at the curb in front of our restaurant known as *Jimmy Hegg's Starlite Club* which read as follows:

"NO SNOWING DURING CAR REMOVAL"

Nobody noticed the sign's strange wording so we called the newspaper. They sent out a photograper whom I think was Russ Bull. The managing editor,

Dave Silverman, liked it so the photo appeared in the Minneapolis paper. This Armistice Day was one of mother nature's most powerful quirks.

WAVES OF MILLIONS OF WATERFOWL
by Donald F. Henkel
Duluth, MN

I can remember the Armistice Day blizzard of 1940 as if it were just last hunting season as it made that much of an impression on me.

As we did every weekend of hunting season for a number of years, my dad, Frank Henkel, my grandfather, Seth Drake, and uncle Ellis Drake, all of Minneapolis, were duck hunting on a large lake and a slough southeast of Buffalo on the farm of Henry Johnson.

We would arrive around 5:30 AM and drive through the barnyard, down across the pasture and down a steep bank to the lake shore on the southeast side of the lake. We would then launch our two-man duckboats and await the coming of legal shooting time, in our blinds after setting out our decoys. The weather was quite pleasant that morning, perhaps a bit warmer than normal for that time of the year, so we were not heavily dressed.

After the initial flurry of shooting of the morning flight, hunting slowed down to an occasional bird, due to the bluebird weather.

Some time around midday a heavy overcast came rolling out of the northwest; the temperature began to drop rapidly and the wind increased noticeably. We should have left the marsh at his time but did not because of wave after wave of millions of waterfowl passing over, riding the front. Ducks reached from horizon to horizon and were so closely packed together that we could hear their wings slapping the wings of adjoining birds. It seemed that all the waterfowl in North America were on the move and were riding ahead of the storm.

We were so interested in this sight that we failed to realize how badly the weather had deteriorated. When we did attempt to leave our blind it soon became apparent that we could not cross the open water to our car. Between the wind, the waves, the flying spray and sleet, our duckboat became unmanageable and resembled an iceberg. My dad strained at the ice-covered oars and we finally returned to the shelter of the cattails on the west shore, where we dragged the boat into the mud and reeds. From there we hiked through the driving snow about one and a quarter miles through the swamp and around the end of the lake to our car. My grandfather and uncle were already at the car as they had been hunting on that shore line and did not have to cross open water. Naturally they were greatly relieved to see us.

By then it was obvious that we could not get the car up the snow covered hill to the farm, so we continued to watch the never ending passage of ducks. We soon became quite cold and wet so we stumbled back to the farm for warmth and food and hopefully to phone my mother in Minneapolis that we could not return that day but were safe.

The following day we got the old Farmall tractor with its metal lug wheels and towed our car back to the farm. Later in the day my dad and I returned to the marsh but could not locate our duck boat in the snow and weeds. In fact, we never did find it even when we returned to the farm the following spring. Also we found only four of our 24 Mason duck decoys, so it was a rather costly trip in lost equipment.

It was worth it, however, as never before nor since have I seen so many millions of waterfowl at a single time. The air was packed full of hurtling bodies and the sound of their wings was a steady whistling roar. Even now, forty-four and a half years later, I can recall their frightened quacks, honks and continuous cries.

My father and grandfather have long since passed on to where the hunting is easy and bag limits quickly filled. My uncle, now in his eighties, is still alive and lives in Arizona.

I have two very young grandsons who I hope will grow up to love the great outdoors and the hunting life as I do.

I'M 78 AND NEVER EXPERIENCED ANY MORE STORMS LIKE THAT ONE.
by John Heryla
Minneapolis, MN

On that day I was working for the Great Northern railroad at the Minneapolis junction roundhouse near the Broadway bridge on Central avenue northeast. I left work at 4 PM, hoping I could make it home to Columbia Heights where I lived on 42nd avenue and Polk street northeast. It was about four miles.

I got to Central avenue northeast where there is a bridge. Cars were stuck every where on the up grade on 17th avenue. Street cars could have moved if automobiles had stayed off the tracks. Cars were criss-crossed everywhere. I helped push some autos to get going, but too many cars behind me went around my car, met some others coming toward them and they all got stuck again. I worked my car to the right as far as I could and walked back to where I was employed.

The second shift boss was glad to see me because his workers couldn't get to work. I was a boilermaker's helper and was now told to be engine watchman, feeding all hot engines coal and water.

At midnight, the same situation. The midnight foreman called to say he couldn't make it to work and the second shift foreman had to stay another shift; I was asked to stay another shift too. About 2 AM I was given a chance to take a brief nap, then finished the night. Of course in 1940 we didn't get paid time and a half. Then I had to stay and work my own shift of 8 to 4 PM. Anyhow, I worked 32 straight hours.

On top of all that I walked the four miles home, stopped at a grocery store to buy milk and bread and arrived home at 8 PM. Was I tired? I'll say. I had supper, went to bed and slept until 7 AM the next morning. Then walked to the street car line and went to work again. After work I took a scoop shovel from the railroad to shovel my car free, then drove home.

That was some storm. I am now 78 years old and darned glad I never experienced any more storms like that one. I put in 42 years on the Great Northern and I'm enjoying my retirement since 1967.

DIDN'T FIND THE PAIL UNTIL SPRING
by Mrs. L.H.Hoeft
Young America, MN

I was 18 and living with my family three miles north of Young America, on a farm.

The morning of the 11th, my father, Adolph Boehmke, thought the weather was going to be bad but needed feed for the animals. He loaded some corn and grain onto the truck and headed for town to have it ground. He told my mother he'd be back as soon as possible and left at about 9 AM.

My oldest sister had taken the car to town where she worked in the local grocery store. At about 11 AM she called to tell my mother that my father and a neighbor had started for home on foot. They had tried to make it with the truck, found they couldn't do so and put it in a local garage for storage. She added that she would stay with our uncle and aunt in town.

Soon after my mother hung up the receiver, our telephone went dead. Then we started watching for my father to come home. The storm was terrible by this time. About five hours later, at 4 PM, I was standing by the south window and I saw two shadows coming around the corner. I knew one was my father because not many would attempt to walk in such terrible weather. Luckily they had worn enough clothes so, besides some frosty eyebrows and red noses, they were fine, but exhausted. Needless to say, the feed didn't get home but we had enough to tide us over. My sister didn't know for some time that my father had gotten home.

Our neighbor rested at our house and then left again for his home, which was about a mile away. My father remarked that the neighbor might have gotten lost had he been alone because he became disoriented at times. What undoubtedly helped the neighbor reach home from our house was that the road followed the property lines in many places.

One rather funny thing happened to me during this storm. I lost a brand new milk pail. Our barn doors faced north and south but we could only use the north one because the south one was burried by a loose hayloft door. We milked by hand and when we were through my mother told me to fill the new pail with drinking water for the house. Heading back for the house, I had to go out the north door of the barn, around the building on the west side because of huge drifts on the east and head for the house. I ran as fast as I could and in the dark ran smack into a big snowbank. Down I went and the pail flew across the road and down the embankment by the lake. We never found that pail until the following spring when the snow disappeared.

BOURBON FOR HALF-FROZEN ACCOUNTANT
by Willard S. Hull
St. Paul, MN

November 11, 1940 started cloudy with light rain. I wore toe rubbers and a raincoat over my jacket and trousers, a felt hat, but no gloves. It was about 42 degrees. The Randolph avenue street car took me to downtown St. Paul where my office was located on the 20th floor of the First National Bank building. Carfare was either five or six cents.

Our work in the accounting department went smoothly until after lunch when it was announced that the street cars would soon stop running because of the blizzard and that the office would close at two o'clock.

One of my friends in the office had driven that day and his car was parked in an open lot across the street from the Main Post Office. He said he and another co-worker who lived in my area had a lot to do and had decided to work until 5 PM. Knowing I was in a similar fix, they offered me a ride at the same time. So, at 5 PM we left the office and went to the car. It was frozen up tight! Finally we got it started but the fan belt broke in the process.

The three of us in the car got to Ballard's garage then located on Kellogg and Wabasha; their repair shop was up a ramp to the second floor with an entry that was about 30 feet square and open on the south and west sides. We needed a new fan belt and a gallon of anti-freeze which Ballard sold us. Many cars were ahead of us for work. It was up to us to install the fan belt and to thaw the radiator. The tools my friend had in the car were barely sufficient to do the job but, in time, the three of us got it done. It was freezing work. When we found the radiator fluid was circulating properly we started for home.

Because the snow was so heavy and the wind so strong, we followed the West 7th street car tracks to the Randolph car tracks and then to Hamline avenue where we turned south to Bayard — where I lived. In less than two blocks cars were abandoned with snow nearly half way up the car doors. My friends let me out and backed to Randolph to continue homeward.

My block and a half walk south to Bayard was manageable but difficult. Turning west on Bayard the wind and driving snow was fierce. In that last struggle to my house I had doubts whether I could make it. Finally, at nine o'clock I got to our front steps and, in a half-frozen condition, banged on our door. It was promptly opened by my dear wife. I went into the kitchen and sat down in a kind of stupor.

I couldn't speak. Sizing up the situation rapidly and accurately, my wife poured a half glass of bourbon and handed it to me. A few sips of the bourbon and I was able to utter my first words and explain the delay in getting home.

The next morning street cars were not running and the snow was level with car roofs on Hamline avenue. This was pictured in *Life* magazine. Tales of people stranded in every possible situation abounded.

This storm was well remembered by thousands.

MY HUSBAND AND I WERE DUCK HUNTERS
by LaVonne Jacobsen
Excelsior, MN

My husband was 28 and I was 26 and we were duck hunters at our duck lease at Benson on Sunday. At 2 PM it started to snow and by 4 PM it was snowing and blowing so hard we couldn't see the flocks of ducks coming in until they were on top of us. We decided to leave our duck boat and trailer and start for home in Minneapolis. At Litchfield the snow turned to rain but we made it home. The next day, Armistice Day, when we left for work we dressed warmly, although I didn't wear overshoes. It was raining and we knew snow was coming. Department stores were expecting a lot of business because of the school holiday so many people were dressed lightly. After all, it was just a light warm rain.

By 4 PM our company, Packard of Minneapolis, Inc., sent most people home except some service department men and me. I had to wait for my husband who worked for Nelson Oil company near Ward's in St. Paul. He called at 6 PM to say he was leaving to pick me up. The temperature was plunging, the snow had thickened, and the wind increased. Street cars had quit running because they couldn't get up hills or because accidents blocked their tracks. People were frantically trying to find cover. University avenue was deserted as my husband drove it. He stopped to pick up a girl waiting for a street car (which wasn't coming). She was dressed in a light jacket and no overshoes. He dropped her off, picked me up and we started from Packard at 8 PM.

We lived two blocks off highway #12 and one block off highway #100 in St. Louis Park. There were 200 cars stalled in drifts between Hennepin avenue and highway #100. The #100 cloverleaf had 10 to 15 cars blocking it. It took days to tow away and clear out all that mess.

We ended going back to Packard's and staying there. My husband slept on a couch in the president's office and I slept in the back seat of a Packard sedan. I well remember that the wind shook the display windows like a terrier shakes a rag and all night I thought the big windows would collapse.

At 6:30 AM the phones started to ring. At 7 I opened the switchboard. Doug and I were the only ones in the building until 9 AM when four service department men arrived. The six of us held down the place.

Eventually, later that day, we heard that things were better so Doug and I went home. We drove circuitously on Hennepin, Lake and #100. Our street, Quentin avenue, had not been plowed because it was only two blocks long but my husband battered the car back and forth through the drifts as far as we could go. He had to carry me the last 50 yards. We dressed and went back to dig out our car, which took until midnight. We eventually got our duck boat and trailer but even a week later the viaducts were only partly plowed with one-way traffic. One had to honk car horns to warn oncoming traffic to wait. We drove through tunnels.

ONE-EYED MAN DROVE 20 MILES IN HEIGHT OF STORM
by Betty Johnson
Eden Prairie, MN

Our family operated a variety store in Shakopee during the forties. Mom was scheduled for surgery the morning of November 11. My stepfather, Bruce McMurray, would be with her in the Minneapolis hospital, while I managed the store. Late in the day, after the storm had become so intense, my stepfather, who had vision in only one eye, drove the 20 miles from the city to Shakopee. He attempted the return trip because he knew I was unable to operate the ancient oil heating system in the store. He told me he drove all the way with one hand on the steering wheel and one hand holding open the door—and trying to see with one eye only. My sister, Mary Sampson, and I look upon that drive as one of the most heroic events of our generation. Both of these parents are deceased today.

WAS I FREEZING TO DEATH?
by Zylph Anderson Johnson
Hudson, WI

I remember November 11, 1940 and I hope and pray it will never happen again to me or anyone.

This particular morning, as I was dressing to go to my job at Young Quinlan company in downtown Minneapolis, I chose black toeless and heelless shoes to go with the black dress I was to wear at work. We had our choice back then of black, brown or navy blue. My strand of imitation pearls added a final touch. I slipped into my spring coat, no hat and black gloves because it was a beautiful morning.

As I did every day, I waited for my Bryn Mawr bus only a half-block away. I lived with a sister and brother-in-law and another single sister. The usual riders were waiting as I reached the very familiar corner and we exhanged "hellos" and "Isn't this a beautiful day?" comments.

Work went as usual, a busy Monday morning, with few chances to glance outside. By 11 AM there were fewer and fewer customers and I ran across to Woolworth's to grab a quick lunch and to window shop. That's when I realized why business was so slow. It had started to snow softly but the wind was picking up and swirling it around. My spring coat didn't seem so warm and my feet were wet and cold when I returned to work, stomping my feet, brushing the snow out of my hair and wondering what this day would bring.

At 2 PM our store manager came to tell us he was closing the store and we were all to go home. He told us travel was bad and that street cars and buses were running late.

When the buses did come by I couldn't read the signs on the front and had to ask the driver. Having waited over a half-hour I was ready to take any bus to get out of the cold and snow — and wind. We hadn't gone many blocks when the bus stopped, the driver turned to us and said "We can't go any further. We are stuck in a drift." He said we were near a bridge. Because there was no heat in the bus and because I am a determined Swede, I decided, with others, to try walking. I knew if it were by a bridge I had only three and maybe four blocks to walk at the most.

Finding the direction was one thing but my feet were so cold and wet I thought they were going to snap off at the ankles any minute. Keeping my coat pulled up over my head as much as possible I plowed through drift after drift, falling, picking myself up, falling again. My purse was gone, somewhere in a drift but as I stumbled, I prayed. I knew someone was behind me and I'm sure there was someone ahead of me, stumbling and falling as well. I couldn't catch my breath, the tears were frozen in my eyes. I just couldn't move to take another step — when a very dim light was literally shoved into my face and a strong hand took my now frostbitten, gloveless hand — as I wondered if this is what it is like to be frozen to death.

I was picked up by a pair of strong arms and carried into an open doorway. It wasn't until then that I recognized two very familiar voices — that of my sister who was crying — and that of my brother-in-law who had been waiting at the bus stop for whomever needed shelter. God had answered all of our prayers.

My sister LaVonne had filled the two laundry tubs with warm water and I was put into one with my clothes still on as she began rubbing my hands, face and feet. Then she wrapped me like a baby in a warm blanket. I lay on the divan, shivering, shaking, crying, laughing, and again my brother-in-law, Banjo Jose Silva, put on dry clothes, took his flashlight with the battery growing weaker by the minute, and went back out into the raging storm. He wanted to help anyone he could and also keep an eye open for my sister, Geri May. She was probably on her way home from her job at Honeywell on 4th avenue.

It seemed like forever; I may have dozed off—when the door burst open and there stood someone looking like a snow man. No shoes, no purse, no gloves. It was my sister, who had made her way from one street car to another, from bus to bus until she too believed those blocks from the stuck bus wouldn't be too far. And she had made it.

The power had gone off so, regardless of being inside, it was still cold. The telephone lines were down. We all huddled into one room warming ourselves by candles. At that time I think we discovered the now-popular layered look because we kept putting on extra socks, sweaters, blankets, anything to keep us warm.

Morning finally came. We were still trapped inside. Nothing moved outside although the wind and snow had died down. The hills in the snow turned out to be cars and buses, completely covered. The smaller hills were no doubt the people who weren't as lucky as we were. Twenty-four hours later a path had been shovelled to the main street, men and women alike being busy shoveling out and checking the cars to see if and who were inside.It had been a nightmare.

Every November 11 I think about this storm and usually decide it isn't necessary to go any place. If we set out for a short trip, needless to say there's always boots, mittens and extra warm clothing available. The reality of this storm may seem bizarre to the present generation but I suppose it could happen again—so be careful out there.

I now reside in Hudson with my husband and with five grandkids to tell this to; maybe just a little warning will brush off.

POUNDING AND SCREAMING AT THE DOOR
by Helga M. Jorgensen
Edina, MN

On my husband's way home at noon it was quite apparent that our snow storm was becoming a full-blown blizzard. He had the good sense to back the car into the garage. We lived in a one bedroom double bungalow we owned at 3235 47th avenue south in Minneapolis and in that neighborhood there are alleys.

To get out of the garage and go down the alley would take all the push a car could muster. Going forward was better than backward.

After a little lunch we decided we might just as well take a nap with our 14 month old son. While the blizzard was raging outside, and we had just settled down, someone started pounding at our door and our good friend and neighbor was screaming that her mother had been killed and her father injured – in a St. Paul hospital.

She wanted our help in getting to the hospital where she hoped to meet her husband, going there from Pig Eye island where he worked.

I bundled up my baby and went to the duplex next door to take care of her two little girls and my husband prepared for the hazardous drive. This is where it was so helpful that he had backed the car into the garage. It was the only way they could have made it down the alley.

There were many anxious hours as the storm raged. I had my hands full with the three little ones, all the while watching the storm and hoping my husband could make the trip and return without incident. He did get her to the hospital but the trip home was even more hazardous because there was no way to see curbs – and intersections were a mess.

We were fortunate that he was able to get home safely but our friend and neighbor was not so lucky. Her father was seriously injured; her mother and another lady had died as their car skidded on a highway just outside St. Paul; the two women had died at the scene. They had been on their way back to St. Paul from a trip to Duluth.

It was a very sad day for all but we have always been grateful that in this small way we were able to help our friends. The loss of my own mother the previous February helped me understand my friend's situation. She and her husband had helped us on more than one occasion and we are still good friends today. I am now alone but they aren't too far away. I thank God for friends.

BROUGHT BABY HOME IN 30 BELOW TEMP
by Ruth Keller
Edina, MN

Late on November 10, 1940 I went into premature labor. We lived on county road #18 just two blocks south of 36th avenue north. My husband and brother-in-law rushed me to Swedish hospital. The weather was wet and threatening and as we drove along, the rain was turning to heavy slushy snow. We got to the hospital where my 3 1/2 pound son was delivered on November 11.

I watched from my hospital window as the storm was progressing, but the men decided to start for home. They slowly made their way up highway #100 turning onto 36th avenue north where the drifts were high and the visibility zero. They shoveled their way for a short distance but cars were stalled ahead of them and the narrow road was blocked.

Seeing a light in a house on the road, they shoveled their way into the driveway and stumbled into the house where, luckily, the owners gave them some food and coffee. Seeing the weather was impossible, those dear people offered their one bedroom, upstairs, which was gratefully accepted. When the men came downstairs the next morning, there were seven other stranded motorists trying to sleep on the living room floor. They still couldn't move onwards but on the third day they attempted it, shoveling much of the way.

My sister had been left in our house with only a pet dog for company. Her food rations were running out and she was just generously dividing her last slice of bread with the dog when the exhausted men arrived, with clothes wet and frozen.

I heard at the hospital that doctors were using skis to get to their homebound critical patients. This was in the days when some house calls were still being made.

My two other sisters were caught downtown in Minneapolis on that Armistice Day, trying to get a street car or bus, whichever came their way. They made their way to the Radisson hotel where they, fortunately, got the last available room. Later, many people slept on chairs in the lobby. The next day they were able to get a bus but it took three hours to get home.

A nurse friend was working at Veterans hospital. She couldn't get a bus on Minnehaha avenue but flagged down a Minneapolis Tribune truck, which got her through. She was stranded for two days at the hospital. After I had been in the hospital for two weeks, I was allowed to take my premature son home but only under the condition that I would take an incubator. Incubators in those days were actually just square wooden boxes with a thermometer and light bulb inside to regulate the temperature. We strapped it to the back of our car and arrived home in 30 degrees below zero weather. My son, Dennis, has now grown to six feet tall, weighs 200 pounds, so it shows that some of this antiquated equipment served the purpose quite well.

DID STORM HASTEN STREET CAR'S END?
by Ruth Kincaid
Minneapolis, MN

I left the house at about 8:30 AM and walked toward the bus stop on 38th street. It was warm and raining a little and I wore a lightweight coat and gloves, a hat but no rubbers or boots because winter had not yet arrived. There had been no snow or cold weather. I put up my new plastic umbrella and remember that a small twig blew through it, although the wind didn't seem strong.

Downtown at Dayton's where I worked at the jewelry department we began to notice people coming in covered with snow, either front or back, depending upon which way they had been walking. It was about 10 AM. We could see outside that snow was getting heavier and by noon it was blowing almost parallel to the street and piling up at an amazing rate. Rumors reached us that street cars were having a hard time and that autos were getting stalled. I didn't go out in that strange white world at lunch time but looked out and wondered how I'd get home. It was early afternoon when we received notice that we would close at 3 PM.

I put on my light coat, hat and gloves and wished I had something for my feet besides my sturdy oxfords, and decided to leave the umbrella in my locker. My friends and I left for various car lines but agreed to meet at the Walgreen drug store on Marquette if we couldn't get a car. I walked out into a much-changed world. Huge drifts of snow lined the streets and sidewalks were buried under many feet of heavy wet packed snow. The first thing I did was to fall because it was so slippery and lumpy in spots. I managed to cross Eighth street and get into the exit of the State theatre. I was sheltered and could await the Chicago car. People waiting there included some who had waited for over an hour — but no cars had come. A few autos were abandoned on the street and once in a great while one would slither by.

I met a friend bound for the bus depot where she had a friend who might give us a ride. She suggested I come along but she was wearing a winter coat and boots and I didn't want to walk that far clad as lightly as I was. Instead I gradually worked my way to Marquette avenue, standing in doorways and warming inside any store possible. I met several friends at the Walgreen store and we decided it was as good a place as any to wait, particularly since we could see both the Chicago and Nicollet lines from there. We sat in a booth drinking coffee and took turns standing in line to call home. I found that my father had gotten a ride home and my high school aged sister had also made it. My father wanted me to go to the YWCA but it was three blocks away and, since payday wasn't until the next morning, I had only 90 cents in my purse, plus a few car tokens. I decided to stay where I was and hope for a way home.

My friends drifted away and about 6 PM I went across the street and again lined up for that restaurant's phone in the kitchen. It wasn't very clean so I decided on a ham sandwich and a carton of milk for supper. There were people constantly watching for street cars but none came.

As I was wondering what we would do if the restaurant closed, a cry sounded that a street car had been sighted on Nicollet. We crossed to Nicollet and there were two cars fastened together and heading south. Neither was very crowded and everyone was able to get aboard. I even got a seat back near the fare box where there was a little stove in which coal was burned. So it was warm. The two cars went along Nicollet, backing up and then shoving slowly ahead. The morning's wet snow had frozen in the tracks and they had to break through that plus the heavy snow atop the frozen mess. The cars roared and shuddered as they moved along. We got to Grant street and slowly navigated the curves but about one block beyond that point the motor of the first street car burned out and we were stranded. Some people went into a hotel and made telephone calls; the rest of us just sat. Some of my fellow passengers had been on cars since 4 PM and it was now nearly 9 PM. It was warm so we all stayed, wondering if we'd have to spend the night there or maybe in the lobby of the small hotel.

We were among the fortunate ones because about an hour later a bus pulled up to the door of our car. Buses were just starting to be used and they were able to get through, not being tied to a track. We pile onto the bus and it made fairly good time out Nicollet and I was at 38th street by 10 PM. Lucky me, the drug store was open and I could again phone home and tell them were I was. And also that I had only to wait for a 38th street bus and I'd be home. They said they'd be watching for me.

In half an hour the 38th street bus came and it was close to 11 PM when I got off at my street. Got off! It was more like jumping off into four feet of unbroken snow. I went in above my knees. The bus moved off and I was faced with a huge expanse of untouched snow between the corner and my home — half a block away.

I lived across from Bancroft school and the wind had blown across the open area behind the school, blowing down the street and packing the snow. I still remember the effort it took to pull up my legs and sink them into the snow ahead as I struggled up the street. At my house I could not locate the steps and floundered up the bank. But ah, the door was opened, light streamed out and I was pulled in by my family. A hot footbath was waiting, and a hot meal. Also it was wondeful to relax and tell my family all about it — and hear their stories. I was grateful to spend the night in my own bed and most fortunate since many people spent theirs on street cars, or in stores, or in hotels and homes which were opened to them. We read all about it in the next day's paper and about those who had died.

I wonder if this storm may have hastened the end of the street car and the change to buses?

I DELIVERED EN ROUTE TO DINNER
by Margaret Klapprich
Wayzata, MN

On that Sunday, November 10, 1940, my husband and I and our three-year old son Paul picked up my husband's brother Robert, his wife Mildred and his Uncle Bernard and started for our favorite restaurant in Stillwater for dinner, a long way from Wayzata.

We had just entered the Minneapolis city limits when I told my husband to drop me off at Eitel hospital because I was having labor pains. I had difficulty in persuading him I was serious as we headed for Eitel.

His brother took the rest of the family some place to eat, but not to Stillwater, while Ed and I stayed at Eitel. I then proceeded to produce a little girl whom we named Joan Marie. After they had dinner, the others came back for Ed and they all returned to Wayzata. At supper time Ed took Paul and went to tell his dad about our baby girl. While they were on the way it started to rain and soon turned to snow.

My sister, Elsie Day, was a registered nurse on duty at Eitel and she came in on Monday morning and couldn't get back to Wayzata until the following Friday. She wore my clothes while hers were being laundered in the hospital laundry.

The only visitors I had during those six days were my sister-in-law, her husband and their two neighbors, who walked to the hospital from north Minneapolis. Even my husband couldn't come in to see me until Saturday because he worked in a filling station in Wayzata; his entire crew had to work eighteen hour shifts getting roads open, cars towed and started, doing what they could to keep people moving. I remember he told me of the snow that was packed solidly under the hoods of cars, driven there by the wind, and how they had to be cleaned out, thawed and eventually started.

Regular snowplows were used but the drifts were too high, so shovels and walking was the order of the day. Highway #12, Wayzata boulevard, west of Minneapolis toward McCarthy's was a sea of stalled cars, many of them buried completely.

Telephone lines were down. There was no mail service, only telegrams which had to be delivered on foot.

I remember how the wind whistled and in my hospital room the hanging light would swing back and forth. It was no fun.

IN AND OUT OF THE DITCHES
by Ernest Klatt
Buffalo, MN

I am an old man 87 years old and I have a good memory. I would like to share my experience of the 1940 blizzard with you. I was a milk hauler for 52 years and had many experiences. We did not have television and did not get the weather report. We had radio but we didn't listen to the weather. As usual, we had our milk trucks running at 6:30 AM outside the garage, ready to start at 6:50 to pick up milk. The sun was trying to shine through clouds. There was a little mist and snow coming down and freezing to the windshield. Not too bad but it kept on getting worse.

I got to my first stop at 7:00 and the farmer said it looks like it is going to be a bad day. I didn't think much about it then but by 9 or 10 o'clock I knew what I was in for. It was getting slippery and I couldn't see very far ahead. I was not going very fast. I knew that if I stopped, I'd not get started again but I had to stop to put on chains.

I always got to my farmers about the same time, but this day I was an hour late to one of my bigger shippers. I didn't see the two brothers at that farm very often but this time they were ready to help me put the twenty-two cans on the truck. The one brother said if it were too bad he would pick up the empty cans, since they lived only about two miles from our place.

I was nearly at the end of my route and saw a farmer run off the road as he was trying to get to Corcoran, so I took my chain and pulled him out and told him if he knew what was good for him he would turn around and go home. I started for Clover Leaf creamery and there down the road was my other truck. He had cut the corner of the drive so I pulled him out and helped him put on chains. Started out again and got to the creamery. They were glad to see me because I was the first one to arrive. I had a fast dinner and started back to Corcoran. Don't know how many cars and trucks I helped back on the road. When I got almost to Corcoran that same farmer was off the road again and I pulled him out once more. Had a lunch, rested a while. Sure was glad to be home.

The farmer came to get his cans and I gave him 30 Twin City cans that had rust on them but anything that held milk was used that day. Two days later I picked up milk in wash tubs and old beat up 30, 40 or 50 gallon stone jars. About four o'clock a farmer who had cattle in the pasture in Corcoran started to put them in the barn. He got a little ways from home and ran off the road. He called me for help. My helper and I put chains on my stock truck. We got stuck and the truck was there for two days before we got it home again. We called him and told him that we would try to get the cattle out of the pasture and into the barn. We took a horse and five of us men got to the cows and the cows followed the horse home, so we got them into the barn. We called the farmer who was very happy to hear that news.

When I got home the telephone rang and it was my son. He had a milk route out of Hamel and Holy Name. He had run off the road with a load of milk and wanted me to come and help him. I asked him where he was and he told me. He said he could stay where he was. I told him it wasn't fit out for a man or beast and when the weather got better I would help him. At this time my wife and I had a little misunderstanding. She thought I should at least try to help him but, after talking it over, she saw it my way. We ate supper, were very tired and went to bed.

The next day the snowing and the driving wind was still with us. Nothing moving. I worked in the garage all day because we had the snow plow there. We worked to be ready when the snow was over. The county had trucks at Hopkins which were not ready for this blizzard so it was a few days before they ever got to Corcoran. It stopped and the wind was going down that night (November 12) so they called to have me get the snow truck out and put on the plow. I had lunch and started up the road. That four-wheel drive sure had the power. It was slow going because the snow was so heavy, wet and thick that many times I had to back up and make a run for it. It took three and a half hours to go about three miles. I had lunch, started out again, went back to Corcoran where I left my man to sleep so he could help plow the next day. What a night my supervisor and I had. We stayed on the main road; road; we'd go a small way and get stuck, back up, and make a run again for it. Nine o'clock the next morning we got to Corcoran. By that time the farmers were coming from all over, bringing their milk—some with sleds, manure spreaders, and stone boats. (Ed.: a stone boat was a low sledge-like conveyance upon which large stones could easily be rolled for moving). About noon (November 13) we started for the Clover Leaf creamery with four large loads of milk. Were they ever glad to see us!

It was about a week before all the roads and the driveways were open. The snow didn't go away until the next spring. We had a half-breed Indian living with us who had said we would have a lot of snow that winter. The muskrats built huge houses and that means lots of snow and high water in the spring.

As I remember, 1952 and 1965 were bad too. 1935 had a lot of snow and cold. It never got above zero for thirty days. We had to use chains on for a whole month.

GIANT MARSHMALLOWS IN THE STREETS
by Mary Kociemba
Fridley, MN

Although I am now a 72 year old widow, I have some vivid memories of
that terrible day, because I spent 7 1/2 hours in two different cars trying to get
from here to there on the snow clogged streets of Minneapolis. Even though
I didn't suffer any serious physical effects, it was a very traumatic and frightening experience.

I was not yet married and lived with my brother Ted in the northern edge
of Fridley, which at that time was a sparsely populated rural area.

Both of us worked in northeast Minneapolis and I rode with him to and
fro my job each day. I was a factory hand at Durkee Atwood company and he
was an electrical repairman for Brede sign company. Both businesses were
located in the general area between Broadway and Lowry northeast, close to
Central avenue.

Because Ted's work took him all over the city and because he had such irreg-
ular quitting hours, I would hike more than a mile to a small hamburger shop
on Central avenue where I'd wait for him.

On the morning of November 11 when we started for work, the weather was
so balmy that I decided to leave my coat at home but did take a sweater.

As I worked through the morning hours, I began to hear that it was misting
outside. Soon it began to sleet, then snow, and by 2 PM the blizzard was in
full bloom. By 2:30 we employees were dismissed to go home. There I was wondering how I was going to walk that long distance to meet Ted when I had only
a light sweater.

I was certainly glad when a co-worker offered to drive me to the hamburger
shop and we mushed through the deep snow to her car. She proved to be a
very inexperienced driver and it took us nearly three hours to travel less than
one mile. We never did make it to the hamburger shop because we got bogged
down behind a mass of abandoned cars on Central avenue, just two blocks
north of Broadway. They were so covered with snow they looked like giant
marshmallows. Ahead of the cars we could see a street car off the tracks with
its rear end resting against the curbstone, so we knew nothing was going to
move in that area, including us. We abandoned the car and waded slowly
through the snow to a nearby home and were warmly welcomed by the middle-
aged residents. Several other motorists had taken refuge in their home too and,
while we all took turns using the phone, the owners served coffee and cocoa.
I tried calling Ted at his shop but there was no answer so I called my older
brother, Dick, who lived at 27th and Pillsbury and told him where I was
stranded. He said that Ted was stranded too, just a few blocks from me and
told me to sit tight because he had just put tire chains on his car and was going
to attempt to get through to rescue me.

By avoiding heavily travelled streets, he somehow managed to get to both of us shortly after 7 PM. My memory is dim about whether he brought along a coat for me to wear, but I remember what a tough time I had walking to where he had parked; my feet and legs felt like chunks of ice.

After picking up Ted we started the treacherous drive back to his house. It took us 4 1/2 hours to drive from the vicinity of Broadway and Central avenue northeast to 27th and Pillsbury south — and it was a nightmare all the way. To this day I don't know how we ever made it.

After being snowbound at Dick's home for three days, we were finally able to get back to our rural home in Fridley.

WE RENDERED A HALF MILLION TURKEYS
by Herbert Kortz
Minneapolis,MN

I was employed by Minneapolis Hide and Tallow company located in New Brighton. The company had three trucks which picked up meat scraps, bones and grease from restaurants, butcher shops and grocery stores. I worked from 1 PM to 9:30 PM, had a girl friend in Menomonie, Wisconsin, and was 22 years old. I spent my weekends in Menomonie.

That Monday morning it started to rain and was very windy. I left Menomonie at 9 AM to drive the 70 miles to New Brighton. I made it all right but the road was very slippery and got worse as I went west into Minnesota. It took three hours to drive those 70 miles.

When I arrived home in New Brighton I drained the radiator and put in two gallons of anti-freeze. I ate lunch and then walked the two blocks to work. It was snowing very hard and only two of our trucks made it to the plant that day.

The next day, Tuesday, I tried to start my car and found that the thermostat had not opened when I put in the anti-freeze and the block and head were frozen and broken. I didn't get the car fixed for two weeks because garages were so swamped repairing cars which had frozen or stalled on the roads.

A few days later many turkey growers picked up their frozen turkeys and brought them to Minneapolis to sell but were stopped by the health department. Then they brought them to our rendering plant where we had at least 500,000 dead turkeys. We started to cook them, 200 in each cooker, feathers and all. We didn't get all those turkeys processed until spring when they started to thaw.

The winter of 1936 had also been a bad one. We had below zero weather from January into February for 42 straight days. At that time I lived on a farm five miles northeast of Litchfield. For two months we had to use horses and a sled to haul the cream to town and to get groceries.

I retired at age 62 in 1980 and since then my wife and I and two grandchildren have toured 49 states in our motor home. I hope I never see another storm like that one of November 11, 1940.

TODAY'S YOUNG PEOPLE COULD DO IT TOO
by June Krull
Hillman, MN

We were living in our first home, a 20 by 22 foot unfinished shack in the village of Fridley, later annexed to Columbia Heights. We were building it ourselves, slowly, so it was unfinished. We had no ceiling, storm windows or anything but rough flooring. It sat on two courses of home-made cement blocks and we had no contact with the outside world.

We had walked to my parents' home on 39th and Reservoir boulevard a couple of days before and they had asked us to join them in a trip to Johnsville. They were to glean their winter heating and cooking fuel from the brush piles left by a farmer. This meant pulling the brush apart, chopping out anything large enough to burn and then burning the remainder for the farmer. We had no car so were going to ride with my family.

I offered to fry several of our chickens to share for the two meals we would eat in the field. No one had refrigeration yet; we didn't even have an icebox. I covered the finished chicken with a towel, on a shelf near my range. When morning came it was nearly all devoured by our big cat. I promptly threw him outside.

This was Monday and it was raining lightly. My husband walked to a neighbor's to call my folks who said if it cleared by 10 AM we would go. It didn't clear but continued to rain and by late afternoon it had turned to snow. The wind blew so hard we could barely hear each other in the house. We heated our house with a tiny wood stove, hauling packaged fuel from a mile away on a sled. That fuel consisted of six blocks of compressed coal dust, wrapped in brown paper. We paid a dollar for those six pieces. The wind blew under our home and through the walls. Everything movable was fluttering all the time. The insulation was batts of newspaper covered with brown paper.

As the day progressed, the storm got worse. We survived by wrapping our feet in newspaper and by putting on boots heated in the oven. We were lucky to have electricity. Our stove obviously wasn't big enough for this storm so my husband walked to his parents for a bigger wood stove which was in the garage there. He and his dad laced it to a sled and pulled it back the 2 1/2 blocks to our place. Drifts were over their heads but the sled didn't break through the hard crust on the snow. It was a long and tiring trip up and over those drifts.

There was a large dance hall and beer joint next to my in-laws home and it was filled with stranded motorists. They slept on booths, bars or just sitting up.

Their cars were buried and had to be dug out by hand after the storm abated.

We didn't get a paper for a week. Daily they told of more tragedies and horror stories, of whole families frozen to death even though they had burned all of their wooden furniture. Of farmers who never made it to their barns, of parents trapped away from home and whose children died.

My husband was employed on one of the public works projects near Crooked Lake and it was more than a week before his driver could make it out there with his carload of workers.

All of my canning was stored on the ground under our house. I reached it by removing some of the floorboards. It all froze, causing a real hardship. To make ends meet, we paid a farmer 25 cents a gallon for raw milk and made our butter from the cream at the top of the jug. Also we allowed four dollars a week for groceries for two and from that I was also able to pay all medical expenses until after our first son was born in May of 1942. I remember that the doctor bill for the delivery was $35 and the hospital bill for ten days was $60.

I hear a lot of older folk say they don't believe young people of today would be able to survive under those conditions but I believe they would be just as resourceful as we were. Some might even welcome the challenge. I do not regret one day of my life and am thankful I still have my husband with whom I can reminisce. God has been good to us.

WALKING IN TOWN AS BAD AS IN COUNTRY
by Sylvia D. Kubes
St. Louis Park, MN

I was working for my room and board plus $1.00 a week carfare while attending vocational school, taking postgraduate courses in cosmetology. My mother had come down to the cities to spend some time with her sister and we planned to meet in Dayton's fourth floor rest room before shopping and having lunch.

I left home at 50th and Colfax about 9 AM; it was raining and sleeting so I wore high-heeled rubber overshoes, black rayon slacks, a blouse and a black raincoat. No hat and cotton gloves. It was slow going downtown but I finally arrived at Dayton's to find them putting sheets over everything. I hurried to the elevator, rushed to the fourth floor and, of course, mother wasn't there. A clerk said the store was closing because of the coming storm. I called my aunt, who had no word from my mother and we decided I should return home.

I got onto a 54th and Bryant car but it was barely moving, then stopped. I sat on it for two hours and it got as far as 10th street. I was almost frozen stiff because there was no heat on the car. I got off at 10th and went into a bar to use their restroom; got back on the car and it hadn't moved an inch. We sat in that cold street car, dressed for forty above temperature, and sat there until about midnight. We had gotten as far as the Basilica when a city bus took us off and continued on the route. I was the last one off at Bryant and 50th.

The wind was howling, snow was up to my hips and the signs were swinging in the wind. I didn't know which direction to go so went to the corner store and wiped the snow from a sign on the door. It said *Taystee Bread* so I knew where I was. I headed west, plowing through snow by swinging my leg sideways over the snow and sinking each time up to my butt. I went west one block, then south one block and finally saw the lights at the Luger house. They were all waiting up for me and I was greeted with hugs and kisses. It was about 1 AM and I never was so glad to be home. I then called my mother who was worried sick and I put my feet in a pan of hot water. The very worst part of it was needing to use a bathroom in all that time, and no place to go. When I got home, I couldn't, until I had thawed out for about an hour or so.

Street cars had rough going in snow and that may be the reason they got rid of them in the cities. Now they are talking about light rail transit as if that were something new. I think they should have kept the street cars and used buses as extra lines like they used to do.

TALE OF A YOUNG HOUSEWIFE
by Ann Lester
River Falls, WS

The weather this morning (December 29, 1984) was so much like the weather that November 11, 1940 that I was struck with the similarity. This morning our driveway was black and shiny with rain, the snow almost gone from the edges of the driveway, and the lawn almost bare. The thermometer registered 42 degrees, remarkably warm for this time of the year.

That 1940 morning there was no snow, nor any hint of any snow to come, certainly not as much snow nor with such violence.

We were living on fourth avenue in Minneapolis at the time. We had been married the previous January and were living in an old house, somewhat of a mansion in its day, which had been made into small apartments. We had a one-room furnished apartment and shared the bathroom and an icebox in the hall. In the apartment we had a Murphy bed which folded against the wall when not in use, a library table with two straight chairs, a rocker, a wardrobe for our clothes, a dresser, a lavatory which served as a sink with a small cabinet above it, a small metal stand where we stored our pots and pans and which held a two-burner gas stove, with a small oven to be used on top of the burners — and a narrow metal cabinet where we kept our groceries.

At the time Bill worked at the Minneapolis athletic club where he washed pots and pans. I took care of a little girl about a year and a half old. Our joint income was $120 a month.

We lived about a mile from the Athletic club so Bill could walk in nice weather. A light rain was falling and he took the street car about two blocks away. The weather was so mild he wore a suit jacket, his work pants and low shoes. I don't think he wore a hat or gloves. Since it was Armistice day, a holiday, the people for whom I worked didn't need me so I stayed at home.

I had planned to spend the day sewing a winter coat. I had bought an old Singer treadle sewing machine at an estate sale for $10 and had bought the material for the coat. After Bill had gone to work and I had cleaned up the breakfast things, I went to work on the coat. I cleared off the library table, cut out the coat, folding each piece with the pattern still thereon, opened up the sewing machine and sat down to sew. Between basting and sewing I kept busy enough to be unaware that it was getting colder until I had to get up to turn up the heat. When I looked out I could see the wind was rising. The first snow began to fall when I stopped to have lunch. It was fine snow slanting from the north. As the afternoon wore on, the snow fell faster and heavier, the wind rose and the temperature fell; it was obvious we were in for a severe storm.

I turned on the radio which confirmed the blizzard conditions. I didn't begin to worry too much about Bill until I heard that the street cars had stopped running. Then I realized he would have to walk home, dressed as lightly as he was. I put away my sewing and waited for him.

He came but much later than usual. When I heard his footsteps on the back stairs I opened the door to help him inside. He was shaking severely from the cold, gasping for breath from the wind, staggering with exhaustion. I led him to the rocker, knelt to take off his shoes and socks, chafed his feet with a dry towel and covered him with a blanket. After some time the warmth began to seep into his body; he stopped shivering and started breathing normally. Finally he could speak. "It was terrible. Terrible!" he said. "I never thought I'd make it."

The next morning we read in the papers about the extent of the storm and the disaster which stemmed from it. The duck hunters who had died on Lake Pepin, the people marooned in their work places, spending the night there because they couldn't get home, the people with small flocks of turkeys who had carried them into their houses rather than let them freeze to death. That was an historical storm. Everyone has a personal story to tell.

A friend had gone to a movie theatre at eleven to take advantage of the lower rate. When she came out three hours later she walked into the blizzard. I don't know how she did it, but she got home and survived.

WCCO RADIO TOWER MAN
BRAVED STORM TO HELP US

by Patricia Lonkey
Brooklyn Center, MN

I remember it well; we were living in Anoka county near the WCCO radio tower. The house was being remodeled because it was not insulated. However, we had a good oil burner in the living room and also an old cook stove in the kitchen. We had two small boys, ages two and four. My husband worked in St. Paul and tried to get home when the company closed early. He got as far as Como park where the highways were patrolled and he was not permitted to go any further. He got out and walked, not even knowing the street directions, finally getting to a house to call his brother and mother; they got a taxi and drove to pick him up, after which they all went back to their apartment.

I realized how hard the wind was blowing when it blew out the fire in the oil burner and I couldn't light it again. I took things that I needed, and a large lounge chair, into the kitchen. Luckily we had some 4 x 8 foot sheets of *Firtex*; I took a sheet of that and put it over the doorway in the kitchen; then I started up the old cook stove and heated the kitchen. We were lucky to have lots of wood, mostly boards, and it was just outside the door where it was easy to obtain. During all of this I worried about my husband because I could see that things were getting bad and I heard on the radio that the highways were closed.

During the evening someone rapped on the door. I was afraid to answer it. The man outside asked if we were all right and I said yes and that we were warm. Then he told me that my husband had called the WCCO radio station nearby and he had told him he'd check on us. He also offered to take us back to the station with him; I declined, saying that as long as we were warm and had plenty to eat I didn't want to take the chance of going out. I forgot to thank him but think of him very often. Just to think what could have happened to him! It was a good block each way from the tower to our house, yet this superb man made this great effort to check on us. How could I ever forget it?

At least I now knew that my husband was all right and I could feel a little more at ease. It was still a couple of days before we were plowed out but that was nothing compared with the situation of the duck hunters who died due to the suddenness of this storm. It was also made difficult because transistor radios weren't on the market at that time.

I think of this nightmare very often and I thank God for being with me.

THOUGHT WE'D NEVER SEE LIGHT OF DAY
by Dorothy V. Lundin
Minneapolis, MN

I don't recall being aware of the changing weather conditions during the day. I was working as assistant head nurse on obstetrics at St. Barnabas hospital, Minneapolis and I know the weather intensified sufficiently that at 3 PM my supervisor told me I could go home. That meant going by Chicago avenue street car to Hennepin avenue downtown, then transferring to a St. Louis Park car. It was 5 PM before the Chicago car reached Hennepin in the heavily blowing and accumulating snow. I was able to telephone my husband at his Lake street office and he was going to try to pick me up at 7th and Hennepin, the corner from which I called him.

He was able to get there and we started our trek on highway #12 toward Louisiana avenue. I don't remember the time it took to reach highway #100 — the *Beltline* but I do remember that cars were off the road on both sides of two-laned #12 all the way to #100. It was obvious that we would not be able to get through the maze and confusion of cars on and off the highway ahead. In his attempt to turn around, Carl couldn't see the traffic lane and slipped off the highway. Only through his skillful driving and pushing the car was he able to get it back on the road headed back toward Minneapolis.

The windshield wipers couldn't remove the crusted ice and snow so Carl got out to scrape it off manually. When he got back into the car I touched his face, only to find it glazed with ice which his body heat hadn't melted. I thought then we'd never see the light of another day. But with our youth, a new car — a Chevrolet, Carl's driving skills, and a lot of good fortune, we arrived back at St. Barnabas hospital at 10 PM — from where I'd started seven hours previously.

I was very cold and a night nurse whose name I no longer remember was preparing for the night shift. She ran a tub full of warm water for me and gave me her dorm bed for the night. Carl returned to the office where he'd started. Residents in the apartment above the office provided him with bedding and he made a bed on the office desks. When morning came, my presence *in residence* was really appreciated because some day shift nurses were unable to get to the hospital. So our mothers and babies were not without nursing care.

I recall that our hospital administrator snow-shoed in from Franklin and Nicollet avenues to St. Barnabas, which was across the street from the present Metropolitan Medical Center.

It had been a day and a night and a blizzard to remember.

THOSE FINE OLD STREET CARS
by George R. Martin, MD
Minneapolis, MN

Nobody dressed for cold weather that morning. I drove my parents' car to the University and the storm came so rapidly I didn't get home until after midnight. The Nicollet hotel was the finest and busiest hostelry in town and it was at the curb in front of that fine hotel where my car broke down. It remained there for three days, being no impediment to traffic. Besides, it was under an eight foot snowdrift. I made it home on one of those fine old street cars, but it took four hours to make the trip to 33rd and East Calhoun boulevard. I remember the spectacular showers of sparks when the trolley jumped off the wire. This was caused by the accumulation of ice on the trolley. The conductor then had to get off and replace the trolley. This occurred so frequently it drastically increased our travel time. The next morning I put on my arctic clothes and walked all the way downtown, stopping occasionally to warm up. It was a ghost city; even the trusty street cars had quit trying. Nobody was out; nothing was moving. The wind had produced monstrous drifts and the temperature had reached far below zero levels.

WOMAN REFUSED USE OF TELEPHONE
by Genevieve R. McInerny
Edina, MN

I remember that blizzard because I was out in it. I had left my work about four o'clock and waited for my street car at 5th and Hennepin avenue for quite a long time. Finally it arrived — it was the 28th avenue south and Olson highway car.

We went along smoothly until we were near the court house and as we turned on fourth avenue the car went off the tracks. The poor motorman worked so hard on the trolley and couldn't move it back. We were stalled there for what seemed to be hours. He called the street car company which sent out a bus. We got going fine again until we got to 28th avenue and 42nd street. The poor chap turned on 28th avenue as the storm was getting worse. We got as far as 44th street near Lake Hiawatha, so he turned the bus left. The wind was blowing and the snow drifting so badly that the bus got stuck. He couldn't budge it and he had a full busload of people to worry about. He kept that bus running and opened the door every once and a while to provide fresh air. Not one person complained to him. No doubt everyone was very hungry with nothing to eat since noon.

Eventually he said he'd try to get out to see if someone would let him use a telephone to call for help. How he ever made it to that house I'll never know. When he returned to the bus, he said the lady wouldn't let him use the phone and refused to make the call for him. She thought he was a burglar. He said "I told her no burglar would be crazy enough to be out on a night like this."

So we were in the bus all night long until about 8:30 AM when the company sent out another bus and took us all back to 42nd street and 28th avenue. I got off but can't recall if the others did. I called home and my brother picked me up.

I was sorry I didn't get that wonderful bus driver's name. I hope we all thanked him for keeping us warm so none of us froze. I surely hope so. I lived in Minneapolis until 1982 at 2812 E. Minnehaha parkway.

BOY FRIEND SLEPT IN BABY'S CRIB
by Henrietta Mortenson
St. Paul, MN

Working in a downtown St. Paul store on Armistice day 1940 started like any other work day. By mid-day rumors were coming around about how severe the weather was becoming; it had been such a mild spell we gave little or no thought to the severity.

As closing time approached, some of our supervisors had gone outside to check on the blizzard and were asking us if it were possible to contact some one to take us home. I'd called my boy friend but he wasn't too sure he'd be able to make it in his 1936 Chevrolet. Everyone was calling for rides and transportation was grinding to a halt.

I left the store in less than adequate clothing and walked into a blinding white, blowing blanket of flakes so thick I immediately walked head-on into one of the pillars in front of the old Golden Rule.

I was stunned to say the least and as I groped my way I heard the honking of a car horn but was unable to make out the form of the vehicle. "Rats", I thought, "some nut-nut is trying to pick me up." What a time for exigencies. Much chagrin when I heard my boy friend's voice urging me to get in the car.

We struggled along blindly going west on Seventh and turning north on Cedar as the easiest way to avoid driving into someone. I suggested we try to make my sister's place on Jackson by the museum. We could proceed to only one block short of her house and left the car. She, my sister Lucille, lived on a steep hill.

Her husband had called from South St. Paul to say that he'd be late for supper. We didn't see him during our two days' encampment, stranded and unable to proceed further. The telephone lines had not gone out yet so we were able to notify my parents of my location.

That night my sister and I took the two babies and settled down in her bedroom while we'd put a rocker and a chair together for my boy friend. Next morning I was aroused by my sister's loud laughter. She'd found my boy friend had climbed into the empty crib in the nursery and was sleeping like a baby, all curled up like a new born infant. He was exhausted because he had gone down in the storm to shovel out his car and with the help of the neighbors had pushed his car up the hill to her house. When he arose he had to walk to a coal store to get some fuel for the house which was bitterly cold. During the previously mild weather there had been no reason to stock up on coal. Luckily my sister was an excellent cook and made us a fine stew and baked some bread. After the fire started up and with all the cooking we enjoyed a fine time.

The second day after the emergency the plows had opened downtown St. Paul. I walked down to the store to find a party-like atmosphere. Everyone was trading stories of where they had spent their time during the storm. Drifts piled up over our heads and finally the street cars started up the main streets — and I finally got to my home and back to mundane living.

Nobody had spent the night in the crib. Just a few hours.

WE WAITRESSES WORKED FOR TIPS ONLY
Elsie Moselle
Minneapolis, MN

I was a young girl employed at Smith's Colonial inn on Excelsior boulevard and caught my bus daily at the Greyhound bus depot. Smith's was a very popular eating place specializing in fried chicken dinners and southern pecan pie. I was a waitress, receiving no salary, working for tips only. We had to spend 35 cents a day for a clean uniform, five cents for a clean apron and pay the busboys 25 cents as well. Jobs were hard to find. We had a busy luncheon schedule but by 11 AM many cancellations were received. The roads were blown over, drifted, and most of us spent the night at the restaurant. By noon the next day the highway looked much like the picture so frequently seen of the bridge by the Minnikahda club — very drifted over. One of the men who worked in the nearby service station drove us back to Minneapolis, driving wherever he could, backtracking, but eventually making it.

SUBSCRIBER RUDE TO PAPER CARRIER BOY
by George V. Nass
Brooklyn Center, MN

I was 15 years old and a paper carrier for the Minneapolis Tribune. I will never forget that day for a number of reasons.

I started from my parents house to do my routes—I was carrying two routes because another carrier quit. I didn't get very far even though, for traction, I had rope around the rear tire of my bicycle.I decided to walk to pick up my papers. They weren't delivered near your home as is the practice today. I walked from 19th avenue and 36th street to Lake street and Cedar avenue, six long and three short blocks, about three-quarters of a mile. It was a very cold morning and I really appreciated being able to sit inside a stairway to fold my papers.

The two routes to the best of my knowledge were from Lake street to 35th street and Bloomington avenue to Elliott avenue.

It was slow going, plowing through four foot snowdrifts. I arrived at one house at 9:30 AM and was met with "It's about time you delivered this paper!" He couldn't get to work because of the snow and, I suppose, took it out on me. Today I would have told him where to put the paper.

I came home very wet and extremely cold but I had delivered the papers. About two weeks later the Tribune awarded certificates to carriers who had delivered papers that day. I was the only carrier who delivered papers from our paper station. (The only thing that bothered me was that the carrier for whom I delivered the other route, also was given a certificate of appreciation.)

Later that day my father was able to get his 1936 Ford started by cranking it with a hand crank. It had two frozen cells in the battery so couldn't be started otherwise. He then took me to Kaplan's on Franklin avenue (which is still in business) and bought me a sheep-lined coat. I don't know where he found the money to buy the coat because money was scarce.

About a month before that big blizzard our Boy Scout Patrol of Troop 120 was transported to an overnight Scout camp by a man whose car had a rumble seat. That man died in the Armistice Day storm, having been found in his car near the cut at the Minikahda golf course.

Some years ago I retired from employment at a company after 32 years. Upon my retirement I had accumulated 1,600 hours of sick leave that was not used and was paid over $7,000 for one-half of that unused time.

I have never regretted the years I carried a paper route and feel it was an excellent experience. Early in life I learned if you have a job to do, do it to the best of your ability.

BUSH LAKE EPISODE
by Lloyd Nerburn
St. Louis Park, MN

I was 27 years old and employed as a boys' worker at the B. F. Nelson settlement house in northeast Minneapolis during the evening and attending the University of Minnesota during the day. On weekends I would go to Bush lake where Miss Frost, the head resident of the settlement house, rented a cabin each year. There I would study in peace and quiet. I recall that on Sunday, November 10, it rained. On Monday I went outside to get wood for the fireplace and began tidying the cabin. It was beginning to snow and I recall going down to get into my car and cleaning off the windshield and other windows which were covered with snow. This snow was falling rather heavily and a brisk wind was blowing.

I got only about 200 yards from the cabin when my car bogged down in the ground, softened by the previous day's rain, and got stuck. There I was, stuck, with no one to help me; the few other cottages were unoccupied. Dressed only in a light topcoat, I trudged through a couple of feet of snow to a beer tavern about a half mile away and called my boss, Miss Frost. She drove out to get me in that blowy, snowy weather. After we got back to the settlement house I realized that the weather was so bad I couldn't get home, so decided to sleep there at least overnight.

Virginia, now my wife, was working at Goodyear, also in northeast Minneapolis. She got a ride with a co-worker who drove her to a friend's home where she stayed overnight. There was no way she could get a ride home by street car. Her father got a ride from where he worked into downtown Minneapolis, where he finally was able to sleep in the lobby of the Radisson hotel. Virginia's mother was unable to get out of the house and said the only people who got through to her were the milkman and the iceman.

Five days later my brother drove me to Bush lake to get my car. I was worried that it might be frozen since I had put in very little anti-freeze. We located the car, which was completely buried under the snow. We dug it out and when I turned the key it started immediately. That amazed me. We couldn't drive it out of the deep snow but, luckily, there was a hill to the left of the road which was windswept almost free of snow. We had to take down a section of barbed wire fence and, after considerable effort, got the car up the hill, replaced the farmer's fence, and were able to maneuver the car onto the highway and home. Wow! What a storm.

SO TIRED NO COLOR IN HIS EYES
by Mrs. Janet Norman
Minneapolis, MN

My dad was a driver for the Minneapolis street department and took his job very seriously. He was home that Armistice Day because it was a vacation day for city employees. About noon he went to get gas in the car to be sure he could get to work. We had recently moved to 44th avenue off Lake street so he still drove from the Currie avenue garage. We had lived in north Minneapolis previously. By 3 PM dad could wait no longer and left for the Currie avenue garage.

Meanwhile the chief dispatcher was in Chicago and no one wanted to give the order to dispatch drivers and mechanics. Several dispatchers and certain drivers and mechanics were duck hunting. However, it was almost 6 PM before they called dad to come to work. He was high on the seniority list so he would have been among the first called.

Dad arrived at the Currie avenue spot about this time and he found that there were no plows attached to any trucks. Besides, the plows for the whole city were stored there. Dad was a strong union man and mechanics were supposed to attach plows, but that night he helped with the first plows, then got out on the street himself.

Dad worked that night, the next day, and the following night before he came home. When he did arrive there was no color in his eyes. He was exhausted. They had transferred him from the truck to a grader equipped with a plow, to try to burrow through the drifts. On our corner I am sure the drift was 20 feet or more.It was up on the telephone pole.

On Tuesday, the next day, my brother skied from the Lake street bridge to downtown Minneapolis. He and a few others got to work and simply notfied branch offices of their firm that they would have to carry on for a few days. He got back home about dark.

We were excused from work at 3 PM. I was home by 6 PM. I was lucky to have the Chicago-Lake and Selby-Lake street cars for my ride home. The cars were packed but everyone was in a good humor. The passengers would get out and push cars off the car line and then get back on. Like so many others, I had gone to work with a short jacket over a cotton dress and had sandals on my feet. I was very wet and cold when I got home.

THE MILK OF HUMAN KINDNESS
by Annabell Norregaard
Shakopee, MN

Forty-five years ago I was Annabell Boegeman, living on a farm in Credit River. It was a nice day when our school bus picked up my sister and me at 7 AM to take us to school in Lakeville.

At 11 AM that morning we were excused from school to go home because of the storm. The superintendent didn't know the storm was so bad. To us it was neat: no school for the rest of the day.

Our bus got about four miles out of Lakeville when it got stuck. You could not see a thing in front of the bus. We didn't know the direction of the last farm drop-off so the driver left the bus to look for it. He came back, feet and hands frozen, eyes and brows all frosted. Two times after that he took two boys with him but returned both times, unsuccessful. Every time he left he told us that no one should leave the bus.

About seven that night we saw a yard light a half mile away; two of the boys and the driver followed that light to a farm house. They soon came back with the farmer and a team of horses. There were a lot of happy tears when we saw them. The snow was so deep it was even hard for the horses to stand, or walk.

We were to go to the farmhouse. The driver instructed us to form a chain and never let go of the hand we were holding. He assured us that the horse had a good sense of direction and that we would make it safely. The boys were first in the chain to make footsteps which we girls could follow more easily. We got to the farmhouse about nine o'clock that night. They had no telephone so the school superintendent nor any of our parents knew where we were.

When my dad learned we had left school at eleven that morning, he started looking for us in a horse-drawn sleigh. Alas, the snow was so deep that the horse couldn't make the route my dad knew so well. He had to go back home. My parents and sisters and brothers all prayed for us.

When it started to get dark all of us on the bus also had started to pray. It had been getting cold in there too as the ice built up on the windows. The driver had us do exercises to keep warm.

There were about 35 on that bus, all dressed like I. Short skirt, anklets, light jackets, no caps or gloves, nothing on our legs. All of us had frostbite on fingers, toes, ears and most of us were frozen on the calves of the leg. We got back to Lakeville in a sled the next day at 3 PM.

The lady of the house where we stayed said she didn't have any food. Yet there were pails of eggs, apples and milk on the steps going down to the basement. Some of the boys swiped some apples but were caught and that was the end of the apples. She did make coffee for us the next morning. She would pour ten cups, then add five more cups of water. By the time we got it, it was more like colored water. When we got back to Lakeville we were taken to a restaurant and told to order anything we wanted. *Wow!* Anything you want and you don't have to pay for it! Because we hadn't had anything to eat since the previous day's breakfast, most of us ate too fast and too much. Most of us got sick.

We all got to call home *long distance* and the superintendent placed us in different homes in Lakeville. People gave us clothes to wear. We didn't get home until November 15, four days later. We had a ball in Lakeville. Farm kids staying in town. Another *Wow!*

I thank my God I'm here today. Yes, we were very lucky.

CEDRIC ADAMS ANNOUNCED SHE WAS OKAY
by Elsie Olmanson
Golden Valley, MN

My husband and I had been married about two years and he was working on our new home which was being built on Roosevelt street northeast. We both had the day off, since it was a holiday. His aunt, Mrs. Ann Loftness, was visiting us from Gibbon and she and my mother, Mrs. Helen Benson, and I went downtown shopping. It was a very nice mild day as we went into Dayton's where we had lunch and spent about four hours shopping.

About three o'clock clerks and customers were rushing around in great excitement. We heard fragments of comments about the store closing and that the street cars had stopped running. We looked outside and were shocked to see a full-blown blizzard raging, and that a huge amount of snow had already piled up.

Mother called my dad, who worked at Massey Harris Harvester farm machinery company. He left work early and drove his 1932 Chevie down Fifth street where the three of us waited on the corner of Fifth and Nicollet. He drove that old dependable Chevie in one set of auto tracks and didn't stop until we got home at Logan north and 29th. He *gave her the gun* to get down the alley, shoveled to get the garage doors open, drove the old car in and gave her a grateful pat. We all gave thanks to have arrived home safely and trudged through deep snow to the back door. Once inside the four of us had to change to dry clothes and drank hot coffee. How good it was to be home safe and warm.

I called my husband who had arrived safely at our apartment at 39th and Penn north. But his aunt Ann Loftness couldn't reach her husband, John in Gibbon to tell him she was safe because long distance lines were down.

However, my mother called Cedric Adams, asking him to announce that Ann Loftness' name be included with the list of others who were safe in Minneapolis and wanted their families to get the word. There were so many such messages to announce over the radio on the 10 PM broadcast that Cedric didn't get to talk about Ann until the third night after the storm. She was already back in Gibbon. That night she and her husband were listening to Cedric and heard him announce that "Ann Loftness is safe with friends in Minneapolis". Many of their friends and neighbors heard that announcement and called to hear of Ann's blizzard experiences.

Rotary type plow taking second cut through a drift between T.H. #10 and Bethel in Anoka County. *(Minnesota Historical Society Collection.)*

See Richard Bren's story "Needed 8-Foot Probe to Find Pickup." *(Photo by Richard Bren, Sr., 1940.)*

Streetcar stuck in snow during Armistice Day blizzard. *(Minneapolis Star-Journal photo. Minnesota Historical Society Collection.)*

Snow accumulation from Armistice Day blizzard at unidentified grocery store. *(Minneapolis Star-Journal photo. Minnesota Historical Society Collection.)*

Automobiles stuck in snow following Armistice Day blizzard 1940. Believed to be Highway #12. *(Minneapolis Star-Journal photo. Minnesota Historical Society Collection.)*

Hunters who died in the Armistice Day blizzard, November 11, 1940. *(Minneapolis Star-Journal photo. Minnesota Historical Society Collection.)*

School bus several days after the storm. See Claude Seal's story: "Drifts Three Feet Higher Than Bus." (*Photo by Claude J. Seal.*)

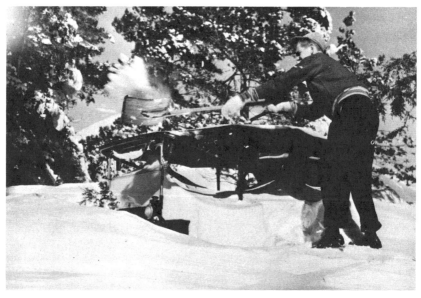

Swede Londeen, Minneapolis, shoveling out his 1917 Ford Model T touring car on November 12, 1940, where it had been parked in back of Myron Fieldhouse at Gustavus Adolphus College, St. Peter, where Swede was a student. He had been duck hunting east of St. Peter. (*Photo courtesy of Swede Londeen.*)

Looking west on Excelsior Boulevard toward Minikahda Golf Club. Several authors comment on this jumbled mass. *(Minneapolis Tribune photo. Minnesota Historical Society Collection.)*

Spot on Sturgeon Lake, Prairie Island, from which Abe Kuhns repeatedly launched his small boat to cross open water to save freezing hunters. See Larson-Nelson story: "Abe Kuhns, Hero Extraordinary." *(Photo by the editor. 1985.)*

Clearing snow out of Memorial Stadium, University of Minnesota, following
November 11, 1940 blizzard. See story below. *(Minneapolis Star-Journal
photo. Minnesota Historical Society Collection.)*

WE SHOVELED OUT MEMORIAL STADIUM
by John S. Merrick S.
St. Paul, MN

I was a junior at John Marshall high school in southeast Minneapolis. For
boys my age about our only source of income during the winter months was
shoveling snow. The University of Minnesota still had one or two football
games to be played before the season was completed and Memorial Stadium
seemed half-full of snow. Three of my friends and I skipped school for three
days and shoveled out the stadium, as part of a crew of about 200. We could
work all the hours we wanted and were paid 50 cents an hour. I think I made
more money during those few days than I did all the rest of the year . . . and
was glad to have the work.

FIGHTING OFF BELLBOYS ALL NIGHT

by Mrs. Marguerite Olson
Lindstrom, MN

I'll never forget how terrified I was. I was 21 years old, working at the Creamette company, a couple of blocks west of Washington avenue. I was let off earlier than usual because of the forecast of bad weather: it was two o'clock but it wasn't early enough.

I walked to Washington avenue and Hennepin to catch my streetcar to go home—I lived south. The snow was blowing so hard it hurt my face and legs. We wore skirts in those days so even standing still was bad. I waited about thirty minutes then decided to walk up Hennepin to try to catch a car to my aunt's house. Once there I telephoned my parents and my boy friend. The boy friend said he'd try to come to get me from where he lived in northeast Minneapolis. We were to meet on the corner across from the Milwaukee depot on Washington avenue. I started walking there, frozen, wet and scared. I could hardly see in front of my face and walked close to the buildings. Even then I fell many times, tripping over curbs, trying not to look up because of the blowing cold snow, guessing as to just where I was.

I met a girl who was as frightened as I was who was heading for Washington avenue to get a streetcar to north Minneapolis. Together we made it to the Milwaukee depot area and stepped into a cigar store on a corner to telephone. My boy friend had started to pick me up, had gotten half way across the bridge where traffic was at a complete stop, so he turned around and went back home. This other girl couldn't make any connections with her family either so we decided to make preparations for the night. There were no cars or taxis or anything moving by this time.

The hotel was right across the street so we headed for that. We got the last room. We went to a telephone to call home but there was a line of people a mile long. We waited for an hour. By then there were people everywhere, sitting, standing, lying down, all shivering and wet and tired and scared.

After getting the phone calls made, we headed for our room, expecting to dry our clothes and relax. We put our clothes on the radiators to dry and went to bed. We had barely done that and there was a rattling at the door. In walked a bellboy who actually crawled in bed with us. We got rid of him, got dressed and decided not to sleep. We sat up, all bundled up with the blankets, tired, cold and disgusted. We truly fought off bellboys all night long.

The night was finally over and we went down to the lobby. A few taxicabs were around but you had to hail them. We went outside and hailed and hailed; after about two hours we finally got a cab and went to the other gal's house. There I waited until the streetcars started again and went home—still wet, cold and tired, but glad the whole terrifying experience was all over.

IF YOU WANT TO LIVE, STOP AT SHAKOPEE

by Sophia Oltmann
Minneapolis, MN

We had gone from LeSueur to visit friends in Minneapolis. My husband and I and son, Eric, age 3 1/2, left Minneapolis that November 11 afternoon for our home in foggy weather with snow beginning to fall. Visibility was poor but we continued on. After all. "It isn't that far."

When we approached Shakopee on #169 we saw cars in the ditches. That was the first signal that the weather was alarming. It had suddenly turned cold which just as suddenly made the highway slippery. We continued through Shakopee but were stopped by the driver of a big truck coming from Savage and Jordan. He stopped us to tell us that if we wanted to live we should not go on. He said he had gotten through because of the weight of his truck but passenger cars were not making it. We listened to him and found a room in the Shakopee hotel where we stayed for two nights. Most of the homes with gas furnaces were without heat but the hotel was warm. They must have used either oil or coal in their furnace. When we went out to eat we had to form a chain with other hotel guests. Recently I asked my son, age 3 1/2 at that time, if he remembers the storm and our stay in the hotel. He said all he could remember were the artificial flowers on the table.

On Monday we were ready to leave for home. I have never seen anything like the driving conditions. There was a path on the highway with drifts on either side high above the car. It was like driving through a tunnel. In certain stretches only one car could get through while others waited.

My sister, Irene Matchke, recently told me that in the evening of November 11 a transformer blew out about two miles from Montgomery. Her husband worked for the REA (Rural Electrification Administration) so he and another lineman walked down a railroad track to the farm and hooked up a transformer. When he got home he told her that if a train had come along they would never have made it but would have been buried in the snow along the tracks.

There was no warning of this terrible storm.

WE WRAPPED IN NEWSPAPERS TO KEEP WARM

by Dan Opperman
Waconia, MN

Our family was returning from vacation in Sheboygan, Wisconsin. As we came closer to Minnesota, at about Baldwin, we stopped for gasoline and were told a bad blizzard was coming. We continued to drive our 1936 Chevrolet and the weather got worse as we approached the state line. The heater didn't work too well so we wrapped ourselves in newspapers. Road conditions got even worse but we made it to Hudson where we got the last room at a hotel; the whole family had to share one room; my sisters and I slept on the floor.

Early the next morning a group of men met in the lobby of the hotel to discuss the weather and the chances of making it to St. Paul. They called local police who said the road was open to the best of their knowledge but recommended no travel as yet. However, the men decided to form a caravan of seven to ten cars to try to make it. So the caravan started at about 11 Am. It was slow going because we stopped to assist caravan cars when they had trouble. The group reached St. Paul at about 4:30 PM and then broke up.

Our family decided to try to get home in spite of Twin City streets being almost impossible. We made it through both cities until we reached the Minneapolis golf course where we were stopped. The road was completely closed so we turned around with difficulty and stopped at a gas station to ask about hotel accomodations. The young man on duty had heard that all hotels were filled but would make a telephone call to see if he could help. He returned shortly with an address but told us we would have to walk the six blocks. True, we were helplessly stuck.

When we arrived at the address we were welcomed and found that the young man had given us his home address and had talked with his mother. We stayed with them for three or four days and when it was time to leave they wouldn't accept any money, until we insisted they at least take some for food.

Then we had to get our car out of the snowbank and start for home at Bongards, MN. We made it through the big banks of snow at the golf course, had a slow trip down highway #212 and got to the Chaska hill on #212 where there was one-way traffic through the high snowbanks. When we got to Bongards we found 10 to 20 foot deep snowbanks in our yard. We were indeed happy to get home.

ALMOST LOST LIFE HELPING STRANGER
by Mrs. Milo Ostermann
St. Paul, MN

My husband and I lived on a huge hobby farm south of the Twin Cities where he was the bookkeeper. These were the days of the great depression and we were having a hard time living on his meager income. A free house went with the job. His monthly salary was divided into three parts—food, heat, and gas for the car.

The afternoon of the blizzard a stranger came walking up the road and stopped by my husband's office, begging for a ride home. "Only about one mile up the stretch" he said. Although sleet was just beginning to fall and we were low on gasoline, my husband, who was wearing a light jacket and loafers, loved adventure and agreed to take the man home. He dropped him off in his driveway and turned the car around to come home. After a short distance he realized the car was out of gas. He could have walked home but the snow storm had now become a blizzard with zero visibility. He returned to the house he had just left. He was frightened for his life and was worried about me. He remembered there was a mailbox at the end of the driveway. He tried to walk and sometimes he crawled until his hand touched the mailbox and soon he saw a light in the direction of the house. When he finally got there the people let him in and they all huddled around the kitchen stove.

Soon a snowdrift formed across the kitchen floor. They decided to walk across the street to a neighbor's house to wait out the storm, because it would be warmer. Finally, about 11 PM the wind died down and my husband was given warm clothing, including a sheepskin jacket, for his trek home.

In the meantime, back on the farm, my neighbors were aware of the catastrophe. Two dear neighbors invited me over and, as the evening progressed, bedded me down for the night. Unbeknownst to me, the single fellows in the bunkhouse next door were making bets. Would my husband be found dead or alive?

The next day, November 12, was my husband's birthday and he would be 24 years old. This is what I kept telling myself: "Oh, Lord, don't let him die so young." I prayed constantly, and the Good Lord must have heard my prayers because not too much later he arrived home safe and sound.

My husband, Milo Ostermann, would probably be writing this account of the blizzard but I sadly report that he passed away a year ago at the age of 66. Ironically, the man whose life my husband tried to save took his own life a few years later.

OUR UNFINISHED SHELL OF A HOUSE
by Margaret M. Parker
Maplewood, MN

That spring my husband, Bob, and I had bought a piece of land on McMenemy and what is now Roselawn in Maplewood. My brother had purchased the whole piece and sold the corner to us for pennies down and the rest when we could pay. He built a finished house on his piece of land. We had no money but talked a lumber company into about $800 worth of lumber to put up a shell to live in until that was paid.

We had a seven year old daughter and a son just born the previous month, October. We had worked all summer putting up this shell and had moved in on July 1. We kept building around ourselves. We had an oil stove for heat with a small tank outside (the biffy too). The windows and doors were set but had no trim outside or inside to seal them.

I'll never forget that storm. I was 29 then and will be 73 next month. It was raining in the morning. I bathed the little son, fed him and put him to sleep. About 10 AM the wind started blowing like mad and I knew I must get some milk soon. There was a dairy farm kitty-corner from us and nothing else in three directions except our brother's place.

I grabbed my milk cans and went across the street. By the time I started back with the filled cans I skated home with a two-gallon can in each hand. The street was sheet ice. A half hour later it started to snow and the kids were being sent home from school—on foot because there were no buses. Our daughter came in looking like a frozen icicle. I called my husband at work and told him to bring home some oil because our larger can was empty.

The snow was blowing in around the windows and doors clear across the front room into the kitchen. I was having a heck of a time keeping the little one out of the snow and the stove was burning but not giving out much heat.

Bob made it home without the oil, thinking he could go back with an extra can, but he never made it. He got stuck on Wheelock parkway and the car was there for three days. He walked back home.

It just got worse and worse and colder and colder with more and more snow getting inside the house. My sister-in-law got home about 3 PM and got stuck trying to get into the yard. My brother came straggling in about 5 PM and got stuck right behind her. We were supposed to have a little party for my husband's birthday but we were too busy trying to keep the kids warm. When we ran out of what oil we had our party consisted of moving our kids, our dog, our bird and all our canned goods and food into my brother's house at 3 AM. There we *camped out* for three days. Each day my husband walked to work on Third street near Mounds Park Bank at the Northern Pacific railway commissary, a distance of five or six miles. The third day he came home on Wheelock parkway and found it had been plowed, so he returned and shoveled out his car. We had already shoveled the yard and our road had been plowed the second day. St.Paul was always the last (and still is) to plow and we still needed heating oil. We got it late the third day and the next day moved back home.

It took us 16 more years to get our house done. We did it all ourselves and paid for everything as we went along.

We had another bad storm which I remember vividly. I think it was the winter of 51-52. My husband couldn't drive to work then either and walked in for a few days. That was the year of the big flood in the spring, and almost all the commissary had to be moved to Minneapolis to get away from the river.

My dear husband left me in 1969 but I am still living in *The House That Bob Built* as we always called it. It will be 45 years on July 1, 1985. Here I will stay until I can no longer cut the grass and shovel the snow. Maybe even after that because my son and younger daughter live nearby.

WE LUCKED OUT AND STAYED IN A CASTLE

by Ellis Peck, Wayzata, MN
Albert Colby, Excelsior, MN
William Gresham, Webster, WI

On November 10 I hunted with a group at Lake Emily and killed my first two geese — two beautiful Canadian honkers weighing 12 and 13 pounds. What a thrill!

The next morning, Armistice Day, it was raining and we decided to start for home. A lucky move for us because hunters who stayed didn't get home for three days and some perished. It started snowing before we got home.

Ray Johnson, manager of the NSP, called, telling me to come to work to fix Rufus Rand's transformers which had burned out. So we three who are writing this loaded a transformer and left for Rand's beautiful new home on Gray's bay, Lake Minnetonka. It was a castle. We were pleased that the transformer was inside the house because it was snowing and blowing hard. Mr. Rand, a very democratic man, said we could stay overnight at his home, saying "I'll bed you down". So we thought we had it made until Ray called telling us to get over to Navarre sub-station because Spring Park and surrounding areas were without power. Mr. Rand said "You can't go out in this raging storm. I'm going to call your president, Mr. Pack", which he did. Mr. Pack was glad to know where we were because they had crews out of whom they had no knowledge of their location.

Again we thought we had it made. Then Ray called again and told us to get to Navarre. Our foreman, Albert Colby, was sweating it out. Between the president of the company saying he was glad we were safe, Mr. Rand telling us not go out in the storm, and Mr. Johnson telling us to get over to Navarre, Albert didn't know what to do. I suggested to him that we'd better get to Navarre because people were out of power and heat, so we bundled up and left. As we did, Mr. Rand handed me a flashlight saying "You'll never make it. If you don't, come back here".

On our way out of the driveway we met a man walking to Rand's. He said "This storm sucks the breath out of you". Before we were out of the driveway we slid into the ditch. So back to the house we went.

Everybody was happy to see us, including Mr. Rand, who had said we'd never make it. We had dinner with the maids and a nurse. Colby said he thought he had a fever and before he could say anything else the nurse had a thermometer in his mouth. It was funny watching the nurse trying to keep him from talking so she could get a reading. He was excited because of the pressure he was under as foreman of our crew.

Of course Colby called the manager to tell him what had happened. The manager asked if there were extension telephones in the house. I suppose he was wanting to change places with us. To pass time, we played cards with the maids. I also remember that it was Mrs. Rand's birthday and they had planned to go out that evening, but because of the storm that plan was cancelled.

At bedtime Mr.Rand showed us where we could shower, which felt so good after having been in the cold so much that day. We thought he would put us up in the servants' quarters but instead we were ushered into the guest rooms. Hudson Bay blankets on the beds and foot-thick carpets on the floor. We certainly fared better than many others caught in the storm. I remember hearing of a farmer who took in people from the storm, fed them all the food he had, and then one of them stole the plateful of money that was collected for him.

When I got home, there were my geese hanging outside my window, covered with snow and frozen stiff.

It took me a week to get over the thrill of being Mr. Rand's guest in his beautiful castle.

THEY TOSSED HER IN A SNOW BANK
by Irene Peterson
Minneapolis, MN

November 11, 1940 began as a typical Minnesota winter day, not extremely cold, as one could tell by my attire as I walked to the street car stop at Nicollet avenue and 19th street. I was wearing a light weight wool gray skirt with a matching short sleeved sweater, a black cloth coat with a small fur collar, cotton dress gloves, high heeled black leather pumps and a black Empress Eugenie hat with a gray feather about five inches long.

At 35th and Nicollet I left the streetcar to walk east a short half block where I was employed as a companion and light housekeeper for Mr. and Mrs. Campagna. She suffered from a heart disorder and he didn't want her alone when he was working. She loved to cook so, as usual, I found a delicious breakfast awaiting me.

It began to snow as I performed my various tasks. After lunch, as we were making Thanksgiving plans, there was no improvement in the weather. Normally I would stay until after dinner and tidy the kitchen but I asked to leave early today and Mrs. Campagna consented.

So at 2 PM I left to brave the wind and blowing snow. The scheduled street car was no where in sight. After a while I decided to walk one block to 36th street to wait in the corner drug store. What a long block that was! The drug store was packed with people like sardines in a can, right to the door, but they squeezed me in. It had taken me 40 minutes to walk that one block.

The store was cold from the pack of wet people. My legs and hands were very cold and the lower part of my coat and my shoes were soaked.

At 3:10 a young man came in offering to take as many as possible in his enclosed van provided they could make their way from Nicollet and their nearest street. At age 22 I thought I could chance it so, with five others, climbed into the rear of his vehicle. At Franklin avenue three people got out and at 17th I left after profusely thanking the driver and his companion.

Meanwhile, in the basement apartment where I lived with my mother and a girl friend Jo things hadn't been dull. My brother, Kenny, and his wife, Elaine, were managers of the apartment complex. Jo's boy friend, Ken, stationed at the army base, had come in for the day. Kenny and Ken had spent the day shoveling and helping people dig out their cars. Mom and Jo were making hot coffee, chocolate and soup for the workers and the freezing tenants who made it home.

From Nicollet avenue nearly to the front of our building the lowest drift I fought through was over my waist. Fortunately, Elaine was looking out the window and opened the door for me. My hands were so cold I couldn't manage the knob. Thus I walked into my apartment at 5:50 PM with legs that felt numb, two hours and 40 minutes after I left the drug store. The last block and a half had taken nearly two hours to walk. While mom fed me hot soup, Kenny and Ken massaged my legs. Finally the feeling returned.

Jo, in a facetious mood, said "If you three snowmen were smart like me you would stay inside where it was warm." Although she was dressed only in a cotton house dress and fuzzy slippers, it didn't stop Ken and Kenny from picking her up bodily and carrying her out to throw in a snow bank.

When I felt better and had quit feeling sorry for myself I regretted that I didn't learn the names of the good samaritans who brought me closer to home. I would have liked to repay them in some way.

Although my hands and feet are susceptible to cold, even now I can be grateful. So many were not that fortunate.

STRUGGLING TO MY APARTMENT
by Kay Peterson
Minneapolis, MN

I was working days as a waitress in a horse-and-a-half restaurant in the warehouse district just north of downtown Hennepin avenue in Minneapolis, a farm girl from northern Minnesota trying to make it on her own.

Whether I was working from six to three or the later eight to five shift that day I don't remember. It took hours in freezing, blowing snow to get home to the housekeeping room in the Kenwood area that I shared with my cousin. The last several blocks I traveled on foot because the street car had given up at the foot of Lowry hill after many futile frightening stabs at the climb.

At that time there existed the Plaza hotel which I later learned had wall to wall people all night, even sleeping in the lobby. Their homes were probably further west and south—say the end of the Oak/Como-Harriet line or the Bryant-54th & Penn, or Morningside. I knew I couldn't afford any kind of hotel accommodations so continued onward.

I stumbled uphill in the dark and the blizzard, trying to get to 908 west 22nd street. Thank God there was electricity and occasionally I could see a light through the blowing thick flakes. Stopping at door entryways to get my breath and to relieve the terrible chill, puff, puff, shiver and stomp my feet, turn from the wind but keep moving. Keeping moving was the main secret—but I made it finally.

My cousin, who worked at Dayton's employees cafeteria, had made it home first. That was the night our dear landlady, Mrs. Harris, broke her own house rule and made us, her *children*, her babies as she called us, a real hot toddy.

We gained a third roomie that night. A little sparrow had come in through the air holes in the old storm windows. That bird was part of our small household until it chose to face its natural world again.

Nobody went to work the next day. It was only a couple of blocks to a grocery store, so we didn't go hungry; we were warm and comfortable and very lucky.

It was certainly a surprise blizzard. Some of my farm relatives from fifty miles away from Minneapolis were in town that day. You know how farmers keep tuned to the weather—but they were caught unaware and barely made it home that afternoon.

THREE HOURS DIGGING PATH TO OUTHOUSE
by Mary Reiter
Richfield, MN

A tiny cottage without electricity on the shore of Bush lake was our temporary home. The fall of 1940 had been so pleasant that we had extended our stay until November 15, at which time our new home would be ready.

Our two boys were ages three and two months. That afternoon it started to blow as the temperature zoomed downward. Fortunately, it was Armistice Day and my husband was home. By 6 PM we knew we could not leave.

Since there was no heating stove in the cottage, we opened and lighted the three burners of the kerosene cooking stove. I can still smell that kerosene. But that necessitated opening a window and we could all see our breaths.

The snowing and blowing continued all night. When morning came we opened the single door to see a wall of snow. We had to bring some of the snow into the house in order to start shovelling. The old Auburn car was completely out of sight. To show the extent of our being remote, my husband spent three hours digging a path to the outhouse.

Our first need was for water. We started to melt snow and found that it took a great amount of snow to make a small amount of water. We also needed water for the baby's diapers, so melted more snow, and hung the diapers on fishline from my husband's reel.

As we were doing these things, a man appeared on snowshoes, carrying two quarts of milk. He seemed like an apparition but was a nearby farmer named Cooper who had become concerned for our children.

We all worked at digging us out. Almost a carnival atmospshere developed as other neighbors appeared. We shall never forget some of their kindnesses, and the hot dishes and more milk.

Mr. Cooper hitched up a pair of mules and plowed a small road. Three days later we heard the blessed sound of the Bloomington snowplow. It was over.

None of us caught cold and the baby didn't develop any rash from the skimpy diaper washing technique we had to use.

WHO SAYS MIRACLES NEVER HAPPEN?

by Thelma J. Ronay
St. Paul, MN

We had two guests for dinner the evening of November 11, 1940. Fortunately we had enough room to accommodate them for a couple of days, because by the next day we needed help badly.

Our 6-month old son, Jim, had just been discharged from Children's hospital and it was essential that his formula be prepared with homogenized milk, a common thing today, but not so common then. After his 6 AM feeding I realized I had only enough for the 10 AM and the 2 PM feedings. In those days one fed one's baby every four hours and we were instructed to do so on schedule.

After breakfast my husband, and Cliff, a friend, went on foot in the waist-deep snow looking for a store where they could buy at least one quart of homogenized milk. I had called Jim's doctor who had given me a prescription that *might* be okay but he preferred homogenized milk. Fortunately, I found someone at the drug store who could accommodate us if someone could pick it up.

The first stop by the boys was the drug store and the second was Hove's grocery; a janitor was there but they had no homogenized milk. They walked up and down Snelling avenue, down the cross streets where they knew there were stores, even stopped at the bakery on Snelling and LaFond — but no homo milk. They tried east and west on University avenue. No luck. After about six hours they returned home, tired, discouraged, soaking wet. We fixed them something hot to eat and drink while they got out of their wet clothes and discussed any other possible action.

I fixed the last bottle of milk in Jim's formula and said a few more prayers.

We had just finished the bottle when there was a tap on our apartment door. Thinking it was a neighbor in need, and with Jim over my shoulder, I went to the door to see what I could do.

A miracle happened!

Standing at the door was our milkman with a quart of milk for our baby. He knew of our problem with Jim and had walked — from I don't know where — just to be sure we could feed him this blessed milk. Oak Grove dairy was one of the few dairies that handled it in those days.

Who says miracles never happen?

DAD LAUGHED, SAYING "THIS IS A REAL ADVENTURE"
by Betty Jane Schutte
Minnetonka, MN

I swung jauntily south from Dayton's department store, headed for McPhail college of music for a day of lessons and an evening of chorale practice. I eagerly awaited evening because our choral group was singing the tone-poem *The Highwayman* and I loved it.

My spirits soared and the hazy, pinkish glow in the western sky, the close, unusually warm weather, kept my spirits hovering around high C.

In my spring-fall, black and white Chesterfield coat, no gloves nor overshoes, I felt fortunate to enjoy such a balmy day in November, as violins, voices and horns wailed a cacophony of sounds I enjoyed as I entered the white, rectangular building.

It was, of course, November 11, 1940.

Classes hummed along so busily all morning that it was noon when I chanced to glance out a window and see snow hurtling down. Having experienced 20 cold, snowy Minnesota winters, I thought nothing of it and concentrated on afternoon harmony-ear training classes.

After lunch, during music history class, our instructor informed us the college would close in 30 minutes, around 4 PM, due to unusually snowy conditions.

My friend, Alta Jean, and I sauntered to the lounge or waiting room next to the first floor office and found it teeming with students of all ages, teachers, clerical workers and some parents. Everybody was anxious about the snow storm which had gathered momentum while I was absorbed in classes.

Alta Jean and I made our way to the huge east wall to check on the storm. Near zero visibility greeted our eyes. Hazy promises of yellow lights flickered through the snow in apartments across the street. Drifts of snow piled up on the curb as winds twisted and twirled screens of snow through the street and against the window. Occasionally a car sputtered past, a few making quick stops to pick up a music school student.

The office administrator circulated a plan for us to stay there overnight in the large lounge. The office radio warned folks to stay inside because this sudden, unexpected storm was dangerous. We could use the office phones to call our loved ones and inform them we were safe.

Alta Jean could get no answer at her St. Paul home. I reached my mother to tell her of my plight.

"Stay there," she insisted. "Dad is on his way home from St. Paul now. Call again in half an hour."

It was several half-hours later when I could get the phone and dad was now home. I told him that we were staying overnight.

"No", he wouldn't hear of it. "I'll come to get you."

"No, don't come out in this storm," I objected. "It's too dangerous."

"It's almost five now and mother and I will be there by six. Watch for us," he insisted.

It was no use arguing. My dad, George H. Scherven, was dauntless.

Alta Jean still could not reach her family and was beside herself with worry. I invited her to ride with us as we lived on Dorman drive near the Marshall-Lake street bridge, close to St. Paul; it would be more convenient for her parents to pick her up there.

We fretted through two hours of anxiety when at about 7 PM dad's 1936 four-door Ford pulled up and parked in a foot of snow outside the school entrance. We hustled out and into the steamy-windowed car. Mother said "We would have been here earlier but you know your dad. He stopped several times to help people and cars in trouble."

Dad laughed. "This is a real adventure" he said and laughed again.

The faithful Ford plowed and skidded along at a snail's pace, the frosted windows being opaque and requiring dad's occasional stopping to brush away small mounds of snow. I'd venture we were one of only a half-dozen cars braving, or challenging, the storm. Sixteen inches of snow covered the roads and we were forced to drive in the middle.

Miraculously, after more than an hour, we chugged home and shoveled our way into the garage.

Alta Jean and I didn't sing that night, but she stayed overnight with us and, although we had to forego the pleasure of chorale practice on *The Highwayman*, we were to have our real life, courageous highwayman rescuer in our midst.

HOW DID TRIBUNE DRIVERS MANAGE TO DELIVER THOSE PAPERS?
by Jim Seiter
Plymouth, MN

My home was at 2113 Portland avenue and I had a morning newspaper route in the apartments on Third avenue and 24th street. For delivering my papers that morning, I received a certificate from the president and circulation director of the Minneapolis Tribune newspaper company. My three sons have gotten a lot of mileage out of this certificate by ribbing me about how "tough it used to be".

However, that storm made a lasting impression, because I can remember everything about the day of the storm and the day after. I remember it very vividly.

I was in ninth grade at De La Salle high school on Nicollet island and we did not have school on Armistice Day. The school gym was open, however, and basketball tryouts were being held. A group of us walked from south Minneapolis to De La Salle that morning. It was warm and raining very lightly.

We walked home after the basketball tryouts and by 1 PM it was getting much colder and the rain had turned to sleet. I mentioned to Tom Kelly, also a ninth grader, that I might have trouble delivering my papers the next morning and he said he would help me. (Tom has been a detective on the Minneapolis police force for 30 years or so and probably remembers the storm as well as I do.)

The next morning I picked up my papers at 5:30 AM on 4th avenue and Franklin and Tom was true to his word. He met me at the corner and together we had all the papers delivered by 10 AM.

At 5:30 AM there were stalled, abandoned street cars and nothing moving. I don't know how that Tribune driver was able to get the papers to 4th and Franklin, because nothing was plowed. He must have been able to manuever around the drifts and avoid getting stuck.

When we returned to my home after delivering the papers we learned that school hd been cancelled for the next two days, so we enjoyed some hot chocolate and planned our activities for those free days.

THE NIGHT JIM'S CAR GOT PAID FOR
by James P. Shannon
Minneapolis, MN

I was a senior at the College of St. Thomas and owned a 1931 Model A Ford, for which I paid $150.

On November 11 the rain started and turned to sleet and heavy snow by mid-afternoon. I left the college, drove home to South St. Paul and posted myself at the end of the street car line. My high clearance Model A with snow tires was going to prove valuable.

I ferried many stranded commuters to their homes, never asking any of them for money, but they all gave me generous tips, enough in fact to pay off most of the balance on my note for the car.

My father was in the cattle business and had aout 50 cattle on feed on a leased pasture in St. Paul Park, across the river from South St.Paul. We knew by 5 PM that the cattle would die unless we could get them under cover by nightfall. At about six o'clock dad and I drove my Model A over there even though the highway department had warned all travelers that the roads were impassable.

When we got to the farm several of the cattle were stranded far from the barn, in snow deeper than their legs. Dad and I opened a path for them by foot into a barn where we broke out hay and straw for them. A few of them were so weakened from trying to leap through the snow that we had to carry two of them about 50 yards. They were only yearlings. By the time dad and I got back home at 8 PM my dear mother was worried sick about us.

In our family folklore that night is referred to as "the night dad and Jim saved the cattle, worried mother almost to death, and got Jim's car paid for."

But that's the lighter side. The terribly sad part was typified by a dramatic photograph which appeared in the St. Paul Pioneer Press or Dispatch of November 12 or 13 showing six or eight cars totally submerged in snow on highway #8 near New Brighton, some with only their radio aerials visible above the snow—with all their occupants dead.

PASSED OUT—WOKE UP IN SNOWDRIFT
by Clara Shoultz
Golden Valley, MN

I had quite an experience that day. When I left for work in the morning it was a beautiful day. I was wearing open-toed shoes. Suddenly the blizzard came through. All the stores and offices in downtown Minneapolis closed.

I had four blocks to walk, after getting off the street car. With only open-toed shoes, walking in that deep snow was terrible. I fell down and passed out, then came to. When I opened my eyes I was laying in a snowdrift.

I looked up and saw a neighbor's house. I got up and walked around the corner to our house; I crawled up to the back door and scratched on the door.

Our children happened to be in the kitchen and heard the scratching and opened the door. My husband, Hank, came to carry me into the house. We lived at 736 36th avenue northeast.

ONE OF FEW WHO EXPECTED THE STORM

by Donald Skoro
St. Louis Park, MN

I'd like to pass on to you a story told me by William Schutte who, until his death a number of years ago, worked in the sales department of The Colwell Press in Minneapolis. At the time Bill Schutte called on me, I was with Reach, McClinton & Co. with offices in the Baker building in Minneapolis. We had a mutual fascination with the weather and it was with great delight that he told me this story:

On the morning of November 11, 1940, Bill Schutte left his home in St. Louis Park near highway #100 bound for his office in downtown Minneapolis, observing that it was a particularly fine morning for so late in the season. Soon he realized that he was taking a far greater interest in the weather than usual, a concern born of his many years as a private pilot. By habit he had developed an awareness of what was happening in the atmosphere for his own safety and peace of mind while piloting his small aircraft.

About 9:30 AM Bill decided to call his wife at home to check on his barograph (a self-registering barometer). Mrs. Schutte reported that the instrument must be broken becaue the recording needle had dropped so low that it had left the graph paper on the drum. This report prompted Bill to call a friend at the U.S. Weather Bureau office at Wold-Chamberlain field. His friend told him that the needle on the office barograph also had moved completely off the drum.

With growing apprehension, Bill left his office and returned home. He found his tire chains in the garage, put them in his car and drove to a neighborhood service station. He asked the attendant to mount the chains on his wheels and fill the gas tank. This was done with a great deal of ribbing and joking because the attendant was working in shirt sleeves and thought Bill must have lost his mind. When the work was finished, Bill clanked and clattered back down town and put his car in the company garage.

History tells us what followed. By the close of the business day the blizzard had descended upon the area with all its fury. Bill told of the crowds of people, lightly clad, huddled at the street car stops waiting for street cars that never came. Bill left his office and began an evening-long process of picking up the stranded office workers and driving them home. Late in the evening he was forced to return to the company garage and spent the remainder of the night sleeping on a desk.

This is a true experience which has fascinated me for years.

THE RACE FOR THE HOSPITAL
by Estelle Smith
Maple Grove, MN

What a day! Snow and blowing snow, drifting and piling up everywhere. Phone calls from loving relatives and friends concerned about the imminent arrival of Smith #3. All seemed fine to me but I did love talking to someone. Dr. Holzapfel called about 4:30 PM saying not to worry. He was taking his nurse, Martha, home with him so everything would be okay. Now I started getting a little nervous. Having a baby at home with two other children around was not the way I wanted things to go.

Dad came home later than usual and soon after that his dad stopped at our house on his way home from work. He decided to stay so we'd have a car if we needed to get to the hospital.

About 3 AM Baby Smith the third decided it was time for her to show up. Al called the doctor who said they would be at our house within 30 to 45 minutes. He called back to say he couldn't get his car going but he'd called for an ambulance to pick me up. A few minutes later he called to say there was no ambulance available but he'd called the police and they'd get there as soon as possible. However, we should get some water boiling and sheets ready just in case. Al and a very nervous grandpa were very busy and Jacquie, 4 years, Eddie, 2 1/2 years, slept soundly, thank God.

About 5:45 AM the doctor, his nurse and two policeman came in the door. They had gotten to within two blocks of our house. The doctor examined me and decided we'd try to make it to St.Mary's, a long way from our house on a good day.

The two policemen made a crossed-hands seat for me and carried us to their car. Two policemen, the doctor, Martha the nurse, two or three shovels, and me — no room for Al or dad. No time for bargaining. All the way to the hospital my only worry was where would we put the baby if she couldn't wait to get to the hospital.

At 7:20 AM we arrived at St.Mary's. Heaven couldn't have looked better to me right then. While the doctor was prepping, Patti could wait no longer and was born at 7:45 AM, November 12, a beautiful, healthy, normal seven pound ten ounce girl. The nursery staff called her *Snow White* while we were there. Dr. Holzapfel was marooned there, on duty, for a couple of days. No other doctors could make it to the hospital.

Patti Anderson is still quite a gal. She has a daughter and two sons and a darling grandson. She is the second of four daughters and has four brothers — a great family.

I WALKED FROM SEVEN CORNERS TO 32ND STREET AT HEIGHT OF THE STORM

by Violet Johnson Sollie
Mound, MN

I had been working part time for Local 292 I.B.E.W. and that office was to be closed November 11 because it was a holiday. I had also been working part time on a research project with Mrs. Gladys C. Blakey at the University. We had decided to take advantage of the holiday to get in an entire day on our project, working in a little room off the inner court of the fourth floor of the University library. We brought our lunches so we wouldn't have to go out to eat.

It had been so warm the day before, Sunday, that I had picked some flowers for the table. The chrysanthemums were still blooming. When I left that Monday morning, I wore saddle shoes, a camel's hair fall coat, a hat (we wore hats then regardless of the weather) and kid gloves. It was starting to drizzle but it was still warm when I got to the library.

We worked in this little inner room, mostly undisturbed except for an occasional graduate student telling us it was storming. We really had no idea it was getting bad. At 4:30 Mrs. Blakey left and I lingered briefly. I intended to catch a 5:10 bus from the Greyhound station for Mound and thought I had ample time if I left the library at 4:40.

When I left I was surprised at the fury of the storm. However, I saw a street car down Washington avenue and ran to get on it and rode it to Seven Corners where it stopped because of stalled street cars ahead of it. I decided to start walking, expecting the express bus along any minute, but it didn't come. By the time I reached the old Milwaukee depot I was sure my hands were frozen. I stopped in the ladies room at the depot, pulled off those kid gloves and ran cold water over my hands. They had been numb but they began to hurt and tingle and the color started to return. I gave them some hard rubbing, had my second wind by now, and decided I could make it to the Greyhound depot at Seventh and First avenue north. It still hadn't dawned on me tht my Mound bus would not run.

It really was not too bad walking from the Milwaukee depot to the bus depot. I could get out of the wind sometimes because there were a lot of buildings along the way. When I got there, the place was packed. The information person said no buses were leaving for any destination. An announcement was made that those who wanted to do so could cross the street to the Alvin burlesque theatre for a place to sit and for shelter. All hotels were full. I considered the Alvin's offer but I was hungry so I went back to a little sandwich shop on Hennepin for a hamburger and a cup of hot coffee. While the hamburger was being prepared, the girl on the next stool said she wondered what to do. She lived near 32nd and Hennepin but there was no transportation and she had found all downtown places full. I had two sisters living at 32nd and Girard, which was near her home, and told her I had made it walking from Seven Corners and believed we could get to 32nd. So we decided we could make it together to 32nd. I assume it was about 7 PM when we started. I was afraid of the bottleneck where Lyndale and Hennepin used to meet and traffic was usually snarled, but there was no traffic. Nothing moved. It was cold, but we made a block or two at a time, occasionally stopping in the entryway of an old home to get our breath. The wind was worse than the cold but with every block we were a little heartened and when we parted at 32nd we had made it. (Ed.: She had walked 4.7 measured miles.)

There was no security system on apartments then and I went up to my sisters' apartment. The younger one came to the door but the older one had gotten a room at the Radisson hotel downtown. My sister was shocked to see me, but made me take a hot bath, which I did, while she made another hamburger, heated some stewed tomatoes and made a pot of coffee. I was shivering but the hot bath and food helped.

In the morning street cars were still not running. I called my office no one answered, so I assumed no one could get there. I raided my sisters' closets, got some skating socks, a sweater and scarf and when the street cars started, rode downtown. I went to Dayton's, which was nearly deserted, and bought some overshoes and warm mittens. Then back to the bus station to see when buses would start.

When the first bus for Mound left at 2 PM it had two drivers and a shovel. We turned off Hennepin to Wayzata boulevard to find an auto graveyard. Cars were everywhere. We went on the sidewalk by Dunwoody because abandoned cars blocked the street. By the time we got to Mound it was dark again. The bus had not gone into my road, through the island, but one of the drivers said he had friends on the island where he planned to spend the night, so he would walk home with me. He did—and we found those roads better than those we had gone through. But I was glad to be home, and there on the table, were the flowers I had picked Sunday, still fresh. I did go to work the next day.

ALCOHOLICS ANONYMOUS GREW OUT OF STORM
by Rolf Stageberg
Northfield, MN

I think this story is different because this experience provided immense benefits which are still benefitting people today.

I was an assistant probation officer in the Minneapolis municipal court offices. It was a relatively short period after I had read the story in the Saturday

Evening Post written by or about a drunk in Detroit who, in desperation to solve his own dilemna, dreamed up the idea of something he called Alcoholics Anonymous. It was of special interest to me because most of the people referred to our office were having problems with alcohol. I was an earnest social worker trying to help with the problem but scoring zero. I was terribly frustrated over the whole matter.

But then came the storm. The leading actor of this story told it to me himself so I know it is true. A friend for many years, Pat Cronin said that on that day there were three Chicago drunks in Minneapolis. They were socked in because of the storm, frustrated over having nothing to do and decided to go to General hospital to visit the *snake pit*. They hoped to find some prospects there on whom they could try out their new conversion to Alcoholics Anonymous. So they went there and, as Pat told it to me, they found a miserable drunk, a successful salesman who had drunk up all his assets and was teetering on the edge of personal oblivion. But he still had one asset. He had intelligence and the capacity to listen. Pat listened to the story of these drunks from Chicago who called themselves *alcoholics* and he bought the story they told him.

The result was that Pat became the one-man AA missionary in Minnesota. To anyone who would listen he talked of the typical resistance people put up to excuse their alcoholism. He recruited five men to become his first squad and they rented a small apartment on Franklin avenue from which they carried out their outreach. I remember the names of two of these men but won't give it here. The main thing is that from Pat and this small group grew the AA programs and squads all over the upper midwest—the Dakotas, Montana and possibly other neighboring states. Pat may properly be called the father of AA in the upper midwest.

So out of the terrible storm grew this effective tool for treating the destructive forces of alcoholism.

(Editor: Mr. Stageberg went on in later years to become the superintendent of the Minneapolis city workhouse from 1956 to 1972.)

ANTI-FREEZE COST 3/4 OF WEEKLY SALARY
by Cliff Stone
Wyoming, MN

It was a dull gray, misty morning in the fifties as I drove to my work at the hardware firm of Janney, Semple, Hill & Co., on south Second street in Minneapolis. I was thinking ahead to the evening when I would add alcohol to the radiator of my 1930 Chevrolet coupe, which was the reason I drove that day, instead of walking as was usual. It had been so mild that fall that normal winter preparations had been postponed. With temperature in the high fifties, alcohol would soon boil away on longer trips, leaving plain water as protection against freezing. Prestone was available at approximately ten dollars a gallon, that amount being about three-fourths of a week's wages at that time.

I parked on Second street facing east to Second avenue south, just off Marquette avenue.

About 10:30 light snow started falling, which increased in intensity during the day. By 3 PM the wind was blowing horizontally down Second street, still from the west, causing many anxious glances from windows and comments by us. At 5 PM quitting time I went to my car, expecting to drive away as usual. I had been in snow before, my car had good traction, and I saw no reason for concern.

Turning the key and pushing the floorboard starter button produced only engine noise but no firing in any of the six cylinders. I raised the left side of the hood and was shocked to find the engine compartment completely filled with snow. It had entered through the hood vent slots on both sides, those slots acting as scoops for the blowing snow. I tried to clear away the snow as best I could from the spark plugs and carburetor, but without results.

After accepting the fact that I had a dead car, I pondered my next action. I had worn only light clothing and the normal low shoes. Public transportation was now halted. The only choice was to start walking to where we lived at 2012 Oakland avenue south, near Franklin. I don't remember much about that two mile walk except that I walked close to the buildings along Portland and on the lawns when advisable. My thoughts were on my car and what I should do about it. I managed to avoid dwelling on exactly how wet and cold I was becoming.

After eating and changing to dry clothes (we didn't have much available in town because we were still spending some time at our lake cottage), I began the hike again. I was determined to get the car off the street.

On my way back to the car I stopped at a little garage on Third street and Third avenue south across from Charley Hall's chicken shop. I told my tale of woe and requested help and, although he was literally buried with work, he consented to assist me, a consideration I never forgot.

The tow truck made it through the deepening snow (it was now getting very cold as the temperature kept dropping); the driver hooked up the tow line and began pulling the car. As we reached the intersection of Washington and Second avenue, the tow line parted, leaving me and the car on the street car tracks, a precarious position. The tow man was very verbal about this happening, leaving me fearful he would abandon me as he left for his shop. I was left alone with my wild visions of being there all night. Eventually, maybe only fifteen minutes, he returned, hooked up again and took the car to his garage where it would be parked overnight. It was shoved into a corner out of the way. It was about 9 PM, about three hours since I had left home. I left, promising to get the car the next day, and started walking that two miles again, in 12 inches of snow. As I recall, the total snowfall was about 16 inches.

I walked to work the next morning. Excuses weren't accepted readily in the forties. Only a few people had made it to the office or the departments. Transportation was still bogged down. Only a few cars having chains mounted on the rear wheels were moving freely. Our stock of chains had been exhausted the previous day when the storm started.

I don't remember when the street cars stated operating again; I do know that I walked home again that afternoon, ate and walked back to the garage. My gruff friend remarked about the mess my car had made on his floor. I thought the water was from melted snow but it was from the engine. I had started to fill the radiator with water and heard water running out, coming from the block behind the carburetor. The garage owner said that the frost plug had popped out, something I had never heard about. I even found water inside the car from a ruptured car heater, one of those things you installed yourself. That had to be by-passed before proceeding with the radiator.

Since repair of the block was impossible then, I reinserted the frost plug, holding it in place with a stick propped against the carburetor. I wasn't permitted to leave the car any longer so water, alcohol and a can of radiator solder were added. No serious leaks were seen so I paid the kind owner his requested three dollars for all his trouble of the previous night and for storing the car for 24 hours, and drove away.

The car recovered. I had no more trouble during the 1 1/2 years I drove it after the big freeze.

SO BUSY MY POCKETS
WERE STUFFED WITH MONEY
by Arthur Teslow
St. Louis Park, MN

I was running a Standard Oil service station at 24th and Bloomington. It was a nice, mild morning until it started raining about noon. Then the weather really deteriorated. The rain changed to snow and there was a terrific cold wind. Then all hell broke loose at my station.

At that time few people used Prestone because it was a new product and quite expensive for those days. Everybody had to have alcohol for their radiators. My helper, who lived across the street, was duck hunting so I was left alone. Of course, when they came in for alcohol they also filled their gas tanks and I was checking and adding oil.

The snow started piling up and soon I was pushing cars away from the pumps so somebody else could get serviced. Luckily, the passengers and other people helped me push cars in and out of my driveway. I had a moneychanger strapped around my waist and put the bills in my pockets. Before long my pockets were so stuffed with bills there were no remaining pockets. Money was sticking out the top of pockets because I didn't have time to put the bills in the safe.

Pretty soon the entire driveway was full of stuck cars and people pushing their cars up to the pumps and then away from them. This continued until after dark before things started slowing down.

I then started thinking about how I was going to get home; I lived at 4734 Vallacher avenue in St. Louis Park. I closed the station at 9 PM and started for home. I got as far as the cut through the Minnikahda golf course on Excelsior boulevard where the whole road was completely blocked with dozens of cars whose owners had just abandoned them and gone home. I was able to turn around and go back to Lake and Hennepin. I tried the Carling hotel which was full by then, it being after 11 PM. I went to a bowling alley on Hennepin between Lake and 31st street and was truly concerned about where I would sleep. I talked with one of the fellows there who lived in a rooming house on Girard avenue. He called his landlady who had an extra mattress and bedding. She put it on the floor and that is where I spent the night.

FARM FAMILY HOSTS 20 KIDS 3 DAYS
by Eileen Beckius Wagner
Apple Valley, MN

It was misting that morning when our bus driver, Rollie Flynn, left his mother's farmhouse and walked to his big 42-passenger orange school bus that glistened like a pumpkin.

Rollie was wearing a light jacket, no gloves, and high shoes, but no boots. His mind wasn't on that 7 AM meandering run from farm to farm into Jordan as much as it was on the previous day's events. The bans of his marriage to Betty Martin had been announced in St. Catherine's Catholic church. They had set the date for the end of November.

He started the bus, swung the big machine onto the narrow gravel road and for the next two hours was busy turning, twisting, and filling the bus as he picked up his 32 riders. They ranged from little folks to high schoolers—like the Sheas, the Gradys, Klehrs, Ryans, Wolfs, and the Beckius children, Eileen, Larry and Jean. He was going to remember the Alex Beckius farm before the day was ended.

As Rollie down-shifted to descend the long hill into Jordan, it startled raining heavily and there was the feel of sleet.

As soon as he dropped the children he drove the bus to Ben Engfert's garage to have the radiator repaired. It had been leaking and Rollie had been babying it the previous week but knew it needed repairing now.

"Sure, we can fix it but it might take 'til noon," said Ben. "Okay, go ahead; I'll wait" replied Rollie.

By 10 AM that morning the rain had changed to sleet and snow. In another 30 minutes school superintendent Al Wurst was calling the garage and telling Ben to shake a leg with that radiator job. The weather reports were bad and school was going to be dismissed, and Rollie's was the only bus serving the school.

It was noon when Rollie loaded up his passengers and started up that long hill. I was one of those on that bus.

When we got to the top of the hill, WOW, we couldn't see a thing. Just blinding snow and wind. Rollie Ryan and Jim Shea, two of the older boys, opened their windows on opposite sides to watch and make sure the bus didn't go in a ditch. We girls were not dressed for a storm. We had on bobby-sox but no boots, no gloves, no scarves . . . and it was getting colder on the bus. It felt as though the heater had quit working. Rollie managed to make four stops at farms before he came to our farm road. It was 4PM and he had gone only four miles since leaving Jordan. The bus wheels would spin through the ice, hit the gravel and inch forward. Then they would spin and we'd do it all over again. Sometimes the big boys would get out with their shovels, but their efforts were in vain.

Some children were starting to get frightened. The little first graders started to cry. We were very lucky even to get to our place. My dad saw the bus coming down the road through a screen of snow and plowed a path to the bus door with his tractor.

"You can't go on, Rollie. Night is coming and it's getting worse. The radio says the whole state is halted. People have been lost already, phone lines are out, power is still on—but for how long? Come in and warm up. We've got plenty of room, just butchered two hogs Saturday. Let's get these kids out of the blizzard and into the house where they'll be safe."

My dad and Rollie carried the little Grady twins through drifts that were already waist high. Some children were so anxious to get inside where it was warm that they ran through the snow in their stocking feet. They had taken off their shoes to keep their feet warm by sitting on them.

After all 20 plus kids got in the house, we sat around the kitchen cookstove and warmed up—and thanked God we were safe.

After that front door closed behind us we didn't go outside again until Wednesday, three days later. In the meantime, the electric wires snapped—so no lights. My dad got out the kerosene lamps and the gas lanterns. In the evenings my mother played the piano and we sang songs; we played card games. Dad and mother sat up all night refueling the wood furnace and were there if the younger children needed them. We had a big two story house with five bedrooms upstairs and one downstairs. Most of the little ones slept in beds while the older boys and girls slept in chairs or on the floor. Dad was very worried about a fire or sickness.

Bathroom facilities were something else. We had a two-holer outhouse but nobody could get to it. The snowdrifts were higher than the house. There was a commode upstairs but, with 20 plus people using it, it filled in no time. So it had to be emptied many times. I cannot remember who had that job.

Much credit goes to my mother. She kept calm through all three days.I think she and my sister Angie spent that whole time in the kitchen making meals. They baked bread, cakes and cookies for all of us every day. My mother is now 88 years old and is in fairly good health; she remembers this event as if it were yesterday.

By Wednesday the storm had gone and the sun was shining brightly. The air was noisy with the sounds of plows working. My brother Virgil arrived bringing bread, butter and a few goodies. As the day went on, some parents came with horses and sleighs to take their children home. Others weren't able to get home until the next day. Rollie got his bus out of the snowdrift and was on his way home, thankful to be alive.

Many months later, after the snow melted and spring was in the air, my dad found one of the Grady twin's shoes. He held that shoe while thoughts raced through his mind of those chaotic and exciting days back in November 1940.

CAR BURIED AT CEMETERY GATE
by James W. Wakefield
St. Paul, MN

We had been married only a couple of months and started for Hudson, Wisconsin, where our parents lived. It was a bad day, wet and drizzling cold. We got as far as Tanner's lake and decided it was too slippery, so we turned around. I put on the chains because I had to pick up my sister at the Union depot. I followed the street car tracks and had no problem.

The next morning I started for the National cemetery at Fort Snelling where I worked. I got as far as Fort Snelling and called the superintendent who told me to walk the rest of the way. I couldn't understand what I would do even if I got there, so I turned around and went home. I don't know how many people were hanging on to that old Ford trying to get to town. I know there wasn't room for any more.

I think it was three days before I made it to the cemetery. I never shoveled so much snow in my life—before or since. We tried to make a snowplow but it broke right away. The drifts were so hard that we drove over the tops of them. There was a car buried by the cemetery gate but we didn't even know it was there until the owners came to dig it out about a week later.

A lot of hunters were caught in the storm and died, some of which we buried.

One thing I remember is that I found out that was no job for me. I transferred to the post office in June as a janitor, letter carrier and clerk.

THIRTY-FOUR BELOW AT JORDAN
by Russell A. Welch
Rochester, MN

My home was on grandad's farm about two miles from Jordan 44 years ago. I was employed in Jordan at the Juni hardware store as a journeyman plumber and on November 10 had just completed installation of an automatic hot water heating system in a remodeled home.

The morning of the 11th the electrician and I returned to the job to fill the system and recheck our work. At about 10 AM when I was letting air out of the radiators on the first floor, I noticed it was snowing fairly heavily. There had been no snow on the ground and none had been indicated. When I got to the second floor the snow was coming down very heavily and I couldn't see the house 50 feet across the alley. When I had completed my work and went to the truck for a testing guage I found eight inches of snow. This was about 11 AM. We spent some more time checking the burner, then went to the door to find about 18 inches of snow on the ground.

I said to Lloyd, the electrician, "Let's pick up the tools and go" to which he replied, "The hell with the tools. I'm going now." So we did. I was driving a 1929 Model A Ford about two feet off the ground so made it the eight blocks to the shop. The snow had now accumulated to about 20 inches.

When I finally got the truck in the garage I saw that the other truck was gone. The boss had taken everyone home at 11. I was the only one left in the shop.

I was certain I wasn't going to make it the two miles in the country to my home and, knowing I would need food, plowed across the street and bought bread, lunch meat and a quart of milk. Returning to the shop, I noticed that my tracks in the deep snow and drifts were already completely covered. I spent that afternoon listening to Cedric Adams on radio, looking out the window and enjoying a warm shop.

At about 1 PM my boss, Howard, called and said that if I thought I could make it to his house four blocks away, I'd be welcome and to come on. I told him I was okay and not about to venture outside. At that time I would guess we had something like 24 to 30 inches of snow; it wasn't blowing too severely but the temperature was dropping fast.

I slept that night on a workbench on a big comforter we used to cover appliances when delivering them.

Of course I awakened still worried about my family on the farm but, with no phones working, I couldn't communicate with them. Neither could I find out if my friend, Lloyd the electrician, ever made it home. That morning the temperature was 34 below zero and the wind was blowing hard. I had a sandwich and some milk and looked at the snow through the windows.

At 2 PM my boss called (local telephones seemed to be working all right) asking if I were considering trying to go home. If I did, he said, go to the sports section of the store and get a pair of Cruiser snowshoes, a pack, a match case and matches, along with something to build a fire, just in case, and some food for the pack. I told him I was going to make the trip.

With all of that equipment, I set out for home and, because of my CCC (Civilian Conservation Corps) training, I managed the snow shoes well enough that I made the two-mile trip home in 2 1/2 hours.

I didn't see the new heating system for about a week. It took the city that long to remove cars and trucks so the streets could be cleared. There was no place to put all that snow and it remained a problem all winter.

My grandfather lost no stock but many farmers did. Many people had not put up their winter's supply of fuel. Outside wells froze and some people couldn't get out of their homes. There were no deaths in town but many duck hunters froze. The old timers never recovered from the devastating snow; it was talked about for years. When one can walk on a sidewalk in a pair of snowshoes and look down into windows to see if anyone is inside, the snow is indeed deep.

About 19 months later I found myself in the South Pacific with its monsoon rains and steaming ground. I found myself wishing for some of that snow.

BUS DRIVER MADE U-TURN, TOOK US HOME
by Roberta F. Wesley
Richmond, CA

My name was Roberta Forsyth and I lived with my parents' family on George avenue in St. Louis Park; I was 30 years old. I took my usual Deephaven bus on Minnetonka boulevard to my office in the Northwestern Bank building in downtown Minneapolis. The big old yellow street cars on Hennepin were slipping backwards down Lowry hill — it was terrifying to watch them. When our bus driver saw that happening he made a wide U-turn and headed back to the Park. If he had not made that decision we would have been stranded downtown with all the others.

My dad worked at Northern States Power company on Fifth street. When he stepped outside, his new derby blew off, hit the sixth floor window of a building and he never saw it again. He was headed for the Harbor bar for his traditional Armistice Day drink at 11 AM to host his fallen buddies from World War I. He had to spend the night there curled up on a curved lounge seat.

My mother and sister called for a taxi which got stuck in front of the house; only its roof light was visible. With the driver they spent the afternoon playing gin rummy and drinking hot tea. They never did get to their destination, the Legion hall, where they were to set tables for a dinner party that night. It had to be cancelled anyway.

HANDICAPPED LADY MADE IT TO WORK

by Warren Witt
Minneapolis, MN

My bride and I had just moved into our new home on Meadow Lane North in Golden Valley. My family owned a store, among several, at 4100 West Lake street, now one of Lincoln Del's outlets. We sold it to them. Anyway, my job was running the meat and bakery departments. C. T. Thomas had the produce and groceries.

I put chains on our Ford and took off down Glenwood avenue to Glenwood boulevard. The wind was coming from the east and by driving through Sunset Gables I arrived. The houses had helped to screen the roads.

No one showed up for work. I hung around until noon, sold one loaf of bread to a next door neighbor, and went home. I don't remember the driving at that time as being so difficult.

My father, Ray Witt, ran our store at 705 Hennepin avenue. About one third of our help showed up because many lived within walking distance. I remember that Mary Ford, our phone operator, made it; she lived at the Curtis hotel for 30 years . . . and she was crippled.

Dad went across Seventh street to the Majestic hotel (I believe it burned down during World War II) and rented an entire floor of rooms for the thirty or so employees who had showed up. Benny Haskell sent over the potables. They say a good time was had by all.

THEY SHOVELED THREE MILES FOR CIGARETTES

by Mary Frances Wold
Coon Rapids, MN

Although the 1940 blizzard will be recalled by many with stories of hardship and bravery, there was also a touch of humor.

We had built a garage in which to live while erecting our house in Columbia Heights. On the morning of the 11th the weather was so mild we decided to hang storm windows over the openings on the house to close it in so we could heat it. Then we could work inside the rest of the winter. When my husband

and brother-in-law from Chicago started working on the scaffolding at 10 AM the wind had picked up. I remember that our car was parked in front of the house, facing the wind, which would prove one mistake too many.

At lunchtime the radio was forecasting heavy snow but no blizzard warning was given. They continued to work until all the windows were hung and fastened down by which time the storm's wind and snow were whirling around corners. About that time we received our last phone call from our sister. She was asking her husband to come home because she'd heard reports that street cars were unable to run. When the men tried to start the car the engine compartment was filled with wind-driven snow. It wouldn't start. They gave up and plowed down the hill to our little house which was warm and cozy. Since we had been carrying water from across the street, they quickly filled all containers possible with snow to melt.

That neighbor came over later with a pail of water and told us he had abandoned his car two miles away and walked home. His wife, who rode the street car to work, had to spend the night with a co-worker near their job. This neighbor had bought coal and had been forced to abandon it in his car so the fellows helped him get to another neighbor's where he borrowed enough to last the night. The depression was just ending and people routinely bought coal in small affordable quantities.

Our small oil stove worked mightily to keep us warm, with much banging from expansion and contraction. We had plenty to eat, made popcorn to eat with apples. We kept the conversation light so we wouldn't wonder too much about our families—and we existed.

In the morning we could see out through only two windows, looking over the tops of huge drifts. Both doors were snowed shut. We put a blanket on the floor and removed the inset from the front door. Snow immediately fell into the middle of the room but at least we had a place from which to start shovelling. We did this with my cookie sheets.

Since we had no plumbing, it was imperative that a path was made to the outhouse. It was only 25 feet away but it seemed they had to shovel half a mile.

We spent the morning playing card games while we waited to see if the plows would run. Our milk, bread and other foodstuff was beginning to run low. We thought we could make do with what we had until the men ran out of cigarettes. That did it! The need to get out then became very important. They bundled up, found shovels to help clear their way, and walked or plowed their way to the store three miles away.

It was to be another day before our neighbor's wife arrived home. Everybody had problems. My mother had not been able to get home but had stayed at a downtown hospital. My brother walked from Nicollet island where he worked to northeast Minneapaolis to be with those young ones still at home. He had frostbitten toes, fingers and ears.

We were some of the fortunate ones.

SNOW PRANK

by Helen deLong Woodward
Minneapolis, MN

Have you seen Snow
On his charger the Wind -

    Wild steed bit champing, tossing his mane
    Mad mount driving, traversing the plain
    Dashing hither and yon on the street
    Buffeting all and sundry they meet
    Battering awnings, worrying signs
    Probing crevice and crack by design
    Plucking wild at breaths helter-skelter
    Driving mortals scuddling to shelter
    Hoisting sky high, dirt, paper amd leaves
    Whirligigs smoke and shivers the trees
    Snatching at curtains, shutters and curtains
    Pushing at windows, maddening vanes
    Strewing all forms of file and rank
    Chortling over this frantical prank

Suddenly tired of delirious mirth
Snow stables his steed and covers the earth.

SOUTHWEST MINNESOTA

The Pipestone National Monument

PEOPLE PICKED US UP, SAVED OUR LIVES
by William H. Dittes
Mankato, MN

In 1940 I was school superintendent at Sherburn, MN. I drove to Minneapolis on November 9 to attend the football game between the Universities of Minnesota and Michigan. I left for Sherburn Monday morning at 6 AM, expecting to be there for an Armistice Day program which was to be held in the high school auditorium at 11 AM.

It was raining when I left Minneapolis. I picked up Miss Mable Beck, a teacher at Sherburn. She had visited her parents at their home on Bryant avenue south. A sister, Edna, was a teacher in the Minneapolis system and a brother, Roland, was a dentist. I sang with Roland in the choir of the Wesley Methodist church during the depression when Dr. George Mecklenburg was pastor there. I was doing graduate work at the University and also singing with the Minneapolis Apollo club under the direction of William McPhail.

I didn't have a radio in my car and we were not dressed for winter weather. As we neared Mankato it started to snow. When we left there we were going directly into a sixty mile an hour wind. Half way to Lake Crystal there were large, rolling hills with no trees and no farm buildings in sight. Snow was driving into the car and the hood and engine were compacted with snow. The car stalled and I was able to steer it to the shoulder of the road. I got out and considered walking to Lake Crystal for help. I couldn't have made it.

A large new car came by and stopped. They had a radio and knew about the storm. They advised us both to get our suitcases and they would take us to Lake Crystal, so we did that after locking the car. If those kind people had not picked us up, we would both have frozen to death. The next day several people were found dead in their cars near where we had left my car.

We got out of their car at a gas station and we did not get their name nor where they were from. I have always been sorry that we did not.

People were already at the gas station. We went immediately to the hotel and got the last two rooms available. An elderly Welch couple ran the hotel and were rather reluctant to furnish meals but finally said they would if they could satisfy us. We got along very well during the two days and nights we were there. We guests spent our time visiting and playing cards. After two days we got a truck to go out and pull my car into the garage. After it was thawed out my passenger and I drove on to Sherburn. We found high drifts on the downtown sidewalks of Sherburn.

Mable and I were always grateful to those people who stopped for us and saved our lives. Mable passed away a few years ago after having been a teacher and a principal in the St. Louis Park system. I am fortunate to be alive today at the age of 90.

THANKS, GOD, FOR USING ME
by Dwight G. Drown
Marshall, MN

I was living with my sister and her husband on the west side of Marshall. I believe it was about noon when a Mr. Murdock called to ask if we had any kerosene, which he needed for his stove. He lived in a shack at the ice house which was about a quarter of a mile away across highway #19, alongside the river on an elevated road at the ice house. He was going to come over, knock at the door and we'd get the kerosene for him. We didn't realize how bad it was outside. He did come but we never heard him.

When he hadn't come, so we thought, I put on all the clothes I could find with a scarf around my face and when I had the kerosene in a gallon can I headed for his place. I was 19 years old.

The wind was at my back and didn't seem too bad until I reached the highway, 200 yards away. I was half way there—another 200 yards to the ice house. Because the road was elevated and the wind so strong I had to get down on my hands and knees and crawl those last 200 yards. Seeing was impossible. I just felt my away along that gravel road.

When I got to the ice house I had a chance to get my bearings. I found the shack and had to dig snow away from the door. I found Mr. Murdock in bed with all his clothes on. He informed me he had been to our place but we had no way of knowing.

I put the kerosene in the space heater and got it going. He had a wood stove and I put the stovepipes on and out the window (a metal frame for stovepipes). Then I went outside and found some wood inside the ice house. I broke it up, carried it in and started a fire in that stove. Back outside to get more wood. I believe this was lumber for openings in the ice house that I broke up. I thought I carried enough wood to last for a couple of days and Mr. Murdock thanked me over and over again. He was probably in his late seventies.

I truly felt God had moved me to go help the old man because he surely would have frozen to death in his bed.

Again I had to crawl on my hands and knees because I couldn't stand up in the high wind. It took longer to get home because I was facing the wind. Also I became disoriented in the park across from us and had to talk to myself to determine where I was and how to get home.

I look back and thank God for using me to help that old man that day.

I am a retired State Trooper.

STEERS WANTED TO GO WITH THE WIND
by Jack C. Franklin
Redwood Falls,MN

Dad called me to get out of bed before daylight that morning saying that there was a blizzard raging outside.

We drank some coffee and as soon as we could see we started on foot for a rough 120 acre pasture a quarter of a mile away. We had 25 head of hereford steers and a cow in this pasture. I was scared because the wind must have been blowing over 60 mph and the snowstorm was blinding me. Drifts were already three feet deep.

We found the cow with 13 of the steers at the bottom of the lane by the pasture; we knew we needed to find the rest of the steers but didn't dare leave this bunch because they wanted to go with the storm and that could be disastrous. Already they could hardly see because of ice and snow in their eyes. I told dad to take them to the house, knowing the cow would lead them and they would follow. We forgot to say how we would find each other again in the storm. After dad had started with that bunch I started in the other direction, going with the storm.

I went with my back to the storm until I came to the line fence which then turned south. I followed this fence and came to the 12 steers which were going slowly along the fence, blinded from the ice on their heads. Their bodies were blown full of snow, the strong wind blowing their hair straight out and the snow compacted on their coats.

I got ahead of them and by hollering loudly got them turned into the wind. I had to keep hollering at them because they wanted to turn and go with the wind. I was floundering in waist deep snow and trying to walk, sometimes to run, and hollering. It was beginning to wear me out. I had to lean into the wind just to walk. At times when I was hollering at one end of the cattle I couldn't see where the others were. Had they stopped or turned around on me? So I had to keep running back and forth from one end of the group to the other.

I had been raised here so if I could see trees or a cluster of rocks I knew my location. In fact, I still live at this same place, where I have lived all my life.

I finally got to the bottom of the lane and there was dad walking in a circle trying to keep warm. He didn't dare leave because he didn't know where I was. We made it to the barn with my bunch of steers also.

After all my running and breathing in that cold air and stumbling through the snowdrifts, I was in bed for over a week with a tight chest. I suppose there was nothing tragic about this storm but had we been just one hour later starting after the cattle they would all have died. That's what happened to thousands of animals during that storm. Our cattle would have gone into a ground sag in a fence corner and died there.

They were mortgaged cattle in those days also, just as in farming today.

I forget the number of days of the blizzard because I was in bed, but the roads were blocked for at least 10 days and then it took a crawler tractor to open the rock hard drifts full of black dirt. It also was more than 20 degrees below zero after the storm.

YOUR FEET ARE STILL COLD SAYS HUSBAND

by Helen McRae Hesli
Apple Valley, MN

We were newlyweds of five months and were living in Lamberton, about 140 miles southwest of the Twin Cities. We had gone to St. Paul to visit our folks, the Norman McRaes and Nick Hesli. Our friend, Leonard Coulter, had gone with us to visit a girl friend in Minneapolis. We intended to go home Sunday night until Leonard called and suggested we make it Monday morning so he could go out with his girl again Sunday night.

We left St. Paul about 6 AM, my husband being dressed in a business suit and I in a cotton dress and anklets, regular attire in those days for Monday morning laundry and other chores. We did have coats but no scarves or gloves. My father had given us a rug which we had in the back seat, and we had our luggage in the trunk.

My husband, Gene, was driving; I was in the middle and Leonard sat by the window. When we left St. Paul it was starting to rain which became increasingly disagreeable as we headed homeward. When we reached New Ulm the radio was still saying rain but it was 9 AM and snowing there. Some miles further the snow became heavy and the wind whipped up more blizzard-like conditions. When we went through Cobden and as the road (highway #14) turned more southwesterly, we proceeded under a railroad bridge and our vision became completely obscured. The severe northwestern wind almost blew us off the road. We crept along a short distance until Leonard said we were too close to the ditch on his side — and suddenly we were in the ditch on the other side — the left side.

We tried to get out with the men hanging on to the car, pushing, and I driving, trying to rock it to get up on the road again. We finally had to give up; we couldn't even see the hood of the car. The guys crawled back inside and we tried to keep warm and plan what we should do. Leonard finally decided to go seek help. In about an hour he returned with a farmer he'd found, and a tractor. He pulled us out of the ditch and left us right away. Our car stalled immediately and actually we were worse off because we were on the wrong side of the highway! Our trunk was frozen shut so there was no way to get more clothes. After some more serious discussion, Leonard decided to leave again.

Miracles do happen. He walked three miles into Springfield where he called the highway department and the police. They told him they couldn't take their equipment out in the storm. They also told him there was a farmhouse a mile or so from where we were stalled.

In the meantime my husband and I crawled into the back seat, huddled and attempted to cover up with the rug my father had given us. You can imagine how little warmth there was in an old 9 x 12 carpet. We talked and talked about our love for one another, our future plans and life together, because we knew we shouldn't fall asleep at the same time. I think one car went by and missed us by an inch.

About five o'clock the door was pulled open and Leonard fell into the car. He had a pair of farm bib overalls for me, some scarves and mittens and a pair of high-buckle overshoes. We put them on and prepared to leave the car. By now it was dark and the snow and wind were fierce. We started toward the farm house he had found over a mile away. I could then see why it is easier to freeze than to die some other ways. It was so exhausting with the wind and snow in our faces, we couldn't see a thing and our arms and legs were devoid of feeling. The men literally dragged me, even though we clung tightly together so we wouldn't get separated. In an hour or so we saw a light and stumbled into the farm home.

The owners had gone away for the weekend and were stranded somewhere but their man hired to care for the livestock was there and delighted to have some company. He was also considerate and fixed us some food.The pain was excruciating as we began to thaw at the fingers, toes, cheeks, inside the knees. We tried the old snow-thawing trick but that was unbearable. (Editor: Seems to me it is not recommended today.) My hands were so swollen and painful I couldn't bear to touch anything so I wasn't much help in the kitchen detail.

Now we can look back and laugh at our first night. There was a little, narrow stairway going straight up to the upstairs bedroom and we managed to climb up with our hurting legs and feet. The three of us slept in an old fashioned three-quarter size bed with my husband in the middle and Leonard and me clinging to the outsides. We heard the man downstairs throwing in wood all night in the huge pot-bellied stove; there was a chimney going up through our bedroom and it got about 110 degrees in that small room. The heat made me thirsty and I asked my husband if he would get me a glass of water. He got up and made his way down the treacherous steps. Leonard called out, "Bring me one too." Gene came, making his way back with a glass in each hand, grumbling about the fine thing of leaving the two of us up there alone in the bed.

We were stranded there three days, saying our thankful prayers that Leonard had been guided safely through all of his walks, that we had all been saved and found that farm house. The farm couple arrived home on Wednesday and soon we were able to go home to Lamberton. The telephone lines were down so it was Friday before we could call home to tell our parents that we were safe and sound.

My fingers still hurt when they get cold and my husband says I still have cold feet.

LIKE YOU COULDN'T EVEN BELIEVE
by Eddie Knouft
Minneapolis, MN

I've been an ardent hunter all of my life and at this time I was travelling for the Standard Oil company of Marshall, which is about 150 miles southwest of Minneapolis and 20 miles northwest of Lake Benton.

Dr. Charles McGuiggan, a hunting buddy, Gene Nafziger and Herm Stedler from Rochester decided to hunt Lake Benton for ducks on this particular day.

It was a mild morning and cloudy. If you've ever hunted ducks you know we put our boats in the lake and scattered our decoys: we had our lunch with us also.

Along about noon the clouds got heavier and the ducks started to come into the lake by the thousands. We were probably over a block out in the lake when the wind came up and more ducks started coming in. An ardent duck hunter doesn't leave just as the ducks come in; that's when you start shooting. By about two o'clock at least 25,000 to 30,000 blue bills and other ducks started swooping into the lake ahead of snow flurries. As the storm got worse we decided to go ashore, heading north into that strong wind.

Needless to say, we had a lot of ducks in the boat, but when we got about 200 yards from shore we couldn't move the boat against that heavy wind and waves so we got out of the boat. Two guys were behind each boat to push it ashore. We just pulled them up on shore, threw the ducks into the trunks of the cars and knew we'd better get home. At this time the wind was blowing a real gale and snowing like you couldn't even believe.

Mr. Stedler and my other friend, Nafziger, were going to Mankato but they never made it: they stopped in a motel on the way. But Dr. McGuiggan and I, who lived in Marshall at that time, drove slowly to Marshall. It was about three in the afternoon and it was dark — snowing like you couldn't even believe. All along the road we had seen lots of pheasants, all dead. Hundreds of pheasants. They were standing up in the fields, frozen to death, snow in their mouths. Dead. We had lots of pheasants in the Marshall area at that time.

I dropped *Doc* off at his house and continued to my own house. It was really blowing and snowing — like you couldn't even believe.

A friend of mine, fellow by the name of Bill Bradford, had gone to Minneapolis to a football game and had left his dog in the basement about five blocks from my house. He called me that day from the city after the game and asked if I would go over to his house to check on the dog.

The next morning I put on all the winter clothes I could find and walked over to his house. No one could drive down the main street of Marshall; it was that bad. The doors of his house were locked but, since he wanted me to water and care for the dog, I broke open the door. That poor dog had been there since Saturday noon and it was now Tuesday morning. He had chewed up every telephone book, broom and anything else he could get hold of in the basement. I watered and fed him and took him home with me, until they got home later on.

We were snowed in there in Marshall about three days. At that time we had a little bridge club in the neighborhood so we just sat around and played bridge.

How well I remember that storm — it has been 45 years ago.

I SILENTLY THANKED GOD FOR BEING SAFE
by Stan Morgan
Pipestone, MN

It was early in the morning of November 11, Armistice Day 1940, when Dr. Walter Benjamin, Dr. Fred Yseth, Louis Steinberg and I left Pipestone in my 1939 Studebaker Commander four-door sedan. We were going duck hunting and anticipating a good shoot at Dead Coon lake, about 30 miles north of Pipestone. As we headed northeast on highway #23 we commented that the snow was falling in large flakes, which usually means the snowfall would be of short duration.

There was a little used dirt road which traverses the north side of the lake and another body of water just west of the lake. We drove east and then returned west to a point just below the brow of a hill. Taking our guns and other paraphernalia, we left the car and descended to the lake shore. We stood on the shore and were transfixed by the scene before us. We could see the dark water below but less than 50 feet above it hundreds of ducks were flying against the north wind. When they saw us they retreated into the lake; not a shot was fired and we shortly also retreated to the automobile. It seemed as though within just a few minutes we had become engulfed in a raging, blinding blizzard.

We knew we were in dire straits. We headed west and within a hundred feet we were blocked by a huge drift. We tried to get through it but in our effort a radiator hose burst and we lost all the radiator solution. Doctors Benjamin and Yseth left for help and when they came to a county road turned south a quarter of a mile to the Bakker farm. Louis and I stayed with the car and turned on the car radio. Cedric Adams of station WCCO was on the air saying that there would be snow flurries that day in southwestern Minnesota. Shortly after he said that, the snow drifted over the hood of the car.

Soon our two friends returned with Mr. Bakker who brought his tractor, but was unable to move the car with it. He informed us that he could take care of only one person at his house, so Louis hung on to the tractor seat and was pulled along to the Bakker home.

Since Mr.Bakker had told us of a farm about a quarter of a mile north, we felt we should try to reach it. Because visibility was down to about ten feet, the three of us felt our way along the line fence until we came to a cross fence which we followed another quarter of a mile across a plowed field. By sheer luck we bumped into the side of a barn, opened the door and were met by two men of the Schuler family; they were milking their herd of about 30 cows. The sweet smell of silage and the the other animal smells were very pleasing to us.

We made our way to the house where Mrs. Schuler directed us to the basement where we shed our wet clothes. I silently thanked God that we were now safe, and I am sure the other two did the same.

Dr. Benjamin phoned his wife and told her to contact the other wives so they would know where we were and that we were safe. He then attempted to call his nurse, but the line went down in just that short period. We again gave thanks that we could reach our families.

We were cared for by these families for two nights and three days while the blizzard raged on. I only wish I had kept a diary of the experience.

We three certainly must have interfered with the rhythmical operation of the farm. The family was having trouble enough battling the storm without caring for three uninvited guests. We tried to help with some of the chores such as operating the cream separator, but running around in our rubber boots made it a clumsy operation to say the least. My recollection is that we spent much time in the basement, trying to stay out of the way, and making life at least a little less strenuous for this fine family.

It must have been November 13 when we put on our boots, shouldered our guns and walked the eight miles to Tyler over hard-packed drifts, some eight to ten feet deep. There we found that highway #14 to Florence was blocked at the viaduct which carries highway #23 over #14. Dr. Benjamin then called his friend, Tracy Hicks, of Hicks Motors in Pipestone and told him of his problem, asking if he could meet us at the viaduct. We then hitched a ride from Tyler to the viaduct where Tracy was already waiting for us.

As we made our way home, we observed that only the cross arms of the telephone poles along the highway were above the snow banks.

My three companions during the hunt are now dead, as is Mr. Hicks. As the only person from this group still living it is impossible for me to check every detail but I'm reasonably sure this account is fairly accurate.

I am ashamed that I did not follow through on the whereabouts of the Schulers and the Bakkers. The Schuler farm is now occupied by the Clinton

Halling family and the Bakker farm is owned and occupied by the Arnie Sorenson family. I am eternally grateful for these gracious people who were so friendly and helpful to us during this harrowing experience.

WE SPENT THREE NIGHTS IN THE PACKARD
by Robert J. Munson
Minneapolis, MN

On the Saturday morning preceeding the storm my grandfather, Bob Seiberlich, and I left Glen Lake and drove a 1938 Packard to the Lac Qui Parle slough between Appleton and Milan. The weather was very warm and humid. At the university, Minnesota was playing Michigan featuring Tommy Harmon, the All-American.

We arrived at the Lac Qui Parle slough and hunted the rest of that day. Toward the latter part of the day the weather changed and I actually believe the wind was coming from the southwest. The temperature was dropping and my grandfather decided we should get off the lake, now known as the Minnesota river, and go to Appleton to spend the night with a relative, Elmer Benson, former U.S. senator and Minnesota governor.

By the time we left the lake and were ashore we noticed that hundreds of mallards were lighting in the water and wouldn't acknowledge our presence. Two other hunters came along with shotguns and told us they had shot 144 mallards on the water.

Luckily we were able to get to highway #7 and did return to Appleton. The weather was deteriorating so rapidly that my grandfather wanted to return home to Glen Lake. We started and made it as far as Milan where the Packard became stuck in the snow which had completely drifted over the road. It was evening and we had no place to go so decided to spend the night in the car.

I recall that my grandfather was a heavy smoker and had to have the car window open slightly. Occasionally he would tell me to clean out the exhaust pipe so we could run the motor to keep warm. Fortunately, being an old hunter, he had brought along enough warm clothing for us; we also had some sandwiches which my grandmother had prepared. These were in the trunk of the car and were frozen but we managed to eat them. During this time Cedric Adams was talking on WCCO radio about the problems duck hunters were having in the Wabasha area.

During that night we managed to run the car because my grandfather had just filled it with gas. The next day we sat in the car, running the engine every once in a while just to keep warm but still conserving gasoline. We spent three nights in the car until the weather finally cleared, which I believe was Tuesday. We saw a snow plow coming from the southwest on highway #7 going toward Milan and it seemed almost a day for it to get to our car. There had been other cars stuck behind us and when the plow finally reached us my grandfather went to a farmhouse with others and let our family know we were alright.

I also remember that during the course of those three days, one farmer went out to check his cattle and got lost between the barn and his home and subsequently froze to death. This was near Appleton.

I also recall hearing that Max Conrad, a famous pilot, would be flying over the Lake Pepin area dropping whiskey and food to surviving hunters in that area.

Pheasants were very plentiful in those days. After the plow had gone through we could see the tail feathers of the pheasants sticking out of the snow drifts. I personally picked up 21 pheasants that were half frozen and put them into the trunk of the car. When we got home we put them in the chicken coop. Needless to say pheasants and chickens do not get along together.

DUCKS WE KILLED SURE DIDN'T SPOIL
by Stanley Pivec
Hopkins, MN

We were ready for a big weekend of duck hunting at Heron Lake. This was our favorite spot, which always paid off with many enjoyable wild duck dinners. I picked up my hunting partner, Hugh Coyle, one of the better shots in Hopkins, and we were on our way. We got as far as Mankato and a very light snow started to fall. There was no wind so we didn't get concerned. We got excited because usually this weather condition created good hunting. We arrived at Herman Becker's in Heron Lake early on Sunday evening. Herman lived on Heron lake on a farm with lots of lake shore. We were given a room and Mrs. Becker fed us for the duration of the hunt. Herman also was our very capable guide. We went to bed early so we would be well rested for the next day.

The snow fell lightly all during the night, and a light northwest wind was blowing when we got up in the early morning. The conditions made us expect good hunting. We ate a good breakfast, got all our gear together and to the lake we went. We got to our platform blind, set out our decoys and all looked perfect. The ducks decoyed well and we shot fifteen in no time.

In about two hours something strange started to happen. The whole atmosphere seemed changing. The light snow we'd been having began to fall much heavier. The winds started to pick up, getting gustier by the minute, and blowing the snow. The ducks started to fly with absolutely no pattern; they were confused. Herman said "I have lived here all my life but I have never seen anything like this. Let's head for shore now; there's no time to pick up the decoys. We'll get them later." We prayed that my five-horse motor would run and get us to shore. Herman used some of the extra clothes we had taken to wrap around the motor so it didn't freeze. Without that motor we would have been stuck.

We got to shore and the storm was still getting worse. The snow was falling very heavily and the winds were horrible. At this point it was a matter of survival. Herman suggested we turn the boat upside down and huddle underneath it, letting the snow cover us until the storm was over. Before we did this Herman walked a little ahead of us, hollered for us to come there; luckily he had found a line fence that went close to his house, which was about three-quarters of a mile away. By now we couldn't see ten feet in front of us. We agreed that following the fence would be our best chance of staying alive. We couldn't see but with the fence to hang on to we covered our faces and started the long walk, taking one careful step at a time. After what seemed to be hours, what a happy moment it was when Mrs. Becker opened the door and we walked into the warm house ALIVE! Herman was the stabilizer who kept his head and kept us alive by making the right move at the right time. We sat down and had some delicious hot coffee, then went to the barnyard to help Herman get his sheep inside. We had to pull big chunks of ice from their faces; otherwise they would have died from suffocation.

The next morning our car was completely covered with snow. We ate breakfast, dug the car out and got ready to start home – on this Armistice Day 1940. By this time the storm was calming down, the plows were working, so we decided to start for home. We got as far as Vernon Center where we had to stay. The roads were completely blocked. People were staying and sleeping in churches and the pool hall. I spent the night on a pool table. Of course there was no way we could get word of our safety to our families. A traveling band, also stranded, played music to help us cheer up and the sense of humor of some of the other people stranded there helped us all. They even made us laugh a little. God bless them.

About this time we were also beginning to think we should have stayed put back at Herman's.

When we did get through to an operator she explained that the lines were down and no calls could get through. We explained our problem and she took down the telephone number and our information, telling us she would keep trying. We later found out she kept her promise. After we had left she was able to get through to my wife to let her know we were alive and coming home. I'm thankful to her even now, 45 years later.

Late at night some big plows went through town and we followed them almost to Belle Plaine; they had come to a big cut they couldn't get through and had to wait for heavier equipment coming from Jordan. While we were waiting, we were walking on top of the banks of the snow. One of the men saw something sticking out of the snow. It was the radio antenna of a car. The highway crew dug out the car and found two men inside, dead, probably from carbon monoxide. They weren't as fortunate as we were.

The road was finally opened all the way and we got home. What a reunion! Neighbors came over to hug us and everybody's eyes were full of tears. I was back with my family. Two days before I wasn't sure I'd ever see them again. I'm thankful today I'm here to tell my story.

We did bring ducks home, a full limit, and they sure didn't spoil. They were frozen like rocks. We all said many prayers for all the hunters and others who didn't make it home.

SWAMPED BOAT NEAR ORTONVILLE
by William B. Swartwood
Minnetonka, MN

It was the day of the Michigan-Minnesota football game, Saturday, November 9, 1940. My friend Jack and I were going duck hunting at Ortonville with two other fellows as soon as they returned from the game. (Minnesota won by one point). Ortonville because a girl friend of one of the fellow had offered the use of her family's lake cottage, probably at Big Stone. After a rainy night we awoke to three inches of new snow. We decided to go north to Lake Traverse where hunting was supposedly good.

At Traverse Jack and I decided to hunt from one small boat, to save money, while the others each took his own boat. Jack and I rowed south to a reedy spot, quietly watching the ducks in the middle of the lake. After about an hour the wind became stronger with more snow which seemed to arouse the ducks. Some came our way, we knocked down a few as the weather got much worse. Heavier snow, more wind, with more ducks flying over us. We shot more birds but couldn't find all of them in our reedy location. We soon decided we should lose no time in getting back to camp.

When we pulled from our sheltered spot we found that the wind and snow were even more severe than we had realized. The boat was pitching with water sloshing into it. One of us bailed while the other rowed. Although we both worked frantically, we still had about a mile of this now treacherous lake to navigate through. In the contest, the waves were winning, so we decided to head for the nearest shore. As we turned the boat to shore the waves surged over the back of the boat and we got our worst drenching yet. We were struck with our helplessness and thanked God for the fairly nearby shore. Just then we were swamped by an enormous wave, so clambered out of the swamped boat into the icy water. It was up to our hips but we were glad to traverse those last 50 feet and to drag the swamped boat onto the shore, saving our guns, ammunition, birds and ourselves.

Cold and shivering in our soaked clothing, loaded with our guns and ducks, we hiked back to camp, leaving the boat behind. The camp didn't provide rooms so our only shelter was the car, a canvas-topped convertible. The heater generated some heat for the front seat, already occupied by the other two fellows. They had not been as unlucky and weren't as water-soaked as were Jack and I.

By now we realized we were in a severe storm and decided to return to Ortonville. Visibility was so bad we couldn't tell what road we were on. My next recollection was that we had wandered into South Dakota (Ortonville is on the state line) and had to retrace our steps to the Minnesota side. After many experiences we did reach Ortonville and our friend with a girl friend there arranged for us to stay overnight with her family and a neighboring one. What bliss to get into a warm house, to get fed, to get out of our wet clothing into a warm bed.

We awoke to mountains of snow and impassable roads. How were we going to get back to Minneapolis, about 200 miles away? We were young guys making this trip on a shoestring and our money had nearly run out. Our only hope was the train, the Olympia, a top of the line train which, on this occasion, was fortified with two engines because of the storm. I had barely enough money for my ticket and the others boarded by grace of loans from friends. The car had to be left in Ortonville. Relieved to be on our way, accompanied by the good samaritan girl friend and her girl friend, also returning to Minneapolis, we settled on the comfortable seats of the Olympia, convinced and grateful that the dreadful ordeal was over.

Ah, but it wasn't over.

A few miles past Montevideo, in the night, the train rammed into an enormous snowbank, rocked and shook and settled as dead as a doornail. We were marooned thereon all night; in the morning we climbed off to see what kind of a mess we were in now. One side of the train was buried in snow to the top of the roof. We did learn finally that we would be transferred to a local milk train running on another track parallel to ours but on higher ground not yet blockaded. We waited. We were hungry. We ran out of cigarettes. Finally, the local rescue train arrived and we boarded. At the next town the conductor announced a ten-minute stop. Two of our fellow hunters jumped off to buy a candy bar each, with more borrowed money. They ate them quickly before rejoining Jack and me who had no money for such luxury and were left with growling stomachs. The seemingly endless journey resumed, with tedious stops all the way back to Minneapolis. Although we were ravenously hungry, we knew we were lucky to be out of the blizzard and on a warm train.

Finally we reached the Milwaukee depot in Minneapolis and rushed to get a streetcar to get home as fast as possible. Surprise! No streetcars were running. We tried to get cabs but they refused to take any fares beyond the downtown area. More waiting. At last word reached us that the Nicollet streetcar line had opened. When it came I used my last dime, hoarded for that purpose rather than spending it on a candy bar, and reached home.

The ducks Jack and I had shot in that miserable weather had been lost in a poker game to the other two hunters while we were back in Ortonville. This had been the most adventurous, though exhausting, trip of my life and it was some time afterwards before I fully realized our danger during that 1940 blizzard.

SOUTH CENTRAL MINNESOTA

THE BACHMANS FIND LAKE JEFFERSON BAD
by Stanley F. Bachman
Minneapolis, MN

Monday, November 11, 1940—the day of the great Armistice Day storm and
a day I shall never forget. It started at 3:30 AM when my father, Henry Bachman, touched my shoulder. "Stanley! Time to get up!" I was sixteen. Dad and
I were going on a long-anticipated day of duck hunting. I dressed hurriedly in
the unheated room. I could hear the rain falling outside, usually a good omen
for duck hunters. I was soon ready, and dad and I climbed into his new Buick
with the guns, ammunition, lunches and thermos bottles of coffee and hot
chocolate which mom had prepared for us. We set out in a high state of anticipation.

The drive took us from Minneapolis southwest toward the Ward Kluntz farm
on Lake Jefferson, near Cleveland, about 70 miles from the Twin Cities. The
Kluntz family had been friends of our family for many years. As we approached
Shakopee, the rain turned to snow and dad, the enthusiastic hunter that he
was, said, "This is going to make hunting good. The bluebills should come
right into the decoys." As we reached our destination, Lake Jefferson and the
adjoining sloughs on the Kluntz property, the snow continued. We set the
decoys in front of the blind I was to use and dad continued to a large slough
area, through canebrake and cattails, wearing a pair of bog shoes he had made
himself, especially to reach this site, which he considered to be a prime hunting
spot.

Daylight was just beginning and the hour to begin shooting arrived. Snow
was falling more heavily than ever by now. A strong wind was starting to blow
and I could feel the temperature dropping. As I recall, neither of us fired a
shot. Hours went by, but no birds were flying, or if they were, they couldn't
be seen. The fast-falling snow had penetrated my clothes, and ice was forming
on my cap and collar. I could barely make out the decoys, which were globs
of white about 50 feet ahead. Nearly three hours had elapsed since dad and
I had separated. I realized by now that we were in a really big blizzard and I
began to feel anxious about dad and our situation. I was excited by the drama
of our predicament, but also worried, and I hoped dad would come soon and
say we should head for home. It was about 10 AM when I finally saw him
trudging through the blinding storm, looking more like an animated snowman
than a man. When he came nearer, I was amazed to see that his collar was
covered with red ice! It was from cuts on his neck caused by the chafing of the
ice on his collar. A strange sight, but he was unaware of any discomfort.

We agreed to leave the decoys and begin the trip home as soon as possible,
never thinking that we might not be able to make it. The car started nicely.
We had about three-quarters of a mile of pasture road between us and the
farm, followed by another 500 feet or so to the gravel road.

We could only see a few feet in front of us and the car didn't go very far before being stopped by a drift which reached halfway up the grill. We decided to walk to the farm, thinking we could borrow shovels and dig our car from the drift. Then, if we could get the cat to the farm, we surely could make it home.

The wind coming at us as we walked was so strong it was nearly impossible to move forward, and drifts were already waist high. Our minds turned from shovels and getting home to just reaching the farmhouse. After struggling ahead for what seemed an eternity, we were nearly exhausted and very thankful when we saw the outlines of the buildings and were able to make our way to the farmhouse. When we arrived there, several other hunters were already there, too. By nightfall there were twelve stranded people crowded into the Kluntz home in addition to Ward and Francis Kluntz and their five young children.

Fortunately, Ward's livestock were all inside buildings and were safe. His chickens, however, were scattered about the yard and buildings, so we all set out to catch them and put them into their coops. It was quite a feat with the chickens flopping about in the snow and squawking when we would lunge for them. In quite a short time we managed to gather up all that we could find. Toward evening we pitched in helping Ward with his chores of milking, feeding and cleaning. This was helpful to him and took our minds off the severity of the storm. As luck would have it, one of the trapped hunters was a cook at St. Peter's State hospital. He took over the kitchen with its big wood range and, with Mrs. Kluntz's grateful agreement and help, made sure we had plenty to eat. Pancake batter was mixed in a big dishpan. The pancakes were our meal that first night and the next morning as well, along with hot oatmeal.

After eating, that evening, Mrs. Kluntz brought out all the blankets she could find and we each staked out an area on the floor. As I remember that night, and those that followed, there was no thought of entertaining ourselves after supper. We ate, talked a bit, and went to bed. Sometime later we were awakened by a room half filled with smoke. Someone said that the chimney was on fire. There was a lot of commotion while it was determined how to put out the fire. The wind was howling, the temperature was probably minus 20 degrees, and there were nineteen people in an old two-story wood-frame house. Someone, I don't remember who, went up on the roof and dropped a chain into the flue, scraping around the sides of the chimney to extinguish the fire. It wasn't long before the house was quiet again and everyone was thankful we had a roof over our heads.

By morning the snow had stopped but the wind was still fierce and it was extremely cold. After breakfast we put on our warm clothes and went out to see how bad things were beyond the protection of the yard. Knowing that we might be marooned for some time, we took our guns along, hoping to shoot some game for future meals. The snow was deep in some places, but there were other places where the wind had swept it away, exposing the frozen slush which had formed before the blizzard began.

Our car, which had been left in the pasture, had been blown fairly free of snow on the ouside but the white menace had seeped into the interior and had filled a good portion of it. Together, dad and I cleaned it as best we could. Then we raised one side of the hood and were astonished to find a solid mound of snow covering the engine. Would it start? We scooped and brushed as much away as possible and then held our breaths as dad got into the car, put the key in the ignition, and depressed the accelerator. The engine groaned a few times and began running. What a great sound! We kept it running while we continued to remove snow from all parts of the car.

Feeling satisfied that the car would run, dad and I took our guns and went in search of game. The other hunters were doing the same. When we arrived back at the farmhouse about noon, we found we had pheasants, ducks, coots, rabbits, and squirrels. Several of us helped clean this harvest and then the cook took all the game and made it into a stew with potatoes and whatever vegetables were available. I remember it was very good and we felt quite lucky to be able to eat so well.

During this time our only contact with the outside world was through the car radios, as there was no electricity or telephone. All we really knew was that the blizzard had hit a large area, leaving thousands stranded and many dead. We were concerned with what might be happening at home and by the fact that we had no way of letting mom and the others know we were alive and well. I believe it was the third or fourth day before we were able to use the telephone.

Of course everyone at the farmhouse was anxious to dig out and get home. Through neighbors word reached us that there were many drifts on the roads, some as high as 15 feet, and most men and equipment were concentrating on state highways first. It was on the fourth day we learned that if we could clear one long piece of road, about a thousand feet or so, we could get into St. Peter; from there to the cities the roads were passable.

I remember that I did the driving home with a partially burned out clutch. We drove through many banks of snow higher than the car and saw many tunnels and cuts made into the drifts to rescue cars that had been completely buried. We arrived home tired but savoring the warm and happy welcome that greeted us! We felt so thankful to be reunited with mom and the rest of the family again. Well over 40 years have passed since that day but the memories of a boy and his father and their unexpected adventure come back to me each winter when we hear our Minnesota storm warnings.

MY HUSBAND ROLLED ME IN THE SNOW
by Lucille Borchardt
Fairmont, MN

We lived in Truman and owned a cafe there. We were expecting our first child the latter part of December. We ran the cafe alone with the help of a cook.

At night we closed the cafe and went home to bed. A great many people had gone to the cities for the football game and business was slow anyway.

When we awoke in the morning, November 11, my husband was going up to the cafe to open it but he couldn't get the car going because of the terrible cold weather and the blowing snow. He got stuck. He wouldn't leave me home alone so he made me get dressed and we started walking the two blocks to the business district.

The drifts were so deep that after one block facing that terrific wind I said "I can't go any further." (I was pretty big with child by that date.) so my husband said, "Lay down and I'll roll you over the snow bank." So he did, and we cut across a vacant lot to some friends' house one block from down town. Our friends, the Marvin Spragues, took us in and we stayed overnight. The next day my husband waded uptown to the cafe, which became a haven from the storm for quite a few people, including our dentist, a widower. All of these people were concerned about my having the baby early after that experience in the snow, with no doctor in town. They all kidded the dentist, Dr. McCartin, that he might have to deliver me.

I stayed at the Spragues two more days until we got the snow shovelled out. Mainly I entertained the Sprague children, who had the chicken pox.

Our baby was born on December 29, 1940. Of course he is now 45 years old.

A DUCK HUNTER'S NEAR DISASTER
by The Rev. Ramon Buckley
Goodhue, MN

My story begins at about 4:00 A.M. in the home of my father, Bernard Buckley. Dad arose at this early hour to prepare for duck hunting. Mother also arose, as was her habit during the hunting season, to prepare breakfast and a lunch for my dad.

After breakfast dad packed his hunting gear, the lunch and a thermos filled with hot chocolate into the car. He then started his twelve-mile journey to Swan lake, which is one mile west of Nicollet and three-quarters of a mile north of highway 14. If you had seen the loaded car when he left you would have been sure he had at least one hunting partner because it was so loaded. But dad would hunt alone that day. Included in the load was extra clothing, boots, spare batteries for the flashlight and his canvas hunting coat.

The twelve miles to Swan lake was driven in darkness. Upon arrival, the hunting gear was stowed in the boat lovingly called the *Queen Mary*. With push pole in hand, dad set out for one of his favorite spots on the lake some two miles distant from the dock on Nicollet bay. He put out his decoys and set up his blind in the pre-dawn light. By then the orange streaks were beginning to show in the eastern sky. Looking around he could see other hunters in three different locations a hundred or so yards from his boat. The sun began to show itself over the horizon and the shooting sounded like a small war. The temperature was in the fifties so the flannel shirt over cotton long underwear kept him comfortable.

The flights of ducks were flying high in the blue sky. Each time the hunters would shoot at them, they would go higher. Dad read these signs and settled down for a long day of hunting. The good shots would be limited to the occasional single or the pair of ducks jumped by another hunter coming through with his boat. Dad would take advantage of these occasional shots the way a skilled hunter should and the morning moved along.

By ten o'clock dad had eight birds of his limit of ten. He decided to take a break and have something to eat. Sitting on the seat of the boat, he poured himself a cup of hot chocolate and unwrapped a sandwich. As he leisurely ate the sandwich and sipped the hot chocolate, he looked around, not wanting to miss a good shot. In the northwest he saw a black cloud bank which, as he watched it, spread in two directions. He quickly made a decision to get off the lake.

By the time he had picked up his decoys and stowed the blind away the temperature was dropping and the first snow began to fall. It was about 10:30 A.M. as he headed for the dock. A couple of fellows in a boat which had been two hundred yards away gave him a ribbing as he went toward the dock. The wind had picked up and was blowing snow in his face. Some time later he knew he was close to the dock but was struggling to find the channel into the dock. Docking the boat he quickly returned his gear to the car for the journey home. He wondered about the fellows he had passed on the lake as he left.

The weather kept getting worse so he had to concentrate on his driving and the fellows on the lake were soon forgotten as he had his own problems. The journey to North Mankato and home was much slower than it had been going out earlier in the morning. There were places he travelled at five miles an hour or less because he had difficulty seeing the road. Occasionally in a sheltered area he would see cars off the road. He dared not stop for fear of getting stuck himself. The wind was so strong and the snow so heavy that the tire tracks were being filled in behind the car as it moved down the highway. He finally arrived home some time after noon, probably close to one o'clock. I cannot remember ever being so happy to see dad in my life. We found out later that his car was one of the last to make it into town before the weather completely closed the highway.

I'm not certain of this fact but we were told that three men lost their lives on Swan lake that day. Who they were I have no idea, but the Mankato Free Press did a story later. I do know that many people died in Minnesota as a result of that Armistice day storm. Dad lived to teach me to be a good hunter and sportsman.

REDHEADS OVER LAKE TITLOE

by William E. Gladitsch, D.V.M.
Bloomer, WI

Forty-five years later is a long time to give an accurate account of a snow storm, but when you almost go down, you tend to remember small details and thoughts.

The day before the storm, Sunday, my dad, Ernst Gladitsch, my uncle, Tula Otto, and I were on Lake Titloe at dawn, hoping for a Bluebill shoot. Lake Titloe is in Sibley county near Gaylord, MN. We had our decoys spread out on the southwest side of Grass island and had very few birds come to our decoys. At 8 AM I left my dad and uncle and went to church. My mother had insisted that hunting not interfere with church. She didn't have the same control of dad or Uncle Tula but I listened and when she said "Jump" I asked "How high?" while I was still in the air.

After church I headed back for Grass island taking along some hot chicken noodle soup for dad and Uncle Tula. Mother's soup had big wide noodles about one-half inch wide and six inches long. I also remember a watermelon. A bit late in the year but I remember it. My dad liked to eat well while hunting, not believing you had to suffer to have a good time.

While we sat in our duckboats, all three tied together side by side, we ate our lunch and discussed whether to stay and hope for an evening shoot. It was becoming hazy, not cloudy, but just enough haze to hide the sun — and it was absolutely calm. We could hear a movement of wings overhead but couldn't see a bird because of the haze. In about 30 minutes, the sun cleared away the haze briefly and we identified them as terns. By one or two o'clock the Redheads started coming in to our decoys. We expected Teal, Widgeons or Pintails but they must have gone overhead with the Terns and we never saw them.

As a kid growing up in a duck hunting community I heard a lot of talk about the *Northern Flight* of ducks. Some tales were told going back to the late 1800s. I wondered if I would ever see the mythical Northern Flight. At sixteen, I had been hunting for five years and was beginning to think they were pulling my leg about the abundance of ducks when this flight was in progress.

Today those flocks of 50 to 100 Redheads were flying over the lake, just above the haze: we couldn't see but could hear them. They would smell the lake and come diving out of the haze and plop into our decoys almost before we could shoot. We didn't even stay down in our blinds—just stood there and shot. They showed no fear of us. I would be picking up ducks, away from the blind, and they still decoyed in with me in open water. We quit picking up and kept shooting.

After a half hour of steady Redheads, then Canvasbacks and Bluebills poured into our decoys. My dad asked if I felt like a game hog yet. That hadn't occurred to me. He said, "Let's pick up and go home" and still the ducks kept coming.

I asked the old fellows why we had such a great shoot when it was so quiet and no storm or wind. They didn't have an explanation except that even a blind pig finds an acorn once in a while. So went my first Northern Flight.

It is amazing that we had such poor weather information in 1940 when just two years later our forecasting improved to the point where they could tell us in the Eighth air force what the weather would be over Germany the next day. Now in 1985 we take weather forecasting for granted.

Note, again, that hunting day was Sunday, November 10.

That night I went roller skating at the New Ulm rink. I got home about 1 AM and decided to go hunting to get some more of that Northern Flight shooting. Although word had got around that the flight was on, no one wanted to go with me. Dad and Uncle said no way in hell would they spend a night in a duckboat, so I went ahead by myself, shoving the duck boat into the lake at 2 AM. So I was alone, in my 18 foot duckboat, 23 inches wide. I remember the width because that was the widest board I could buy at the local lumber yard. Planed 12 inch white pine end up 11 5/8 inches and I used two for the bottom. Long and skinny, and quite tippy, the boat went well through rushes and was easy to paddle. It had a deck at each end and under the decks I kept emergency equipment such as raincoat, an eight by four foot hunk of canvas, and a few cookies, apples, candy bars and a summer sausage in a gallon pail.

While I was setting out my blocks, great big snowflakes started to fall. Absolutely no wind. I believe the reason I remember all these details is because this storm was so unexpected. By the time I got the decoys placed it was really snowing. I still had a couple of hours until shooting light, so I laid down in the bottom of my duckboat, on some straw I had there. This was before the days of airmattresses. I then covered up with the canvas and an army blanket and was warm and dry.

About daylight the wind started. It came from the northwest and the anchors on my decoys were not heavy enough to hold the decoys. They started drifting downwind, so I tied the strings together to make a long train, anchoring each end to a different muskrat house.

It finally was light enough to shoot. My first duck was a Black Mallard. When I went out to get it I had a good deal of difficulty getting back to the island because of the strong wind. After that I only shot at upwind ducks which would fall in the tall grass of the island. The water there was only about three feet deep with a large number of rat houses. As the wind got even stronger, I jammed my pushpole into a big rat house and tied my duckboat to it. Again I covered up with everything I had and stayed warm and dry.

I knew I couldn't make it to shore in that wind, so I stayed put. In late afternoon the heavy snow quieted the waves somewhat and they calmed down some. The lake started to freeze and the slush controlled the waves to where I thought I could handle them. I drifted and paddled with the wind to the south shore of the lake. I had parked dad's car on the north shore, so I was on the wrong side of the lake and had to walk home.

The next day we went to get the car and couldn't find it because the snow was so deep. We used an iron rod (actually a muskrat spear) and poked around until we located it. It was about four days before we could get the county plow to open the road so we could take the car home.

That day I took my skates and a gunny sack and skated around the lake, picking up ducks that were still alive. We had to chop them out of the ice. Some we thawed out and released; some we cleaned and saved to eat. We didn't have a freezer then, but things stayed frozen on the back porch.

There was only one other person on the lake that morning as far as I know. It was Tanny Utendorfer; he was on Tree island. He tried to make it during the wind and was swamped. With the wind direction as it was, he must have drifted close to Grass island where I was but I never saw nor heard him. His health was severely damaged by that experience.

Les Kouba did a painting called *Redheads Over Lake Titloe* which you might have seen. Grass island is the one on the extreme right. In the painting the wind is from the northeast.

The time that the storm hit Gaylord didn't coincide with when it hit the Mississippi river bottoms, or western Minnesota. So, if the storm moved about 25 to 30 mph, there should have been eight hours warning from western Minnesota to the eastern border of the state.

In retrospect, I think what kept me from going down was my youth and having a lot of extra gear. Those spaces under the decks of my duckboat were always full of extra gear which a mature hunter would not have expected to use on a warm fall afternoon. The second factor was that when I realized I was in trouble I remembered what my dad said to me once when I was about to do something dumb without considering the consequences. It was "Willie, I hope your ma didn't raise any idiots."

As an avid duck hunter, I am still trying to figure out when the ducks are going south. In 45 years since that November 10th-11th I've only been there for two other good Northern Flights. In both cases I was very concerned about the weather the next day, but nothing materialized.

TWO OF THE CRIDDERS FELL IN THE WATER

by Mrs. Alfred Goltz
Elmore, MN

We had finished the morning chores and didn't have radio in the barn at that time. We went to the house about 7:15 and were eating breakfast with our children, Margaret, 9, Glenda, 7, and Lowell, 4. Our radio was turned to WCCO in Minneapolis when they reported a blizzard raging at Madelia. My husband, Alfred, hurried to take the cream and eggs to town before the storm reached here. The girls went along since they didn't have school that day. My sister, Olivia, came from town with them and before they reached our place the storm hit them.

Snowbanks were building and they got hung up in a snowbank. Alfred walked to a neighbor's place about 80 rods away, for help. (Editor: 1 rod = 5.5 yrds. 80 rods = one fourth mile.) Neighbor George Vikingstad harnessed a team of horses to a wagon and brought the family the last mile home. The car stayed in the snow until the next day.

We had 40 head of Hereford feeder cattle in the field grazing on corn stalks and oats stubble. We were very worried about them. Alfred and I went to search for them, going in an old model Buick that he had remodelled into a pickup truck. The air pressure was so drastic it was a struggle to breathe and we knew we were taking a big risk just to go out there. A dredge goes through our 160 acre farm and has a well-built bridge. We found our way over that bridge and were about 30 rods into the field when we got stuck in about ten inches of mud and snow.

The barometric pressure was at its lowest and we couldn't see our hand in front of our face;. the blizzard was that violent. Alfred decided to walk back home, at least a half mile. He found the fence line, then the bridge, and followed more fence back to our house. He left me sitting in the truck, saying "You stay in this truck until I come back." I took heed and that's what I did. Yet I thought that I too could find my way home, but a guardian angel spoke saying, "Don't do it".

Yes, my husband found home, reported to the family that he had to go to the field and get mom home. He harnessed the sorrel team, Blanche and Lady, to the manure spreader and headed in search of the truck and me. I could hear the chains on the harness hitting the single tree when the rig was about 40 feet to the left of me and gave out a loud yell. "Here! Here! I am here!" He couldn't see the truck but turned the team around. I climbed into the spreader and the team took us home, knowing the way. The cattle were not found that day.

We were chilled to the bone when we got to the house. Our little girls were worried about mom; I went to bed for a while to warm up and being pregnant I too was a little worried about what might happen. But, Praise the Lord, I weathered the storm.

It subsided by midnight, a full moon shining. My brave husband jumped on Blanche the-horse-with-more-than-horse-sense and struck out with our shepherd dog, Doc, in search of the cattle.

The cattle were at the far southeast corner of our farm facing away from the wind. They were iced over their rears and backs, lumps of manure were frozen to their tails and bodies. When Alfred found them they began to move as they heard the crunching of the horses's steps. The ice on the cattle rattled and cracked like glass as he got them started for home. They found the gate and the bridge. The dredge was level full of water which was covered with the drifted snow.

All the stock walked over the bridge except two cridders which didn't follow. They missed the bridge and fell into the deep water. Alfred got one out of the water but there was nothing to do for the other one except to use ropes. There were tree stumps on the banks of the dredge; he got ropes around the steer's neck and around a tree stump and, by struggling and pulling, he finally got the steer out; then he removed his overcoat, put it over the animal's back and pushed him toward the yard and the shed.

The icy chunks had pulled off hair from their hides, leaving large naked spots on their backs.

The next July 9 a beautiful baby girl was born; we named her Roselyn Ardean and she's Rosie to this very day.

I'm writing this story on January 19, 1985, as the *Alberta Clipper* storm is clipping along from the northwest at gales of up to 60 mph with a windchill of 80 to 90 degrees below zero. We do have some cold weather.

MY PINK CLIMBING ROSE WAS BLOOMING
by Mrs. Augusta Johnson
Chisago City, MN

We lived in a small southern Minnesota town called Kasota, three miles from St. Peter and nine miles from Mankato. There were the four of us: my husband, Carl, and sons, Walter C., 9, and Eugene R, 6. Carl was employed as an orderly at the St. Peter state hospital.

November 10 was a beautiful warm sunny Sunday. I had just taken photos of my beautiful pink climbing rosebush and Carl and I talked about putting on the storm windows. He hesitated for a while because it was still so nice and warm but then we decided to put them on, and so we did. In Minnesota that action is somewhat of an admission that winter is here but it didn't seem so on that gorgeous Sunday.

We lived in a small two-room house with a little attic, which we had built from scratch during the depression days. It had no modern facilities then.

The next day, Monday, November 11, Carl had off because he had worked a recent Sunday. We were to be so glad that he was home. The boys had left for school, which was seven or eight blocks away, when Carl went to the barn where he got our drinking water from the neighbor's well. This was about 200 feet away. As he returned to the door he could hardly make it because of the hard wind and freezing rain hitting him in the face. He remarked that it was really getting bad outside and that he thought he should go get the boys from school. He started our Ford sedan but at that moment the boys were left off out in front. He picked them up and a couple of others. Of course they were very cold because they were not dressed for this extreme weather.

We had no radio, not even electricity in our house then, to warn us of the storm. We did have a three-burner kerosene cook stove and a wood burner for heat and we surely needed them. The snow kept coming down fast with a terrific wind and it just kept getting colder.

The next day Carl walked to work because driving was impossible for some time. He and another fellow who also worked at the hospital were glad they knew the train schedules because they had to walk over the train trestle across the Minnesota river just to get to the hospital.

There were people with pneumonia at that time and some died during the storm because doctors couldn't get to them. It took a couple of days before the snow could begin to be removed.

Of course many hunters lost their lives and froze in the lake near there. We had four or five feet of snow, or more. Our boys climbed to the top of the snow on the road and could almost reach the telephone wires. The snow was that deep.

Carl died almost four years ago. The boys are now 50 and 53 years old and live in St. Paul, one working for 3M and one for the Northern States Power company. We moved here in Chisago City 12 years ago to retire.

I NEEDED MONEY FROM THESE 180 DUCKS
by Gordon C. Johnson
Mankato,MN

I was twelve years old and my major recollection was that I had raised 180 White Peking ducks to be sold for Thanksgiving and Christmas dinners. We were rather poor so these ducks were of major importance.

As the storm progressed in the early afternoon my father insisted that we get the ducks together and into safe quarters, mainly the chicken houe. The problem: we couldn't find them or hear them anywhere.

There was an old wagon sitting near our grove of trees; it was somewhat sheltered on the east side by some boards which had been piled up. As the storm progressed, the snow drifted against the boards and the wagon, leaving an open spot under the wagon. The ducks had managed to crawl beneath the wagon into this small place and the heat from their bodies helped create the open space. Ducks, boards, wagon, all were covered completely with snow.

As we hunted and searched for the ducks I came to the wagon and a large chunk of snow fell off the mound into the area where the ducks were huddling. At last! They were no longer lost. I think they were equally as happy to be found as I was to find them. In a short time they all would have smothered.

Humor? Well, it was funny to see my dad and me carrying ducks in a basket to the shed. They didn't seem to be too cooperative. Of course, being the age I was, I thought it was fun. My dad, however, felt very differently.

The neighbors across the field from us had a large herd of cattle. They stayed outside in the winter since most were beef cattle and non-milkers. Their shelter and feeding area was a straw-topped shed created by threshing oats and letting the straw fall onto the shed. It was a warm and cozy spot. The cattle had been checked at 10 AM and all were safely inside. For some unknown reason, one hour later, the next time they were checked, all had left the shelter. If I remember correctly, some 40 head were lost and not found until next spring when the snow melted. Many were found in roadside ditches, frozen to death of course.

These episodes all happened 2 1/2 miles east of Amboy.

THE WOES OF A RURAL SCHOOLTEACHER
by M. Grayce Gegan Kortuem
Madison Lake, MN

Marysburg, where I was a teacher in a one-room rural school, had a church, a school, two houses and a rectory. There were 22 children in grades one through eight. It was located 2 miles northeast of Mankato in LeSueur county. My mother taught school in Ottawa while my sister attended high school in Cleveland.

At 11 AM that Monday morning, Frank Hoven, Ernie Frederick's hired man, and Francis Kortuem, my future husband, came to the schoolhouse. Their purpose was to ask that the four Frederick children be excused from school because of an impending storm. The Fredericks lived directly across the road from the schoolhouse. Of course I consented and continued school.

About noon I became aware of an abundance of nickel-sized snowflakes which were "racing each other for a coveted place on the ground." I immediately remembered that when my sister and I had left home that morning the weather had been so balmy that we had ignored our mother's wise caution to wear our boots.

At noon there was another knock at the door. It was Bill Kortuem to warn me not to leave the schoolhouse.

We continued the day. Noon lunch, social studies, reading, last recess, and language classes. The temperature continually dropped; the snowflakes accumulated rapidly; the wind rose. At dismissal time, I came to the awful realization that the students, nine of them, would be my overnight guests at the school.

Fuel, food and shelter were my main concerns. My upper grade boys filled the empty coal scuttles from the coal shed just a few steps away. An empty five-gallon can replaced the outdoor two-holer; the entryway provided privacy. Because all 22 children had not been at school that day, a sufficient amount of drinking water remained in the earthenware drinking fountain. Had that not been the case, we could have melted snow.

My next problem was food. Like most children who attended rural schools, those who had food left in their lunch buckets, consumed it at the last recess. Fortunately, at sunset, Leo Lyons, a close neighbor, came to check on us. He volunteered to go with me to the Frederick farm across the road to get food. We thoroughly warned the children not to leave the school. Generously, the Fredericks provided me with plenty of warm, nourishing food for ten hungry people. Although the distance returning was short, the wind and drifting snow masked the landmarks until Leo and I believed we were lost. Luckily we spied a clump of plum bushes which gave us the landmark to the building. The food was rapidly consumed and Leo went home with a promise to check on us in the morning.

My next concern was how to keep the children happy during the evening. I'll read to them, I thought. Then *click* off went the electricity. The coals which fell into the ash pan then provided our only light. We could read by that light too, and read we did.

Bed time came. Where would these nine children sleep? Not on the floor. Have you ever checked the temperature of a rural schoolhouse floor in wintertime? A number of tables and desks provided the springs and mattresses for the night.

Did I sleep? No, indeed. I was happy to keep feeding the hungry furnace and keep watching that no coals would start a fire and burn our shelter.

Morning came. The winds had subsided and the snow had ceased. The whole landscape had been transformed into a billowy, white counterpane. Ernie and Frank came with more food for breakfast. Reading and games occupied our time until one-by-one the parents were able to reach the school and give the children a ride home. At 3:30 the last of the children left and Annie White, who lived near the school, invited me to her home. She gave me the best meal of mashed potatoes, chicken and gravy that I have ever eaten. She tucked me into a warm, soft bed where I drifted in dream to the warm, sunny southland.

THIS UPPER-CLASS FILLY OBJECTED TO GEORGE
by Bea Lorenz
Montgomery, MN

I was employed at a restaurant called The Double Dip which was across the street from Miller Motors in Mankato. The place was open 24 hours a day; we rotated shifts and didn't even need a front door key. It was a truck stop. We had no telephone but there was one available across the street at all times since Miller's was also open 24 hours a day.

The story *One Night in a Barroom* couldn't possibly touch on all the events that went on in any block in Mankato that day. It seemed to us that we received the brunt of the storm.

I received a message to start from my apartment at four o'clock because there was so much drifting and blowing. I took extra clothes in a suitcase and started for work. It was so rough going that I had to remove my glasses and put them in the suitcase. I had only about four blocks to walk — from 827 South Front (there is a mortuary there now) to the 500 block of Front — but when I got to work at 5:45 I was wet, cold, short of breath and damned glad to be inside; I went to work immediately.

Mae and Vic Lowe owned the place and they were anxious to hurry to their home also, about two blocks away. There were a lot of people in the restaurant, most planning to eat and then find a place for the night. By 7 PM the word was that every room in town was taken including those in private homes. As the storm got worse there was less incoming traffic but the town was already full of travellers.

At about 8 PM our lights went out and shortly thereafter we had no heat. Except for the cook, four truck drivers, and me, all of the others were strangers. We had one candle so we put it near the order window. To help with our power problem, I called George Demarry of Demarry Electric who obtained some lanterns from a hardware store, filled them with kerosene and brought them to us.

The crowd in The Double Dip was building up. By 9 PM we had so many with children that we made beds and blankets from newspapers and put the children on the floor in the rear of the place. I remembered a friend in St. Paul who had slept in the park when she was unemployed and she had told me how to make a bed and blanket from newspapers. That knowledge came in handy.

We had plenty of coffee to keep serving but bread and eggs were getting scarce, so we stopped serving whole eggs in order to make cakes instead. I asked the truck drivers to help by washing dishes and watching the counter while I made some syrup for the pancakes.

We had a few highbrows but everyone seemed to mix well except for one person. There was a mutt named George which used to leave his master whenever his keeper went on a binge. This little fellow would come to the restaurant and stay outside by the entrance until I finished my shift and then he would walk me home. One of the men at Miller's said the dog wouldn't have anything to do with his owner when he was on one of his blasts. He also thought it interesting that the dog had some way of knowing when I was on duty. Otherwise he never showed up.

Anyway, I heard a weak whining—and there was George. I took him in and made a bed for him back in the kitchen after warming some milk for him. One of these upper class fillies said, "Good heavens, you're not going to bring that mess inside, are you?" I looked at her and answered something like this: "He has feelings and he's all wet and a mutt should be no worse than a soaked waitress, a full-blooded Czech, waiting on you until the food runs out, after getting dried off herself."

Came morning and I couldn't leave at 6 AM because no one came to relieve me. I stayed until 7 AM when the Lowes came; I asked them to leave George there until the streets were clear and he could find his way home.

I couldn't get to my own home by then since there were drifts as high as I am tall. Two of the truck drivers got shovels from across the street and said they'd walk me home, shovelling through the deeper banks. Would you believe it? It took almost two hours for us to get through those four blocks.

I'm 66 years old now and we did have some heavy snowfalls in the years gone by but this one was very different.

I WAS HOUSEBOUND FOR FIVE MONTHS
by Mrs. Frank Manwarren
Fairmont, MN

I was a young farm wife living in the country and we had a prematurely born two month old son who was of much concern to us at that time. He was only two months old.

We had our crops out and chickens all locked in the hen house for the winter, but no coal. Just corn cobs to burn in the furnace. As it got colder we shut all rooms except the kitchen and even moved our bed in there too. We were worried about keeping our small son warm.

Our hot water tank heater was connected. It ran through the cook stove. My husband was milking and I remember firing the cook stove so steadily that the water started to boil in the heater and I thought it was going to blow up. I grabbed the baby and stood by the outside door, thinking I could get out if it started to explode. But it didn't.

There was a turkey farm about two miles north of us and their turkeys were still out on the range. We found frozen turkeys in our grove the following spring.

A close neighbor lost cows and calves that stood in the southeast corner of a field and froze to death standing up.

But the thing I remember most, was that I didn't go any place from November 11 until in March because of our small son. It was a good thing we had company once in a while. Both my mother and mother-in-law lived a few miles away and they both insisted I not take that baby out. So I listened. I love to read, so I sure did a lot of reading that winter.

EVEN OLD NELLIE FROZE TO DEATH
by Bob Mays
Oronoco,MN

I was born in 1930 but remember the 1940 storm very well. We were farming at St. James and I remember that my dad said the night before that it would probably snow the next day. Before I went to bed I went outside; the stars were shining and it was a warm, mild night, for November.

The next day it was a blizzard. My dad and two brothers were out in the barn milking cows and doing chores. My mother wouldn't let me go outside. Finally I talked her into letting me go to the barn which was about 200 feet from the house. I got out in the middle of the yard where the wind and snow were so bad I couldn't see and could hardly breathe. I stood there screaming until my brother heard or saw me and took me back to the house. I didn't go out again for three days.

We lost most of our chickens because many were still roosting in the trees. Even those in the chicken house froze to death. Twenty to forty of our sows froze to death also. A few crawled into a straw stack and lived. One old sow didn't come out of that strawstack for three weeks and had had nothing to eat or drink in that time. Most came out earlier though the straw had kept them warm. One of our horses, named Nellie, froze to death. It was truly very cold.

I remember that we could walk off the roof of our house onto a snowbank which was twelve to fifteen feet high. It was several days before my folks could go to town three miles away. Even then they had to take the horses because it was many weeks before we could get out of our driveway. Some snowbanks were as high as our telephone poles.

These are things I remember. My mother, who is 82, still lives in St. James.

TRYING TO SAVE 100 STEERS
by Donald Miller
Truman, MN

It was my third year working as a hired hand for the Larson brothers at Dunnell, MN. At 5 AM that Monday morning, Fingle Larson called me, which was unusual, because he usually let Floyd Johnson, the other hand, and me sleep until we woke up. Fingle said "Better get up. We have a mess on our hands and have to get in that 100 head of feeder cattle." He was speaking of some 500 pound steers which had just been bought the previous Saturday.

When I opened the door to the barn which would hold the 100 head, the cattle went in but there were only about half the total. We knew we would have to go get the others but, in the meantime, breakfast was ready and we went inside for that. After breakfast we put on gunny sacks with holes cut out for our eyes to protect our faces from the strong wind which otherwise would take our breath away. So we went out into the pasture. With the poor visibility, we had gone only 800 to 900 feet when we lost our way. We had agreed that if that happened, we would put our backs to the wind and drift the few yards to the fence. That worked and we made two or three trips out to pasture using that system. Finally we tok a ball of twine; Fingle would walk along the fence line holding the twine, Floyd would hold the middle of the twine and I would fan out at the end of it. In this manner we moved out across a part of the pasture. But suddenly I was out there all alone with no connection to the others. The twine had unraveled in the strong wind. So I drifted to the fence again and returned to the house where I found the other guys.

I had a 1937 Ford (only three years old then) that I thought I could use to drive all over the pasture because there wasn't much snow on the ground yet. It was all in the air. I didn't get more than 1,000 feet before the motor drowned out; I left it running on two cylinders with the headlights on, thinking I could come back to find it more easily. I returned to the barn, hitched up the team of horses and went into the pasture—and couldn't even find the car. After eating dinner and at about 4 PM I finally found the car and pulled it to the barn with the team. Under the hood it was so full of snow that one more teaspoon of snow couldn't have been packed in there.

We found the cattle about a half-mile east of the gate, in a bunch. Five or six were standing but the rest were down. After finding them we thought we would take half a hayrack of soybean bundles and a wagon box for protection for the cattle out in that pasture. There were no trees there. We got to within 40 rods of the cattle when one side of the sled fell into a washed drainage ditch and flipped the rack. Since we were still 40 rods from the cattle and it was about 4:30 and time to do chores, we gave up on the cattle until morning.

The wind had lessened by morning when we took the team and bobsled to the pasture. Only four or five cattle were standing. The rest were stretched out looking more dead than alive. Mr. Larson went over to examine one and a standing steer charged him. Luckily, the steer's strength gave out after he had charged about 30 feet toward the boss.

With a couple of ropes we had with us, we tied the feet of those cattle lying down and dragged them back to the barn. We were amazed that animals so far gone, after being towed, were able to get up and attack us in the barn. We had to be careful when untying them. We dragged in about 28 that way; of that bunch, we saved 17. Of those we saved some lost their feet and all lost their ears.

The Larson brothers lost a total of 42 head of cattle. They had paid about 18 cents a pound or $90 each for the animals. It wasn't that the temperature was so cold but that the nostrils of the cattle iced up, suffocating them. It was a considerable loss but the Larsons weren't ones to complain. After all, how would complaining help?

Several horses were in the pasture. Mr.Larson went into this creek bottom pasture looking for them. He followed the fence line until he had located them. They looked up at him, appeared startled, and promptly jumped the fence. One four-year old colt nearly cut off his leg on the fence. He later died of blood poisoning.

THE FIRE IN MONTGOMERY, KOLACKY KAPITOL OF MINNESOTA
by Patricia Rynda, et al
Montgomery, MN

Montgomery was visited by one of the most disastrous fires in its history early November 12 when the Westerman Lumber company yard and warehouse, located in the center of the business district, burned to the ground. At 1:15 AM acting policeman John Herman passed the building and it checked out okay but later a brakeman on the M. & St. L. railway smelled burning pine and Herman found and reported the fire; it was in the office section of the yard. Both the on duty and off duty fireman were soon there to fight the fire. When the siren sounded the entire sky already seemed to be a ball of fire and most people awakened thinking their own house was afire. The fireman and hundreds of others fought through the snowdrifts, cold weather and biting wind to keep the fire from spreading. It seemed only seconds before the entire wood structure was completely enveloped in flames. An adjoining warehouse to the north of the yard was engulfed before firemen had a chance to play water on it.

The fighters tried to save the Linberger building adjoining the yard and were successful even after all of its contents had been removed. A boxcar on the tracks east of the burning building was also ignited and lost even though an engine backed and tried to couple and pull it away. The car contained cement and mortar mix.

Due to heavy snow that day, five cars and a truck were parked in and around the building. The E.E.Westerman family car was in the yard and was a twisted mass when fireman came upon it.Cars belonging to Dr. McKeon, Gregory Roach and Ray Sasse were parked on the south side of the building and paint was blistered. The glass was damaged and tires melted before they were removed. A truck belonging to Henry Speikers and a car of Henry Peroutka were on the north side of the building and were total losses.

The heat was so intense that the buildings across the street were damaged. Plate glass on the Ruhland and Washa buildings crumbled and some of the decorative glass was damaged. Also the plate glass in Tupa's pharmacy and the Post Office were also cracked. Glenn Malone was a 17-year old lad, son of Patrick J. Malone. Glenn remembers:

"Dad became concerned for the safety of the U.S. Mail entrusted to his office; we bundled up and trudged there through deep drifts—like in a dream. Huge pieces of slivers of broken glass from store windows were sticking up from the snow like giant icicles. We went into the Post office and proceeded to sack up all the mail we could find; we threw the bags out on the snowbanks in front, theorizing that if the fire spread, it would be easy to load the bags and haul them farther away. We never thought about theft—no one would tamper with the mail in those days. I then went across the street to Linbergers to help carry stoves, etc., out of the building because it was feared that the fire would spread to it. Little did we realize that there were barrels of fuel stored in the building. Looking back now, that moving job was a very *explosive* situation but, fortunately, it was carried out without a hitch."

Lines were strung from the fire trucks and hydrants and thousands of gallons of water were played on the flames from 1:30 AM to 8:30 AM. Huge piles of lumber had to be pulled down in order to get at the blaze and special attention was given the large safes which contained all the firm's records. A special detail remained on duty all day Tuesday and that evening because fire broke out at intervals in the charred lumber.

Mrs. Leo Greer remembers that she had been working as a nurse in the offices of Dr. O. McKeon but had resigned to be married on November 16 to a Kilkennyl farmer, Leo Greer. "Firemen came to my home to get me to open the doctor's safe so that records could be removed to safety. Two fireman had to help me wade through the waist-high snow. Later I went with my friend, Lil Hendrickson, across the street to Franke's bakery, where we worked all night helping serve hot coffee and doughnuts to the ice-covered firemen." We should note that this lady, Ellen, and her husband Leo Greer, did get their ceremony performed on November 16 and will observe their 45 anniversary on that date in 1985.

Philip Dietz worked for Frank Busta, who owned the barbershop directly across from the lumberyard and was city recorder. Philip awoke that night to the sound of the siren and the howl of the wind. The windows of his apartment were purplish from the frozen rain and the light of the fire. Because of the great amount of snow, he waited until daylight to walk to town. He was shocked to see the mass of rubble where once there had been a large lumberyard. When he got to the barbershop he was also surprised to find the door unlocked and the place filled with stoves and heaters from Linberger's across the street.

Monday had been an excellent duck hunting day before the blizzard struck.

Many migrating flocks were caught in the blizzard and some apparently were drawn to the fire by the intense light and dove into the fire. Some sportsmen theorized that the ducks mistook the steam from the firefighters' water as being an area of open water. When Phil Dietz got to his shop he saw several of these ducks waddling around the fire's perimeter. Thirty were caught and placed in a large carton near Louis' cafe, which was a popular gathering spot for the town's sportsmen. Later they butchered the ducks and Mayme Kaisershot prepared a special duck feed.

On Tuesday afternoon there was no school and I (Patricia Rynda) remember sliding and playing on the huge snowbanks. In the afternoon a bunch of us kids walked down to the scene of the fire. The safes had fallen through the floor into the basement of the lumberyard office and we watched as they were pulled onto the street and then across the way to the Citizens bank. I can still see those somber-faced men in long black coats walking into the bank behind the safes. News reports indicated that all of the company's records were safe.

Dr. and Mrs. A. E. Westerman, part of the family, were very concerned about the debris from the fire; as Mrs. Westerman says "The building, as it was old, had one high part. When that started to burn the west wind blew pieces of burning wood over toward our house two blocks east of the fire. Our fear was that some of the burning pieces would set our roof afire, even though it had been damp from the snow. My husband was recovering from seveal heart attacks and was weak and couldn't manage himself. My thought was that if our house started to burn how would I get him out of the house, since both front and back doors were drifted shut? What a dilemna! Soon the burning wood didn't come close to our house any more and we were more at ease. Had the wind been from the east the town would have had many burned homes."

The Westerman building was one of the old landmarks of the city, the firm having been started in 1890, by the late H.E.Westerman. The origin of the fire was unknown but it was thought to have started from shorted wires or the basement furnace. There was much pressure to rebuild the yard, which was done.

It was a fire and a day combined that citizens of Montgomery will never forget. To have such a devastating fire the night of such a severe blizzard made things so much worse, hampering fire fighters and making it impossible for fire rigs from nearby towns to come to their assistance Had the fire gotten out of control for just a short time, the entire town probably would have been destroyed.

WE LOST TURKEYS WORTH $3000

by Florence M. Scholljegerdes
Bloomington, MN

I was a student nurse at St. Andrews hospital in Minneapolis, working night duty; my older sister, now Dorothea Lillestrand, of Bloomington, was a graduate nurse at the same hospital. St Andrews is no longer in existence.

As that Monday progressed we heard of the farmers' problems but it took two or three days of poor communications to hear about our parents. Our father, Fred D. Scholljegerdes of rural Waseca, had a dairy farm and also raised turkeys, at that time having about 1300 market-ready birds. My parents went to the fields to save the turkeys but only got about 50 of them inside. Each lost bird at that time was worth from $2.50 to $2.75 so the uninsured loss was about $3,000. That was a substantial amount in those days. We could only take the dead birds to the rendering plant. We did have enough money to help me finish nurse's training — now I'm retired.

DAD'S OVERCOAT STOOD FROZEN IN PLACE

by Georgia Enfield Schultz
Bloomington, MN

I was home with my parents, eight years old and recuperating from a stay at the Mayo clinic where I had been treated for sleeping sickness. We lived in Mankato at 417 Glenwood avenue.

My dad worked for Miller Motors and as the evening wore on and the wind howled and piled the snow, dad anxiously paced the floor. Miller Motors had a big wrecker called *Tugboat Annie* which was so tall there were three circular steps up into the cab. Dad often drove the wrecker and expected a call at any moment to go to work. He knew that wrecker would be needed to pull cars out of ditches and to help motorists who were stuck. My older brother was across town at a friend's house and called to say he was staying overnight. Shortly thereafter the telephone went dead and the electric lights kept flickering. We finally went to bed.

Dad was up at 5 AM and tried to drive to work. He was stuck within just a few blocks and walked the rest of the way. One or two other men also arrived so they went out in *Tugboat Annie*. Even that monstrous wrecker kept getting stuck until finally, in the early afternoon, they gave up and dad started walking home. He later told us that he could barely lift his legs high enough to plow through the drifts and he walked in the middle of the streets the entire mile home.

Mother and I heard him come in through the basement door and we hurried to the back entry, down the basement steps. I stopped halfway down and sunk onto a step. He was completely covered with snow, looking like a giant snow-man. His eyebrows and hair were frozen stiff and his big heavy overcoat was plastered with frozen snow.

It has stayed with me all of these years—dad walking out of his overcoat. It stood there, all by itself, frozen in place. The coat just standing there was an amazing thing to see. Dad looked at mother and said "Ida, I've never seen any-thing like this storm."

Whenever anyone mentions that blizzard, I can still see that coat—frozen stiff, standing on its own.

DRIFT THREE FEET HIGHER THAN BUS
by Claude J. Seal
St. James, MN

On November 11, 1940 I lived here in St. James, operating a filling station, and running a school bus route with my own bus. The route covered 27 miles which extended north into Brown county, through LaSalle and back to St. James.

That morning I arose at the usual time and saw that it was snowing. Because the ground was warm most of the snow was melting, so I started at 7 AM. The farther I went, the worse it got. When I was one mile into Brown county, which was about 11 miles from St. James, I decided to turn around and start home. I went into the Godahl store and called my wife.

The snow was getting deeper and the wind stronger. Many times I could not see through the windshield; I looked out the side window and followed the grass along the road. Occasionally I had to stop completely, then go ahead again, but I finally made it home.

Shortly after noon the school called to ask me to take three teachers home. So I put chains on my old Chevie and did so, which wasn't easy. On my way back, the visibility was just a few feet when, suddenly right in front me, stood a lady in the middle of the street. She couldn't go any further against the storm. She was a practice teacher and I took her home. She surely was grateful.

About an hour later a friend called and said that he was stalled a few miles from town. He wondered if I would go to his house and get two five-gallon pails, then go next door to his mother-in-law's house and take some coal to his house—because he had not filled his coal bin. Of course I said that I would. There were times I couldn't see where I was walking against the 40 mile-an-hour wind but I finally made it. That was the longest thousand feet I have ever walked. On the return trip, the wind was at my back, which helped immensely.

Later on in the afternoon the electricity went off but that was no real hard-ship because we had kerosene lamps, a propane gas stove and a furnace which operated without electricity. The next day the weather settled down, but it was almost a week before the state rotary plow had the roads open so I could get back on my route. About one mile south of Godahl one drift was three feet higher than my bus. I still have a picture for proof of that vicious storm. *(See page 130.)*

SPENT BLIZZARD IN A 1927 BUICK
by Evelyn McChane Stevens
Minneapolis, MN

The fall of 1940 was an eventful one for me.I became engaged to be married, was graduated from Mankato Commercial college, started my first job as secretary in Redwood Falls, and spent the entire Armistice Day blizzard in a 1927 Buick.

My fiance, Steve, picked me up on Saturday to spend the week-end with his folks near Mankato, to commemorate my upcoming 19th birthday and his army enlistment. His old Buick wasn't a thing of beauty with its enormous wheels and boxcar body, but we thought it was worth the $20 he had paid for it. Extra equipment consisted of a large cardboard to hold over head whenever the rain from the roof got too tiresome — and an old comforter for a shield from the damp chill of an open window made necessary by a badly smoking manifold. It had always delivered us safely until this final battle which it fought so badly, but lost.

Returning we realized the temperature was dropping noticeably and the mist had become a cold drizzle by the time we reached New Ulm. Thankfully I had worn my new winter coat, proudly purchased with part of my $75 monthly wages. However, I was still wearing thin summer sandals. At Sleepy Eye the drizzle became sleet, then snow. A strong wind whipped the snow into blizzard conditions with very limited visibility which added to the hazard of driving on the ice underneath the snow. Suddenly headlights came directly at us and Steve drove down into the ditch and right back onto the road, to avoid the collision. Then, with two wheels in the deep snow on the shoulder and the other two on the icy road, the car stopped and we obviously couldn't move another inch. It was snowing so heavily we couldn't see the front of the car. Steve was going to go find help but I set up such a howl of protest at being left alone that he stayed. We closed the window and curled up in the comforter while the world enclosed us in white.Several times we tried unsuccessfully to start the motor for warmth.

We stayed there throughout the night. The next morning it was clear and calm but not a farm in sight. We saw a grove and floundered through deep snow above our knees, to the farm house, where we were taken in, warmed and dried and treated to a hearty breakfast. The farmer drove us to our car where we discovered the block had frozen and cracked because it didn't contain antifreeze. He offered us $7.50 for the car, saying he could make it into a trailer.

There was no choice, so we accepted. Then he drove us the seven miles to Redwood Falls, all of us being happy he had a truck with chains. Later we realized how lucky we were to have escaped with just the loss of the car and one of Steve's ears being frostbitten. Neither of us caught cold. We were indeed lucky.

THE GIRL AND THE SNOWBOUND MARINE
by G. L. Swanson
Minneapolis, MN

As a fifteen year old girl I was coming back with my parents and brother from visiting relatives in Des Moines.

I don't remember the names of the towns or the people but I do remember what happened as we got closer to home in south Minneapolis.

At the peak of the storm we were literally snow bound. Our car could not go another inch. We had reached a small town about fifty miles from home; cars were stopped everywhere and people were trying to pull each other out of the drifts. The wind was bitterly cold and drifting so you could hardly see. We were dressed warmly enough but had no place to go except for a little cafe. It was very crowded and plenty of hot coffee and cocoa was going over the counter, most of it free of cost. The owners were terrific people and we all called them by their first names at their request. I wish I could remember their names because they were such great people.

We were lucky because there were several other kids about the same ages as my 12-year old brother and me. We had the juke box going constantly and were dancing jitterbug dances. The older folks were playing cards and talking. It was packed to the point where they finally had to turn people away.

I met a soldier there. He was about eighteen. I still remember his name. It was Bob Pope from Coffeeville, Kansas. He was on his way overseas. We grew very attached to each other and stayed pretty much to ourselves just talking and dancing. My folks kept a pretty close eye on us (What could we do?). We wrote letters to each other for almost two years and he even came to see me while still in the service and on his way back home. He was a Marine and had quite a few medals. He also had his girl friend with him. By that time, even though I was with my folks at home, I was already married and eight months pregnant. Not a pretty sight but that shows how our lives had changed. My husband was in the navy at Pensacola, Florida.

When we left that cafe to head out again we ran into more trouble and a family with five kids took us into their home and bedded us down. There were bodies everywhere but we thought it was fun. We played a lot of games, someone played the piano and we sang a lot of songs like *Beautiful Ohio* and *Deep Purple*. Also *Three Little Fishies*.

We stayed there two days and two nights. My mom was a great cook so she helped fix the meals. They even baked cakes and cookies. They smelled awfully good, but better to eat. When we left, my folks insisted on paying them for their trouble, even though they didn't want to take it. With five kids they probably could use the money, particularly since we used the food they had in the house. We kept in touch too for some time but things do come to an end.

I never thought I'd be so glad to see my house again but it sure was good to be home. I have been a widow for fourteen years with grown children and thirteen grandchildren. Time goes on.

THE MISSISSIPPI RIVER AND SE MINN.

KATE AND HAM OPERATORS SAVED MAROONED ALBERT LEA

by Sherman Booen
Minneapolis, MN

I was announcer-engineer on duty at radio station KATE in Albert Lea on November 11, 1940. It was a mild morning until about noon when the sky suddenly became cloudy and a light rain began to fall. I was studying for a pilot's license at the time and was keen on meterology. The station had a small weather station with guages showing barometer, temperature and wind. I noticed that the barometer was falling rapidly but it was just an observation at the time. Then the rain changed to sleet, then snow grains, and the wind sprang up; by midafternoon it was snowing heavily and the winds were at gale force.

I rechecked the teletype which carried our weather forecasts from the Twin Cities but there was no indication of a problem. (Weather reporting was meager in those days — just an official reporting station in Albert Lea.) By 3 PM it was apparent that we were in for a severe storm.

The station manager owned a cabin on a nearby lake, where his young son and several companions had been all day. The island was about a half-mile from the shore, the only transportation being by small motorboat. The manager, Edgar Hayek, naturally became alarmed and asked if we could broadcast messages to his son John to tell him not to try to get back to the mainland. It was against the law then to send messages person-to-person by name, and FCC was very zealous about it, but we did it anyway. direct order to young John Hayek: "Stay where you are. Do not attempt to get back."

By 5 PM little was moving on the streets and the local authorities asked us to broadcast that people should stay off the roads. Then came the report that all communications outside the city were down. Our teletype had stopped receiving and the police advised us that the city was isolated. Within the city some telephones were working and the station began broadcasting personal messages. "Henry is safe at John's;" "Jacobs family: stay where you are" etc. We called them *comfort messages*. The station was supposed to sign off at sundown but we stayed on the air, against FCC regulations. During the night the storm got worse and we finally signed off. I walked home about six blocks and it was almost impossible to see the roads.

When I reported to the station the next day, November 12, the situation was worse although the storm had abated. Wires were down everywhere and we were indeed completely cut off.

The radio station was still operating but no teletype news was being received, no weather reports of any kind, no news. Then we did something that had never been done before as far as we knew, and perhaps has not been done since. We broadcast for direct communication to another radio station. In Mankato,

KYSM. "Hello, KYSM, please communicate with us over your station." Our call was heard and they answered us. For a while we talked back and forth with messages of public service. Mankato still had some telephone circuits but not to the Twin Cities.

There was little we could do and at noon I told the manager that I felt I should go home and operate my amateur radio station and establish communications. He agreed and, after calling the police and city officials, I went home to W9RHT, my home-built radio station on 75 meters. My antenna had been blown down and I struggled through the snow drifts to hang it on a telephone pole. It worked well and in minutes I was talking to Minneapolis.

We were concerned with power companies, railroads, police, telephone companies and health organizations. An amateur radio station in the Twin Cities made contact with these and for the next two days W9RHT was the only Albert Lea contact with the outside world. We carried only priority messages; we dispatched trains, road crews, repairmen, snow plows, and when time permitted, public service messages like "To the George family, Mary is safe in Faribault." At night when radio communication direct to Minneapolis was impossible, we relayed through stations in Iowa and Illinois. The entire amateur 75 meter band just cleared the way and stood by to help. A network was set up and communication direct to Minneapolis was thus perfect. I stayed on the air for two days, grabbing a little sleep at night between calls, eating sandwiches at the radio table. There was no other amateur operator in the city, so no one to help. Although I didn't keep count, I estimated that I carried over 200 priority messages and hundreds of public service messsages.

My telephone rang constantly. We tried to locate stalled trains (M. and St. L.). We called for a railroad snowplow that was lost and we finally located it half way between towns where it was stuck in a drift. The power companies and the telephone companies called W9RHT to distribute and obtain important information. In the meantime the radio station sent thousands of public service messages and everyone was tuned to the station. I stayed at home with W9RHT for three days until the first and only telephone line was established.

Only then did we recognize the magnitude of the storm. We did not know of the lives lost in Winona or events elsewhere.

In retrospect we must remember that we had little in weather forecasting. There was no weather bureau in Albert Lea and little knowledge of the meaning of dropping pressure, frontal systems, etc. As I remember it, there were no lives lost in the Albert Lea area but there was much suffering and many close calls. Station KATE played a key role, telling people to stay put. The amateur station W9RHT became the link with the rest of the world and played a key role in protecting Albert Lea citizens. Other amateur stations outside the storm area, provided instant and accurate service. As is true in any emergency, amateur stations serve the nation well.

THE LEAVING

by Don Bruno
Owatonna, MN

(The final of a series of poems written as seen from behind the desk of the
Hotel Owatonna, when the storm was over.)

The storm was over and the roads cleared.
Some of the guests were not cheered
By the prospect of having to face
The check-out clerk; not having a trace
Of cash left in their purse.
To make matters worse they had never contended
With an ogre like this, with his arm extended,
Waiting for them to deposit therein,
Cash they did not have, and so with a grin
They stepped to the desk as it came their turn
To tell their story.
What they would leave in return
For the lodging they had been provided.
The conversation was really one-sided.
There was no bartering.
Just a statement of facts.
We could tell who they would be by their acts
In the preceding days.
By their habits and ways,
Of avoiding the others, staying in their room,
Probably thinking of the time of doom,
When they must face the situation.
Never believing that we could ration
Our good will around, to all the faces;
An expression that's called, "Touching all of the bases."

For the clerk, this was the hardest part of the act,
As he handled each one with tact.
Some left their watches and some left their rings,
We were loaded with all kinds of things.
All of the offers came of their own free volition,
For at a time like this, who would put a condition
On when they would pay, or if they ever would.
We figured most would pay when they could.

You can believe this or not,
Of all that group, not one forgot
To send their money when they got home,
Probably thinking, "I'll never roam
Out again on Armistice Day,
If the weather is going to treat us in that kind of way."

It was all over.
The storm had been spent.
No matter which way you turned, wherever you went;
The one thought on everybody's mind for some time,
Even the old-timers whose usual rhyme
In past years had been, "When I was a boy,"
That the old storms were only a toy
Compared to the storm that held sway
In 1940 on Armistice Day.

INTO THE WIND WENT MAX CONRAD
by Sally Buegeleisen*
Longboat Key, FLA

With whatever extra money he made, Max Conrad bought airplanes, the new little Piper Cubs that became standard primary trainers. He flew one of these Cubs on what he always considered to be the most extraordinary mission of his life, the flights for which he would like to be remembered, if he is remembered at all.

It happened on November 11, 1940. Armistice Day had started out oppressively damp, unseasonably warm, and cloudy. By midmorning, Max quit working on the new ceiling in the hangar because it was unbearably hot inside. He stepped out for a breath of air and turned his face up into the drizzle that had just begun to speckle the ramp. As he peered up, he caught a glimpse of a formation of ducks making for the river under the lowering gray clouds.

It was Monday, the end of a three-day holiday, and he recalled that one of the students had canceled his flying lesson because he was going duck hunting. Max himself was no hunter, but he did understand the passion of the men who

*Reproduced with special permission from "Into the Wind, The Story of Max Conrad", by Sally Buegeleisen, Random House, Inc., 1973.

took their skiffs out to the sloughs and pools along the banks of the Mississippi to sit uncomfortably for endless hours, waiting for the ducks. Half the town was duck hunting.

That afternoon the wind shifted and the temperature dropped, bringing relief from the heat. Then too quickly, the rain turned to sleet, and Max decided there wouldn't be any flying in this kind of weather anyway, closed the hangar doors and went home.

Betty had planned to go to a concert at St. Theresa's in the evening, and although Max would have preferred to stay home on that kind of night, they went anyway. The wind rattled the windows at St. Theresa's so loudly that the music was drowned out. Three times during the concert, the pianist stood up, shrugged his shoulders, and started to leave the stage, but returned at the insistence of the audience. By the time the concert was over and they had left the hall, the wind was so strong that Betty could not walk alone through the driving snow. The storm worsened and raged all night, from St. Paul to Dubuque. In twelve hours, the temperature dropped alarmingly from fifty-eight degrees to minus six. Before dawn the wind had reached velocities of as much as seventy-five miles an hour.

A little after dawn, the phone's shrilling woke Betty and Max to a world that was white and still except for the howling wind. The hunters had been caught and hadn't come home. Could Max help try and locate them? The wind still blew with such intensity that it was even hazardous walking, but Max recruited some of the students and a few friends, and hurried out to the airport.

He decided to use a Piper Cub. It was almost like taking a canoe out in a gale, but the Cub had been the last aircraft in the hangar and therefore would be the easiest to get out. With Max inside and the engine running, they opened the hangar doors and pulled the plane out tail-first. There was still a fifty-knot wind blowing, and it took ten people, five hanging on each wing, to hold the plane down before the wind caught it and it took off, literally blown backwards. When he took off the first time, Max realized that the snow churned up by the wind made the visibility worse on the ground than from the hundred feet of altitude he held. He could see further than he expected, but the wind was worse. He S-turned toward the river, unsure of what he could do to help or what he would find.

He came to a slough; alongside it was a shallow, newly frozen pool. On the shore of the pool, there was a black dog running up and down near where the willows grew. He recognized the dog but he didn't see the master. The airspeed indicator pointed to eighty, but with the wind coming at him, he was actually covering the ground at no more than twenty or thirty miles per hour. He banked sharply. With the wind to his back, he was rocketing over the ground at a speed of one hundred and thirty miles per hour. But as he turned, he had spotted someone standing in the middle of the pool, frozen up to his waist. The boy waved his arms, then collapsed and fell over on the ice. Max felt a shiver go through his own body and clenched his teeth to stop them from chattering. He knew the boy, and there would be hundreds more like him.

"I flew back again, real low, and this time I saw him plainly in the ice, and right behind him a boat, under the ice, and next to it a body. Then when I was over him, I saw another body, and when I reached the willows, there was another man hanging onto the lower branches of one of them."

He thought of landing but realized that even if he succeeded in putting the wheels down on the ice, the plane would blow away, and a wrecked airplane would be of no help at all. He turned back to the airport, still shaken. Over the field he slowed down for his landing. With fifty knots of wind, his landing speed of fifty indicated would leave him standing still in the air, but in control. As soon as he landed, however, the wind would flip him over. When he greased the plane in on its wheels, men met it and walked it into the open hangar.

Before taking off, he had refused to think about the fury of the wind and the blowing snow. Now there was no doubt that he was endangering his life by going up in that tempest. But he couldn't erase the sight of those men in the ice, and all day he took off again and again, sometimes alone and sometimes with one of his students as a spotter.

He flew low until he saw movement on the ground, and then began circling, to guide rescue boats to where the hunters were caught. He skimmed the ground over channels through which marooned hunters could follow in skiffs. He found men caught on bogs who had been stranded for twenty-four hours or more, lucky to be alive instead of frozen to death. When he spotted them, usually behind the skiffs they had used as windbreaks, he yelled down to them from the open door of the plane.

"Hang on, help is coming!" Then in minutes he would be back to drop five-gallon cans filled with food, whiskey, and matches. Sometimes he could circle the men, shouting, "Start out, and follow me!" They would invariably pick up their shotguns and start, but he would yell, "Leave your guns and take the skiff!"

He could see them breaking through the ice, hanging onto the skiff until they could work it along to thicker ice, and at last, with the Cub guiding them, reaching a rescue boat.

He flew until ten o'clock that night, fell exhausted into bed, and went out the next morning to fly again until the living were rescued and the dead collected. Dozens of men said afterward that they owed their lives to him.

DEATH ON THE MISSISSIPPI*
By C.B. Bylander
Goodview, MN

He was 24 that year, that year when the ducks came and men died, and like most hunters trapped in the deadly Armistice Day storm, he left home wearing only a canvas coat. It was shirt sleeve weather. Fifty degrees. Few had given a second thought to cold weather gear. But few could have imagined the deadly nightmare that would besiege the Upper Midwest that day.

For sure, Oscar Gerth had no idea of what would happen to him . . . chopping up two dozen handmade cedar decoys and burning them to stay alive, the long hours of peering into a smoky fire of dim hope, afraid to walk more than 15 steps in any one direction for fear of becoming lost. No, no one could have imagined the tragedy that befell duck hunters on November 11, 1940. No one at all.

The storm was extraordinary in its intensity and suddenness. This one, the one that baited hunters with a drizzling dawn and beckoning warmth, was rooted far to the north and west. A low pressure system had whistled across the Pacific Northwest, steamed south towards Colorado and took a brief breather over the Texas panhandle, where it sucked in moisture from the balmy Gulf of Mexico. From there it turned north, drenching Kansas with an inch of rain as it ominously eyed the Upper Midwest. The second system, cold and nasty, had swung down from the North Pole. late on the morning of November 11th they collided over the Mississippi river. That, old-timers say, is when all hell broke loose.

At first hunters welcomed the southwest's gusting winds and chill. On those winds was the promise of ducks. "Let 'er rip," they said. But before long the Mississippi river was a swirling tide of unnavigable whitecaps. BB-size snow began pounding flesh—winds howled like sirens, temperatures would soon plummet to 9 degrees.

Mr. Gerth of Winona, 74, didn't forget. Not even if he wanted to. With each sentence he paints a vivid picture of the storm that killed some 161 people, 20 of them hunters between Red Wing, Minnesota and Prairie de Chien, Wisconsin. Gerth is telling how not far from the blind in which he was unloading a man died standing in the water, the thickening ice slowly entombing him, a hand clutching a willow branch. That image causes Gerth to pause in midsentence. He cocks his head the way people do when they are lost in thought, and after several moments of reflecting, he continues.

"Anyone who went out that day, fell in the water or got wet somehow, they

*This article is drawn from the original as published in the *Minnesota Sportsman* magazine, November/December 1984 issue, pages 66-69 and reproduced with special permission of the author, C.B. Bylander.

were done. Hardly anyone could have survived that. The only thing that saved us is that we kept our clothing dry. The cold was bad enough but the wind was something else. It froze so hard that night that the next morning we walked over little ponds, one man in single file right behind the other."

Gerth is among a dwindling legion of hunters who lived through what some say is the worst hunting disaster in U.S. history. He's the kind of man who in a different day might have occasionally told his tales while sitting near the general store's pot-bellied stove, his feet resting on a keg of nails. Today, finding men like Gerth is a hunt in itself.

Drinking coffee in a Wabasha resort is Willis Kruger, 77. He was a game warden here for some 30 years. Nowadays most mornings he can be found at the Wapasha (correct) Resort sipping coffee with 'the boys,' a group of retired men who always know where the fish bite and ducks fly.

Of all of Kruger's stories, two tend to make him shudder. One is the time he was attacked while trying to make an arrest. In the nick of time he stuck a gun in a man's nose. The second is the Armistice Day storm. Five men died in the area he patrolled. "We tried to rescue people that night but . . . we didn't have a boat big enough to handle those waves . . . Everyone knew there were men trapped out there . . . and everyone knew some wouldn't make it through the night."

Ted Beaty, 73, of Wabasha, was 29 the day he walked along a small slough at Robinson Lake near Wabasha. By 4 PM he knew that no duck in the world was worth another minute crouched in a blind. 'On my way back I stopped to pick up a man who had rowed across the lake in a little duck boat. He was just wearing a shell vest and no cap . . . he was just about a goner. He had sat down and fallen asleep. I took off my parka and put it around him. That kind of helped. It was a long hike, the two of us together, and I didn't get home "til pret near nine o'clock. The doctor said he would have froze to death if someone wouldn't have helped him."

There were many heroes and losers in the game of life that day. Among rescue volunteers was Max Conrad, a Winonan already nationally known for his long-distance flying adventures. At dawn on November 12th he eased his Piper Cub into a 50-mph headwind and spent the rest of the day guiding rescue parties to stranded hunters. To some he dropped food, whiskey and cigarettes. To many he was the sign of hope they hd been waiting for.

"I remember him flying over us," Gerth recalled. "I can't imagine how he managed to fly so low. He was just above the ground trying to look under tipped over boats to see if anyone was underneath them."

The lucky hunters, men like Ted Bambenek of Winona, didn't have to worry about burrowing under a boat for protection. Twenty-two then, he was among 17 hunters stranded on an island in Straight Slough. Together they had the strength and resources to build a blazing fire.

"We took turns going out and fetching wood that night," Bambenek explained. "For the most part we just stared at the fire and wondered what the people in town were wondering. Come morning, when we were able to make it to shore, someone brought a bottle of whiskey to us. We were all supposed to get a drink but I didn't. The bottle never made it that far. I think it was dry before it made it halfway around."

The storm was big news across the country and many newspapers dispatched reporters to Mississippi river towns. The Milwaukee Journal sent Gordon Mac-Quarrie to Winona, and in the prose of the times he wove a compelling tale of heroism and tragedy.

"Over in Winona General Hospital tonight lies Gerald Tarras, 17, a survivor. He is a big boy, nearly six feet, and strong. He had to be to live. He saw his father, a brother and his friend die. He has not yet come to a full realization of what has happened, for grief is sometimes far in the wake of catastrophe," he wrote.

Casualties ran so high, in part, because the shooting was so good. Mallards were everywhere, though hard to hit because of the ferocious wind. Winonan Ed Kosidowski, now 70, remembers what it was like.

"The ducks were all over so we just stood there and shot 'em. We had warm clothes—extra socks and all—so we kept firing away. Oh, it was a terrible night. We didn't make it to shore until about 10 o'clock. But that shooting, oh that shooting, you couldn't imagine it."

No one knows exactly how many hunters died along the Mississippi river that day. Their deaths were lumped together with all the others, like the people who died stranded in their cars on the streets of Minneapolis and St. Paul, and the sailors who drowned in Lake Michigan. But some say that perhaps as many as 80 men died in their blinds or boats.

A TRUCKFUL OF FREEZING BEER, SEVENTEEN OVERNIGHT GUESTS, and A COUPLE NOT EVEN MARRIED
by William G. Frame
Northfield, MN

We were living on a farm about 35 miles south of the Twin Cities, half way between Farmington and Northfield on what is now state highway #3. Just north of our farmhouse was an old farmhouse owned by my uncle and just north of that was a newer house where my uncle and aunt lived with their family.

That Armistice Day started not too threateningly. If there were any radio weather forecasts we didn't hear them. It was cloudy with a light drizzle and a little wind. The storm built up gradually during the day with the wind getting stronger, the temperature falling and the rain turning to snow in the afternoon. By early afternoon the wind was very strong and we knew it was a serious storm.

Farmers always have things to do to prepare for a storm so I was busy with odds and ends to make things more secure for the animals. Bringing straw from the strawpile to the barn for livestock bedding was quite a chore. I would start from the strawpile with a large forkful and be lucky to get to the barn with half of it because of the buffeting wind. Our barn had a large haymow door into which the west wind was coming at a great rate. It was hinged at the bottom and was hanging down by the hinges; I had to fasten a rope and pulley to it, then get inside the mow and pull it shut. It was very hard to pull against that wind until it was at least half way up. Then I was fearful that the wind would slam it into the frame with such force that it would be wrecked. Luckily it closed and held. That kept the snow from filling the hay mow.

Before the storm was at its worst I had the farm animals all snug in the barn and henhouse and the hogs were burrowed into the strawpile where they were out of the wind and cold. Many farmers lost lots of cattle and turkeys which could not be protected from the snow and sleet; it covered their nostrils and smothered them.

Because we were planning on a new baby, we had readied the house for winter by putting on storm windows and banking the basement walls. We were as ready for winter as most old houses could be in those days. We usually heated the house with coal but the coal bin was full of corncobs to use until really cold weather came. During that storm I carried many tubs of cobs into the house to fuel the kitchen range and the living room stove, keeping the house warm. My wife was just home from the hospital where she had given birth to a 10 1/2 pound boy and she was quite weak. With three older children to care for, and housework to do, she had all that she could cope with. A woman who had been helping us had just left.

As the storm strengthened during the afternoon, the visibility lessened. The snow got thicker on the road and traffic came to a standstill at about dusk on the stretch of road near my uncle's house. The first people to reach there was a couple from Austin who asked to rent a spare bedroom. Later arrivals were taken in until they had 17 extra people to feed and bed down for the night. About dark a couple of men missed uncle's place and came to our house. They had been driving a furniture delivery truck and came to our door wrapped in those huge blankets used to wrap furniture. We took them in to stay the night, the next day and another night before the road was opened. They were worried about their cars which they had driven to work and left downtown in Minneapolis with no anti-freeze in the radiators.

One of those stuck in the snowbanks was my cousin, Ed, who was driving a truck for Kump of Northfield and had a load of beer which he was bringing back from the city. As he had no anti-freeze in the radiator, he took his jack-knife and cut the radiator hoses to drain the water. He was afraid the beer would freeze if it got too cold so I suggested he light his flares and place them inside the truck, which he did. The next morning Ed walked to the little town of Castle Rock to telegraph Kump to send a wrecker to haul in the truck as soon as roads were opened. Ed returned bringing ten pounds of sugar because he knew we were short of it.

On the second day the plows got through, and all the guests dug themselves out, considering themselves lucky to come through the blizzard alive.

Some of the last people to leave my uncle's house told my aunt that the couple who had first come in and rented the spare room were not man and wife. At that my aunt nearly went through the roof and it was some time before she got over being angry at that couple.

DIPPER FROZE IN THE KITCHEN PAIL
by Mrs. Arthur Hink
Lake City, MN

We were just getting started farming, having rented a farm with a large older house. My husband owned a small flock of about 20 sheep. My father, who was also farming, gave me four milk cows and six head of young stock as my wages for helping him several years and also as a wedding present. My husband also bought 12 head of cattle, a team of horses and a flock of chickens.

On the morning of the eleventh, the weather was quite warm for November but it was misting. We had been busy getting in the corn crop by hand and still had several acres left to husk. I mention that to explain why we had neglected to set up the wood heater in the living room, just getting by with a cookstove in the kitchen. Neither had we put on the storm windows because the corn crop needed to be gotten in first. Of course there was no rural electrification in 1940 in our area. Some people had battery powered radios but we did not since we had very little money. So we had not heard any forecast of bad weather, if there even were one.

The misty rain began to change to snow about noon—and more and more snow. My husband felt we should get the cattle home from the pasture. By now a heavy wet snow was falling fiercly. My chickens were outside and seemed to be stunned by the suddenness of all of this. I started carrying them into the hen house, wet and soaked as I was. The wind changed to the northwest and the snow was now getting knee deep on the level and deeper in drifts.

It was beginning to get dark and our flock of sheep hadn't come home. We lit a kerosene lantern, took a flashlight, and started to the pasture to find them. Eventually, after walking in knee-deep snow, we found what looked like lumps in the snow. They were our sheep, entirely covered by snow; we had to chase them up, their eyes being snow and ice covered so badly they couldn't see where to go. At this time the strong wind blew out our kerosene lantern and, with only a flashlight and in total darkness, we managed to drive most of them to the barn; a few we could not save.

After our animals were safely in barns, we wearily went to the house for dry clothes and warmth—but warm it was not. As a bride I had just papered the walls in two rooms of our rented house and was quite proud of my work. I was shocked to find the northwest walls frost-covered and wet, but still we were thankful to be inside. With only an old cookstove for heat and the wind so strong, we didn't get much warmth. The dipper even froze solidly in the water pail (no running water either). Telephone lines were down so there was no communication. I remember that we huddled in one room all night, covered with all the blankets and coats we could find—but we were alive.

We farmed 37 years on that same farm and never had a storm so early, with such fury, and no warnings. Weather announcements are so helpful now, one of the many things for which we are thankful.

A FRESHLY FROZEN TURKEY FOR A QUARTER

by Alvin Houston
Northfield, MN

I am a retired rural mail carrier; in my early days I drove a team of horses 34 miles every work day on my mail route out of Northfield during the winter months. I learned respect for the weather.

Late October and early November, 1940 were quite mild and November 9th and 10th were rainy days. Monday, November 11th began much like the previous days—rather mild with a steady drizzle. About 10:45 AM I noticed that the rain was beginning to freeze on some bushes and soon the wind was picking up from the northwest. The temperature was almost exactly 32 degrees and destined to go well below zero by 6 PM that same day.

I began congratulating myself that it was Armistice Day, a federal holiday, and that I wasn't serving the mail route for it began to look like the day would be a rough one. Then I remembered that school was in session and the school buses were running. And—because it was a mild morning—few people were clothed for a full-scale blizzard. I was concerned for those children.

The sudden drop in temperature and the wind shift began to worry me and I couldn't forget those school buses. Northfield is located in the Cannon river valley and because of this and the many trees in town, is sheltered from the full force of most storms. To verify to my own satisfaction that the storm was getting dangerous, I climbed into my Ford Model A mail route car and drove out of town a half mile on a familiar county road to open country. Yes, conditions definitely were severe. The wind-driven snow was so blinding that it wasn't even safe to proceed in low gear. I felt fortunate to get turned around and back into the shelter of town.

I drove directly to the high school where school superintendent J. H. Wichman seemed to think that the weather wasn't too bad yet, but said he would telephone the school bus drivers. He would have them report as soon as possible and suggested that I talk to them about the conditions. In about thirty minutes all of the drivers—eleven or twelve, as I recall—and Mr. Wichman and I were assembled in a classroom near the superintendent's office. Superintendent Wichman told the men (our drivers were men at that time) that he would dismiss school at once if they wished to start early getting the students home.

I urged that the afternoon trips be cancelled completely and that we activate a phoning committee to arrange for housing for the children in town that night. Mr. Wichman again stated that he felt the men knew their road conditions better than anyone and that he would cooperate with the drivers in any decision they made. Some of them said that the snow wasn't deep enough yet to be a problem. I agreed but emphasized that, because of the extremely strong wind, visibility was fast deteriorating and it would be impossible to stay on the road. After about ten minutes of discussion, most agreed that it was too dangerous to go out and opted for keeping the students in town. Five drivers said they would take only the students living on main county and state roads and leave the others in town.

A committee went to work telephoning to arrange overnight housing in town, students were dismissed, and shortly after one o'clock the five buses left town for their limited run.

Because of the ice and strong wind all of the rural telephone lines were down, and because short wave radios were not in common use, rural communication was almost non-existent. It was not until Thursday morning, three days later, that the community learned what had happened to the five buses. Every one of them had gone off the roads between three and four miles from town. The driver and students of each bus had held on to each other to make a human chain, and every group made its way safely to the nearest farm house.

Later I talked with one of the host farmers and his wife about the experience of having nearly forty high school students as guests for three nights and three days. He said "We put the girls on the second floor where they slept on the floor, and the boys slept on the first floor. We had plenty of potatoes in the cellar and a herd of milk cows in the barn. The boys helped with the chores and the girls helped my wife with the cooking. The kids had a ball!"

I think we received about 16 inches of snow in that blizzard and the wind must have been above 50 mph most of those three days.

Another incident happened here. There are several turkey farms in our area and thousands of turkeys suffocated and froze to death. In the week following the blizzard, many farmers brought truckloads of frozen turkeys to town and sold them for twenty-five cents each.

IT WAS ROUGH GOING IN 1940
by Florence Graham Johnson
Faribault, MN

That blizzard was an experience I never want to relive.

I was a 22 year old weaver at the Faribo Woolen Mill. We lived 1 1/2 miles out in the country east of the mill. I got out of work at four o'clock just as my dad came to work that day for the four to midnight shift, in the engine room.

I was told by fellow workers not to try to walk home in the blizzard and was offered places to stay overnight. Or I could have wrapped myself in a wool blanket at the mill and just slept there. But I was determined to get home.

First I'll describe the home where I was going. It was on 21 acres which today would be called a hobby farm but our main source of food came from that land. The house was a small two-story five room house with no insulation, no plumbing but—lucky us—electricity. The kitchen had a sink in the corner, without a drain but with a slop pail underneath to catch waste water. It had a cistern pump on it and a pail and dipper for drinking water which had to be pumped outside by hand and brought inside. There was a kitchen range with a reservoir for keeping water warm and two warming ovens above for warming food. In the parlor there was an oil burner for heat, with one small register in the ceiling to heat the upstairs. Under part of the house there was a dirt cellar which you entered through a trap door in the kitchen. Down there were at least 500 quarts of canned goods my mother had put up, plus a big bin of potatoes and other vegetables.

So much for my destination.

I started on my way home through the blizzard and had to go up a big hill past the St. James school (Lower Shattuck) which is now the Wilson Psychiatric Center. The snow was waist deep and the wind very gusty. I had to keep my eyes on the telephone lines and the field fences since there were no tracks of any kind. I finally got home, very exhausted, cold and wet. Much to my surprise and disappointment, mother was not home. She had left a note saying her cousin's wife had passed away and she had walked into town to be with him. The telephone was out of order so I had no communication with the outside world. Needless to say I spent a terrible night and was scared stiff. The fire in the kitchen range was out so I had to start that with wood, kindling and kerosene. We had a big supply of wood stacked up behind the range. I had to fill the heater in the parlor with oil. I did know I couldn't build too big a fire with all the gusty winds or I would have a chimney fire.

My dad and my brother each had a pig which would be butchered later for winter meat. I bundled up again and went to the shed to feed and water them. On my way I could see the chickens standing in the snow, frozen stiff. When I got to the pigs I found one dead. I didn't think the dead one should be left with the live one, so tried to drag it out, but couldn't. So I trudged through the field in that blizzard about two blocks to the neighbors. One of the boys came back with me and got the pig out of there.

Then back in the house to put more wood on the fire and fix supper. Time for bed. The frost was coming through the walls upstairs so I pulled a rocker up to the cook stove, wrapped up in a handmade patchwork quilt, put my feet on the oven door and tried to sleep.Several times during the night I had to put wood in the fire.

I don't remember when my mother came home the next day but I was sure happy to see her. The thing that made me mad after my rough experience was that when my brother found out his pig had died, he blamed me. After all I had gone through I didn't need to get bawled out.

Each time I tell this story I think how grateful I am for my modern home, for the modern conveniences, and that my children have all these comforts.

MAROONED IN THE CAR
by Marvel M. Knutson
Brownsdale, MN

As we left our home in Sargeant that Armistice day afternoon, it was raining. We were on our way to rural Taopi where my husband's older daughter was teaching school. *We* consisted of Ted's daughter. his sister, Ted and me, By the time we got to highway #6 it was snowing and the wind had changed to the northwest. We went on to Brownsdale, about four miles farther. When we got there it was so stormy we decided to return home.

On the way back the engine began to miss and to sputter. The wet snow was getting onto the wiring. The car stalled about three miles north of Brownsdale and it wouldn't start again. Ted decided to walk south to a farm place, so he wrapped two scarves around his head. He walked only a short distance and we couldn't see him any more. After some time he came back full of snow and cold.The folks who lived there had no phone and were elderly as well. So no help could be obtained there.

Then Ted decided to walk north about one half mile, so he left again. I don't know how he made it because the weather was simply terrible. He came back after some time and said he had called the Schmiring garage and they were coming out to get us. That was in Waltham. They got part of the way and could not see the road and went into the ditch. When they got out, they had to go back to Waltham. We didn't know this, of course, so waited and waited, finally deciding just to sit there since it was getting dark.

A car hit us in the back and went into the ditch. It was a man, woman and a little girl from Kasson. They got into our car and we kept warmer that way. By this time we did some crying and much praying. The darkness settled in and it seemed like we might just freeze to death since there was no traffic at all.

Then a thin ray of light appeared right by our side and it stopped. Ted got out and talked to the people in the car. He knew the driver . . . a Mr. Taylor who did construction work around the county. He told us to get into his two-door Ford and we managed to do that. He already had two other men in there besides himself. We were so thankful that we didn't need much room. Ten people, all adults excepting one. We fairly crawled that three miles back to Brownsdale. It was past seven o'clock when we got back there and I still know we were guided that night by a higher power. There was no way any one could see that road; many times it was simply not visible.

When we drove into Brownsdale that night I couldn't believe at first that we had made it. We didn't have a phone at home, so we called a neighbor who went to our house and told my 15-year old sister, who was with our six young children at home. She was overjoyed because she didn't know what had happened to us.

The good people of Brownsdale took us in for the night. The next morning the storm had subsided some and the men went back to get our car. They towed it in and the engine was so packed full of snow it was like an icepack. They thawed it, put in some new wiring, and we started back for Sargeant and for home. The sun was shining and I remember saying "What a wonderful day just to be alive."

It was truly a new lease on life and I will never forget that experience even though it happened 45 years ago.

ABE KUHNS, HERO EXTRAORDINARY
by Milton Larson and
Evelyn Nelson
Red Wing, MN

"I knew this man well," says Milton Larson. "His name was Abraham Kuhns but he was lovingly known to everyone as Honest Abe. He stood six feet four inches and was as strong as a horse. I used to help Abe and his neighbor Harry Hanson fish for carp in the winter time. They had a gigantic net that was a quarter of a mile long. We would chop holes in the ice so the fish could be driven down stream into it. The one haul took us four days to transfer the catch into semi trucks. The game warden was with us at all times, sorting out and returning game fish to the river. I carried some walleyes and northerns nearly as big as I was at that time and put them back into the river. All of this gives you a good indication of what a strong man Abe was."

Abe was a bachelor who lived on Prairie Island, adjacent to the Prairie Island Indian reservation and not far from the now-existing Prairie Island Nuclear energy plant. He was a friend to all who lived on the island, Indian and white alike, and has been described by Evelyn Nelson of the Goodhue County Historical society as "a very kind and gentle man, a man I knew and respected, having also lived on Prairie Island for many years."

I (the editor) stood at the edge of North lake on Prairie Island, Red Wing, along with Evelyn Nelson, and looked across to the spot where two St. Paul hunters had been found frozen to death, buddies who had chummed together, hunted together and now died together. It was a bleak and dreary morning in March, much like that November 11, 1940 day only extremely mild by comparison.

Then Evelyn and I went to Sturgeon lake, still part of Prairie Island, and stood there looking at the exact spot from which Abe Kuhns had launched his life-saving boat. Across this body of water and into the nearby flyways men had fought for their lives that day. Many lost but there were those saved by Abe Kuhns and his tiny boat.

Abe Kuhns had also been hunting that day with a friend named Brestkemp but, when the storm became too severe for safety, these two gathered their decoys and called it quits. As Milton Larson tells the story: "Some hunters had heard some men calling for help from a small island where they were stranded. Their boats had been swamped and they were freezing to death in that horrible blizzard. Abe went across that lake in a rowboat with nothing but a pair of oars and a kerosene lantern. He had to lay on his stomach to keep the boat from capsizing and could take back only one man at a time. Imagine, if you will, what dedication this took on his part under such terrible circumstances. Abe's older brother helped get the men to their warm and comfortable home." There had been six of these hunters, each having taken his own boat to this thin strip of land separating Sturgeon lake from the Mississippi river. Tony Kuhns, brother of Abe, had warned them not to make the trip, but they went anyway. When evening came, Tony told Abe of the situation and Abe "went directly to the landing and bailed out a boat. He set out alone across the freezing white-caps. It was not luck alone that let him row through the hidden stumps unscathed, but years of experience and a natural skill. After he had rescued the first two hunters, he realized that his boat was not large enough to take more than two passengers at a time, so Abe made two more trips, carrying two thankful hunters across to Tony's warm house with each crossing. When the last man had been rescued, Abe went home to finish his chores. Before he went out to the barn, though, he stopped into his own house and thawed out his hands and his face, which had been frozen quite badly. To Abe, it is nothing really unusual. He feels that just about anybody would have done the same." *(Red Wing Daily Republican, November 16, 1940.)*

After this noble event there was a movement in Red Wing to obtain the Carnegie Medal of Honor for Abe. Some people like Milton Larson thought the award was actually presented, but it was not. Although the Red Wing Republican Eagle carried a story that friends were seeking the medal, the Carnegie Hero Fund Commission says it was never awarded. In fact, that group says it was never even nominated, although the same Red Wing paper says the Commission sent its Mr. Irwin Urling to Red Wing to investigate the story.

However, Kuhns did receive the Red Cross' highest award, the Honor Deed Citation, from the Minnesota Safety Council (Red Wing Daily Republican, November 15, 1940) and is still held in great esteem by local people as the city's outstanding all-time hero.

NINE THOUSAND DEAD TURKEYS
by Adele McCoy
Stacy, MN

I was a young wife, 20 years old. With my husband we were turkey farmers on a small farm near Rice lake near Owatonna. My aunt and my parents also raised turkeys; they lived two miles north of Claremont.

It was raining that morning and all of our birds were out on the range, ready for the Thanksgiving market. My father came over that morning; he needed my husband's help because one of his cows was sick and down, so we went home with him not at all concerned about our turkeys. Why should we have been? We had 3,000 birds ready for market.

Papa and Emil were in the barn working with the sick cow so they didn't notice what the weather was doing. Mama, my brother John, a friend named Elmer and I were in the house and we weren't watching the weather either. We didn't have a television in those days and we also didn't have a working radio; hence we had no news or weather report. I don't think there was any official warning.

The temperature dropped and the storm hit so suddenly that we were caught unawares. The moment we realized what was happening, the four men bundled up and headed on foot for the back range where my father's 6,000 turkeys were located. The weather was already so bad they couldn't drive the truck. I suppose the range was about a mile away and there they found the turkeys already in one big pile smothering each other. The men tried to build a windbreak from shocks they carried from nearby fields but they soon realized it was hopeless. The storm was getting so intense and vicious that the only thing on their minds was how to save their own lives.

They could see nothing, not even each other so they had to hold hands or touch each other all the time, or one of them would get separated. They soon realized there was a chance they would never get back to the house and might freeze.

My brother John had a Montana cow-trained bronco named Dusty who was trained to come to his master when he whistled. John figured it was their only chance so he started whistling for him. Dusty was out in the pasture some place. Would he find John by the sound of the whistle? Was he near enough to hear over the howling wind? He did hear and he did come to my brother. The men all took hold of Dusty by the tail or wherever they could hold on. John held him by the mane near his head and kept talking to him to keep him calm.

I don't know how he did it, maybe by instinct, but he led the men to the barn. Needless to say Dusty got a warm stall, a manger full of hay and a feed bin full of oats. I never could ride that horse because he bucked so much but I sure had a lot of respect for him henceforth.

My father lost most of the 6,000 birds. Emil and I couldn't get home for three days and of course most of our birds were dead too. My aunt's turkeys were in a heavily wooded area so most of her 5,000 survived.

The day we got home a neighbor walked to our place and wanted to borrow my riding horse, Bobby, who was a long legged pacer, a Hamiltonian. The man needed the horse because he had a herd of young heifers at pasture about six miles from our place. I let him take the horse. He found his cattle but only two were alive, the rest being dead in a standing position leaning against fence posts. The trip nearly killed my horse. Mr. Sterling spent the night in a barn, rubbing down my horse and came back the next day. Bobby got distemper, ran a high fever, his hooves were split nearly into the quick and he lost most of his hair as a result of the fever. It was a year before I could ride him again.

The family lost about 9,000 turkeys in that storm and, although we had insurance, the loss was so great in the state that we had to settle for about three cents on the dollar. It surely didn't do us much good but we all survived and continued to raise turkeys for many years after that.

I have good reason to remember the Armistice Day 1940 storm.

FIFTY-SIX BUS STUDENTS OVERNIGHT
by Marjorie Kruegel Quiggle
Rice, MN

The sixty passenger orange school bus was almost filled with students in grades kindergarten through twelve. That morning the weather was very pleasant — ankle socks, school slippers, dresses and coats for the small girls. Boys left caps and mittens at home because weather forecasting was not too common in 1940.

I was a bashful farm girl who drove the family car to St. Olaf college daily where I majored in home economics and general science in preparation for teaching.

Rain began falling about noon and quickly changed to sleet while the temperature plummeted, icing everything in a short time. Then followed heavy snow and wind.

I was in class when the professor called my name and told me to pick up a message. This sort of thing was unheard. Everyone's schedule was on file in

Dean Gertrude Hilleboe's office for emergencies and I was completely appalled when told to report to her office immediately! What had I done to deserve such a call? Bootless, I waded without head covering or gloves from the science building about half a block to her office. I was shaking with fear but Miss Hilleboe's pleasant attitude soon put me at ease.

We lived three miles from Northfield on the North Dennison road. My mother had telephoned to ask if I could stay at the college because the roads were becoming impassable with deep wet snow. I almost went into shock when Miss Hilleboe invited me to stay in the Agnes Melby hall guest room next door to her apartment. I couldn't handle the idea of staying in the same room which kings and queens had occupied. I explained that I was sure I could make it home if I could follow the school bus—and the schools were closing about this time. She reminded me of the dangers involved and left the decision to me; I told her I wanted to go home so she gave me mittens and a scarf and I went to my car.

Now I was faced with one of the biggest challenges of my life. I could not get the driver's door open because it was covered with ice an inch deep and I had no tools that wouldn't ruin the paint. Luckily, the passenger door didn't give me any trouble, so I crawled in that side, started the motor to warm it up and help clear the windshield, and then crawled back out the passenger side to clean the outside of the car.

The snow was deep—up to the middle of the hubcaps, but it was fluffy, so I cautiously drove down the hill of the college and proceeded without stopping through town and toward home. The big school bus had left town just a few minutes earlier and I could follow its tracks. Soon I caught up to the bus and I was no longer out in the weather alone. The bus's first stop after leaving town was to drop off my little sister, Marye Ann Kruegel, and my only brother, George Kruegel, at the end of our driveway. The bus tried to stop but it was so slippery it slid out of my way and into the ditch, stuck solidly in the very deep snow bank.

I accelerated the car and proceeded onto our driveway which had no track. I have never experienced such snow driving in my whole life as I did maneuvering that one-third mile stretch of blind road. My folks saw me coming so my dad, Louis Kruegel, opened the garage door and I made it into the garage without incident—and said a prayer of thanks.

Dad then hiked down the driveway to talk to the bus driver. There was no way they could get that bus out of that ditch. Those 56 students and driver would have to be taken into our home. My dad made many trips to our house carrying two tiny children each trip, as did the driver. All shoes and socks were soaking wet from their trek from school to the bus in town. What a pile of wet shoes we had behind our oil-burning Heatrola. Our small two-story farm house was soon occupied beyond capacity.

My mother, Hazel Kruegel, was a former teacher and together we made phone calls to parents, prepared food and called in recruit help from a neighbor across the road who eventually took in the older boys to sleep that night. Together we planned menus. We had plenty of our own milk. Everyone enjoyed the fresh biscuits and bread we baked until our flour supply was depleted. We made plenty of trips to our cellar for home-canned fruit, vegetables and meat. The second day we ran out of bread, so my dad mounted our sleigh and drove our horses to town for supplies. He also took the nearby children home. Finally the rotary plow came clearing the road and soon the Armistice Day storm was a thing of the past.

IF EVER A GUARDIAN ANGEL HELPED . . .
by Raymond J. Rice
Winona, MN

It was about 11 AM that Monday morning when my two partners decided we would go hunting. It had rained during the night and the sun was out for a short period that Monday morning. We did not have to work that day. As I was standing in my back yard waiting for them to pick me up I noticed the mallards were coming out of Lake Winona in small flocks. They would get just above my home, make a complete circle and head straight south. This happened about 15 times while I was waiting. Very unusual indeed. They seemed to sense that a storm was coming.

My partners picked me up and we proceeded to the Stanz boat dock. They rented a boat and I took my own. They got started ahead of me and I couldn't catch them so I decided to go on my own. The wind was already blowing hard. It was now about 1:45 PM.

I crossed Straight Slough, rowing as hard as I could with the waves getting higher and whitecaps being very numerous. I got to the spot where we had decided to hunt but no one was there, so I put out my decoys and went to the blind. I stayed there only about five minutes and decided I'd better get out of there. I picked up my decoys and started for home. This is where my problems began.

I nosed out into the lake and it was really blowing, so I planned my route. I stayed along the rushes, going from the northwest to the southwest across Rice lake and the Twin lakes. Then I had to get out into the thick of it, so I turned the boat around and placed the stern behind a wave and rode across the Twin lakes going from southwest to northeast. I had to keep the boat straight so I would not get swamped. I got to a place called The Forks and grabbed a willow and hung on for a few minutes. A big boat with a fast motor went by on the slough and they yelled at me to go back, saying I would never make it. However, they offered me no help, and I could not go back.

Wind and waves were terrible. Again I rowed toward the southwest, up the slough. It was very hard rowing — I had to feather the oars and make very small gains with each pull. Got up the slough for about a block and again turned the boat around with the stern behind a wave. The wind took me down across The Forks like a bullet. When I landed on the east side of The Forks, I jumped from the boat and when the waves raised it to ground level, I pulled it out of the slough and onto the bank. The waves were rolling over the bank so the ground was covered with about six inches of water. I pulled my boat across the land and in doing so I fell on some brush and got soaking wet up to my neck. I stood up and my clothes froze instantly on my body. I would say that this helped me to keep warm since it kept the wind from hitting me. Then I got behind some willows on the lea side out of the strong wind and then to a small opening to Crooked Slough which was out of the wind. It was now about 4 PM and I decided to rest for a while.

Hundreds of mallards would come in, flying against the wind. They could hardly move, just going up and down and would land within a few feet of me, completely exhausted and wouldn't get up. I shot one, however, and became ashamed of myself because they were fighting the storm just as I was. I put the gun in the case and continued on toward home.

I still had some rough going. Again I had to cross Crooked Slough and go down to what is called Four Corners. Here the waves were rolling five to six feet high, so I stayed along the north side, rowing and staying close to the trees, until I got to the landing. It was about 8 PM. I had made it.

If ever a guardian angel helped anyone, I sure got her help because I could never have made it alone. My duck boat was 12 feet long and three feet wide with a deck. I had less than a pail of water in the boat.

My partners were forced to stay out all night because they broke an oar. They were the last two people to be rescued the next afternoon.

I am now 79 years old but I surely remember that storm of 1940.

MIRACLE SAVES HUNTERS AS BOAT SINKS

by T. J. Strasser
St. Paul, MN

I went hunting for ducks Monday — and death went hunting for me. I got some ducks, and death missed by the whim of a gigantic wave that tossed me within reach of shore after my boat sank under me.

My brother Carl and I were shooting on an island in the Mississippi river near Wabasha early in the afternoon. It was good hunting weather, with a fine rain falling and the wind from the southeast. We had bagged quite a number of birds.

Suddenly the wind shifted to the north, driving in with great force and turning the rain to sleet. We set about retrieving our decoys, which were dragging their anchors.

Then Carl said to me:

"Say, let's get out of here quick; look at that."

I looked. In the open water between the island and the Minnesota shore, waves nearly three feet high were roaring down the channel. We had come out in a small duckboat.

The task of regaining the mainland appeared hopeless, but I knew it was our only chance. The blizzard was already on top of us. I tried to see what the duck hunters on neighboring islands were doing but the sleet obscured everything. I have learned that many of them died.

We abandoned all our equipment except the guns and pushed the duckboat off into the storm. I was at the oars. We knew our only chance was to ride with the waves downstream and edge to the Minnesota shore.

Within two minutes my mittens had frozen to the oars. We were both sheathed in sleet. I was completely blinded by the storm, and followed Carl's directions, desperately trying to keep the boat from swinging broadside to the waves.

We got within a hundred feet of shore and I thought we were going to make it. The boat was only about half full of water and moved with the speed of a power boat on the crest of the hurtling water.

Suddenly the oars were torn from my gloved hands as we were slapped broadside. Water poured over the side and boat sank from under us.

Right then the miracle occurred. What looked like a mountain of water literally hurled us at the shore, and as the boat went down we were able to stumble in through breast-deep water.

I don't quite know how we did it, but we even hung on to our guns. Coated with ice we stumbled into a farm house and the good people inside took over.

Duck hunting is lots of fun!

This story originally appeared in the St. Paul Pioneer Press, November 13, 1940. Reprinted by special permission.

OUR BOAT MOTOR WOULDN'T START

by Byron Swanson
St. Paul, MN

I had an early appointment with a customer at Brandtjen & Kluge in St. Paul that November 11. I was fortunate that I made a quick *sale* for which I was delighted and was rapidly on my way with great expectations of favorable duck hunting conditions. My destination was Red Wing, my boyhood town. On my way I noticed the tree tops were showing signs of snow and ice. Good!

At about 10:30 AM my brother-in-law, Dr. Carl J. Agrell, and I parked our cars on the Minnesota side of the Mississippi and with our 2 1/2 horse motor, journeyed across the river in our light boat to Second Cut, our favorite spot, which was one-quarter mile inland, on the Wisconsin side. By the time we reached our blind the wind and snow had developed in increasing proportions and by mid-afternoon we were battling an unrelenting nature. Having observed only one confused duck, we decided to head for home.

Our motor failed to start and we found it necessary to get out of the boat and push it toward the Mississippi river. An unbelievable condition had occurred; the wind was so strong that the water had dropped about two feet and we were wallowing in soft mud. By the time we were ready to cross the river (motorless) the wind was so strong that a brainless hunter would not have risked crossing.

We must have had a Super Power rewarding us for our past deeds for right at that spot was an occupied cabin where we were invited in for the night. We didn't have a very restful sleep because the Northern States Power company's high electric towers set up such a hum that it kept us awake, plus the heavy fur horsehide blanket curled back my toes so much that they haven't recovered to this day.

With motor operating, we crossed the river the next morning, observing on the way the cruiser of Hjalmer Hjermstad who had been searching for us all night. Fortunately he rescued another hunter from a willow island at the head of Lake Pepin, a hunter who never would have made it otherwise.

All this time I had misgivings concerning my car which I had left unwinterized because the water hoses were soft. I had decided to replace them later and to add antifreeze then. Fortunately all the hoses had burst without doing any other damage.

We stayed in Red Wing three days because the highway was impassable. At that time we also heard that there were seven or eight other hunters, lightly dressed, who had frozen to death. One had sought shelter in a haystack. When we got back to St. Paul we had to walk three blocks to get to our homes; the streets were still unplowed.

No ducks were placed in our freezers that trip.

INDEX